NCI Library

3 9006 01045815 8

PELICAN

POLITICAL

Peter Hain was born in 1950 and brought up in South Africa, until his parents' active opposition to apartheid forced the family

Since then he has lived in Putney, where h

election; he was re-elected as Labour's c

Research Officer for the Union of Comm

married with two young sons.

D1352258

A civil rights campaigner, he first became p

the Stop the Seventy Tour Committee, which organized demonstrations against South African sports tours to Britain. He was also a leading Young Liberal before joining the Labour Party in 1977. He graduated in political science from Queen Mary College, London University, in 1973, and then studied at Sussex University where he obtained a Master of Philosophy.

His other books are *Don't Play with Apartheid* (1971), *Radical Regeneration* (1975), *Mistaken Identity* (1976), *Neighbourhood Participation* (1980), *The Democratic Alternative* (Penguin, 1983) and *Political Trials in Britain* (Penguin, 1984). He has edited *Community Politics* (1976), *Policing the Police*, Volume 1 (1979) and Volume 2 (1980) and *The Crisis and Future of the Left* (1980).

College of Industrial
Relations.
STUDENTS' LIBRARY.

PETER HAIN

POLITICAL STRIKES

THE STATE AND TRADE UNIONISM
IN BRITAIN

College of Industrial
Relations
STUDENTS' LIBRARY.

PENGUIN BOOKS

Penguin Books Ltd, Harmondsworth, Middlesex, England
Viking Penguin Inc., 40 West 23rd Street, New York, New York 10010, U.S.A.
Penguin Books Australia Ltd, Ringwood, Victoria, Australia
Penguin Books Canada Limited, 2801 John Street, Markham, Ontario, Canada L3R 1B4
Penguin Books (N.Z.) Ltd, 182–190 Wairau Road, Auckland 10, New Zealand

First published by Viking 1986
Published with minor revisions in Pelican Books 1986

Copyright © Peter Hain, 1986
All rights reserved.

Made and printed in Great Britain by
Richard Clay (The Chaucer Press) Ltd,
Bungay, Suffolk
Typeset in Monophoto Ehrhardt

Except in the United States of America,
this book is sold subject to the condition
that it shall not, by way of trade or otherwise,
be lent, re-sold, hired out, or otherwise circulated
without the publisher's prior consent in any form of
binding or cover other than that in which it is
published and without a similar condition
including this condition being imposed
on the subsequent purchaser

FOR THE MEMBERS, EXECUTIVE COUNCIL, OFFICERS
AND STAFF OF THE UNION OF COMMUNICATION WORKERS

College of Industrial
5949 Relations.
RN
5949
STUDENTS' LIBRARY.

WITHDRAWN FROM STOCK

CONTENTS

College of Industrial
RN
5949 Relations. RN
5949
STUDENTS' LIBRARY.

WITHDRAWN FROM STOCK

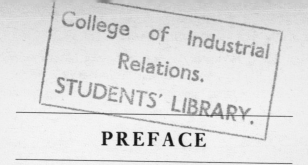

College of Industrial
Relations.
STUDENTS' LIBRARY.

PREFACE

Are strikes always 'political'? Has the changing position of unions made them more likely to adopt a 'political' stance? What are 'political strikes'? Who is responsible for them? What lessons are there in the history of strikes in Britain?

In discussing these questions this book aims to dispel some of the myths surrounding British trade unionism: for example, by showing that the extent to which unions have themselves chosen to act in a militant or overtly 'political' way has been vastly exaggerated. A major theme of the book is that the nature of strikes is determined by the political climate and not simply by the role of unions and employers. The outcome of major strikes is especially dependent upon intervention by governments and other agencies of the state.

But it is not enough simply to concentrate on analysis, as if the role of the trade union movement was an academic matter. Towards the end, an attempt is made to draw together some lessons from the preceding chapters, and there is a discussion of the radical changes necessary to enable modern unions to advance their industrial and political objectives more effectively.

While the book does not claim to provide an exhaustive historical analysis, contemporary strikes are viewed within a long-term perspective so that they can be better understood. The intention is to provide a readable, *popular political* analysis, rather than a text for theorists or connoisseurs of labour history. Inevitably, therefore, it skates over complex issues of debate. And the notes are for reference purposes only: they should not be allowed to interrupt the flow of the argument.

For their help and advice on drafts of chapters, I am very grateful to my father; Andy Batkin; Verity Burgmann; Alan

Clinton; Geoff Hodgson; Maggie Jones; Jean McCrindle; Nigel Stanley; Paul Thompson; and Martin Soames of Penguin.

Thanks also to Pat, Sam and Jake for their understanding and support, not just while this book was being written but all the time.

Peter Hain
Putney, June 1985

1
POLITICAL STRIKES

Whatever attitude they took on the 1984–5 miners' dispute, in one respect at least the British people seemed in agreement: that it was a 'political strike'. Nearly 73 per cent said as much in an opinion poll in the middle of the dispute. In another poll, even 61 per cent of trade unionists agreed that the miners' leaders were 'politically motivated'. But although papers as politically divergent as *The Times* and *Socialist Worker* employed the same description, 'political strike', there was less agreement about who was responsible for having turned it into one. The media overwhelmingly presented the National Union of Mineworkers as the 'guilty' party. By contrast, Labour Party leaders argued that the government had transformed the dispute into a political strike because it was determined to defeat the miners almost regardless of the social consequences or the financial cost.

During the year-long dispute, 'political strike' became an interm – a catch-all phrase also used pejoratively against other strikers, though with little consistency of meaning. For example, dockers taking industrial action over British Steel's decision to use non-dockers to unload iron ore were castigated in Fleet Street editorials and by the government ministers for embarking on 'an even more blatantly political strike'.[1] Similarly, British Rail management were reported as being 'convinced that there is a strong political motivation in the rail unions' threat' to take industrial action against cuts in services.[2]

In November 1984 a succession of businessmen at the annual conference of the Confederation of British Industry condemned 'irresponsible political strikes led by politically motivated trade union leaders'. Individual dockers, railway workers and miners were repeatedly questioned by radio and TV interviewers, not about *why* they were on strike, but why they were indulging in a 'political strike'. Some rank-and-file members joined in the chorus – during a dispute over pay at Austin Rover, for instance, where one car mechanic said: 'This is a political battle. It's not for any of the people on the shopfloor. The union leaders here just want to cause the company as many problems as possible to show they can be a threat in the future.'[3]

Further, the miners were dubbed 'the enemy within' by the Prime Minister, Margaret Thatcher, as she drew parallels with the Falklands War two years before. *The Times* reported on 17 September 1984 that she was 'treating the dispute in terms of a Napoleonic War'. Earlier an editorial in the paper had said that the miners' leader, Arthur Scargill, had 'declared war on British society', while on the opposite page the Secretary of State for Energy declared: 'This is not a mining dispute. It is a challenge to British democracy, and hence to the British people.'[4]

The impression conveyed was of action uniquely threatening and indeed 'un-British', the very use of the epithet 'political strike' giving it subversive connotations.

· 'UN-BRITISH'? ·

In fact much the same thing had been said of previous miners' strikes this century. The 1912 strike, *The Times* declared, was 'the greatest catastrophe to hit Britain since the Spanish armada',[5] while the Foreign Secretary, Sir Edward Grey, wrote: 'this coal strike is the beginning of a revolution . . . power is passing from the House of Commons to the trade unions'.[6] In the 1919 miners' strike, the Prime Minister, Lloyd George, denounced 'Prussianism in the industrial world' and pledged his government's determination to fight it as they had fought it on the continent of Europe.[7] In the 1925 coal dispute, the Home Secretary asked: 'Is England to be governed by Parliament and the Cabinet or by a handful of trade union leaders?'[8] When the Tories called a general election on a 'Who governs the country?' theme during the 1973–4 miners' strike, the Prime Minister, Edward Heath, accused the miners of wanting 'to get rid of the elected government of the day' and their leaders of propagating 'politically motivated arguments' to pursue their pay claim.[9]

There is a certain timelessness about such language. And miners have not been the only targets. In 1966, for example, Labour's Prime Minister, Harold Wilson, said that the National Union of Seamen's strike was 'a strike against the state, against the community' and was organized by 'a tightly-knit group of politically motivated men'.[10]

Consequently, the portrayal of certain strikes as 'political' is nothing new. Similarly the recurring tendency to present picket-line clashes as 'unprecedented' is mistaken. When Labour leader Neil Kinnock described violence in the 1984–5 miners' strike as 'un-British' and when the electricians' leader, Frank Chapple, said it 'had gone further than anything seen before in Britain',[11] they showed how short memories can be, among even the highest echelons of the labour movement.

The violence in 1984–5 pales into insignificance compared with widespread violence during previous miners' strikes. During the 1867 coal dispute in South Lancashire there was large-scale violence against 'blackleg' labour imported by the pit owners to break the strike, and in one incident in Wigan 5,000 miners marched to every pit still at work, smashing property and driving out imported blacklegs. In 1893, soldiers fired on an unarmed crowd of striking miners at Featherstone in Yorkshire; two were killed and thirteen injured. During the 1910–11 South Wales miners' strike, there was mass picketing against blacklegs. Trains bringing them into the area were attacked, and local blacklegs were physically assaulted, their homes attacked and 'SCAB' daubed on their doors. Later, hundreds of strikers were injured in clashes with the police and one was killed. Violence is a normal part of the history of strikes in Britain.

Yet the British seem almost to have a national obsession with strikes. As one study put it, 'the direct consequences of strikes are no more serious in Britain than in other countries; it is not so much the strikes as the hue and cry they attract which is the real "problem"'.[12] A Royal Commission comparison of fifteen major industrial nations found that the United Kingdom's strike record between 1964 and 1966 was 'about average', and later evidence confirmed this.[13]

·STRIKES IN PERSPECTIVE·

The particular obsession of dominant groups with 'political strikes' springs from an anxiety that their interests are more seriously threatened. Of course all strikes can challenge management prerogatives; and if they do so, they can be seen as challenging capitalist interests and hence the 'national interest'. Therefore *every* strike can in principle be characterized as a 'political strike'. However, some are more political than others and it is necessary to clarify first what is meant by a strike.*

One labour historian defines it as 'a collective protest expressed by withdrawing labour from work', another as 'a temporary stoppage of work by a group of employees in order to express a grievance or enforce a demand'.[14] But because strikes can take so many different forms – ranging from stoppages of a few minutes by a few workers to national walk-outs by whole industries – and because they can have such widely divergent impacts, it is not possible to consider a strike as if it were one specific type of action. Strikes occur in different conditions, they can take many different forms and they can have a variety of effects.[15] Strikes are also just one form of *industrial action*, others being overtime bans, the practice known as 'working to rule', selective action and various other forms of work stoppage or non-cooperation.[16]

Between 1969 and 1974 there is no doubt that union successes in winning higher pay rises through strike activity was one factor in widening the recruitment potential of trade unionism, especially

* In Schedule 13 of the Employment Protection Consolidation Act 1978, the official definition accepted by the courts is: 'the cessation of work by a body of persons employed acting in combination, or a concerted refusal or a refusal under a common understanding of any number of persons employed to continue to work for an employer in consequence of a dispute, done as a means of compelling their employer or any person or body of persons employed, to accept or not accept terms or conditions of or affecting their employment'.

among public-sector workers being squeezed by government incomes policies. In this way strikes can be effective 'recruiting agents', especially in sectors where trade unionism has been weak in the past.[17] Similarly, in the 1890s outbreaks of militancy by unskilled workers, previously not organized, resulted in the formation by them of the 'new unions', which in a real sense 'grew out of strikes'.[18] For women workers, strikes were often their first real contact with trade union organization, for example during the late 1880s and from 1910 to 1914.[19] Excluded from the bulk of trade unions which were male-dominated, women's resistance to exploitation resulted in periodic outbreaks of local and spontaneous militancy which then led some to form or join unions.

Bad conditions have often provoked workers to walk out in anger and only then to consider that their interests might best be protected by forming or joining a union. At other times the existence of a union has pre-dated a strike, so that the causal relationship between the two is complex. Nevertheless, there appears to be a correlation between strike activity and rising levels of trade union membership at particular periods in British history, such as the 1830s, through the industrial turbulence of 1910–14 and 1918–26, and more recently from the late 1960s to 1977.[20]

But it is important to get the phenomenon of strikes into perspective. The Donovan Commission reported in 1968 that strikes in Britain were relatively rare and more recent evidence confirms that this is still true.[21] In 1973 it was estimated that, during the previous decade or so (a period of high strike activity), the average union member had only gone on strike once every twelve years for two and a half days.[22] The tabloid press picture of the British worker as 'strike happy' is very far from accurate. Consequently, disproportionate weight should not be given to the fact that British unions do strike – and that at particular periods, such as from 1910 to 1914, 1918 to 1926, or during the 1970s, they have done so on a large scale.

Compared with other reasons for lost production, strikes are also less significant than might be supposed from the media attention they attract. In 1970, for instance, when striker-days reached a new post-war peak of just over 10 million, sickness and industrial accidents cost 20 million working days.[23] By the mid 1980s official unemployment levels were equivalent to nearly 700 million working days each year whereas strikes were costing under 5 million days on average.

·STRIKES AS VEHICLES FOR POLITICAL CHANGE·

Since unions were first properly established, there have been those who have seen strikes as vehicles for political transformation. For example, in the 1830s there was a demand for what some Chartists termed 'a national holiday', in which all workers would strike for a 'sacred month' to force the government to concede universal suffrage. But it gained very little trade union support.

As socialist ideas began to spread, political activists and trade union militants from time to time advocated intensifying class conflict through strikes so that they became part of a strategy to overthrow capitalism. In 1844 Engels saw strikes as 'the first attempt of the workers to abolish competition', thereby threatening the existing social order.[24] Marx argued that strikes were forms of class struggle which could be generalized through a political party into a national class revolt. And Lenin wrote: 'Every strike reminds the capitalists that it is the workers and not they who are the real masters . . . Every strike reminds the workers that their position is not hopeless, that they are not alone.' As one militant later put it:

The great advantage of a strike is that it increases the enmity between labourers and capitalists, and compels workmen to reflect and investigate the causes of their sufferings . . . The fruit of such reflections would be a violent hostility against the capitalist class; and the new converts would be prepared to second the efforts of emancipation made by labourers in other quarters of England.[25]

However, despite important roles played by Marxists in the trade union movement from time to time, the impact of their ideas in Britain has been relatively small.

Then there were syndicalists who believed that a socialist society could be achieved through a simultaneous strike of all workers, with trade unions, rather than the political parties, being the key agencies. A leading French advocate, Georges Sorel, wrote that syndicalists 'restrict the whole of Socialism to the general strike; they look upon every combination as one that should culminate in this catastrophe; they see in each strike . . . a preparation for the great final upheaval'.[26]

British syndicalists such as Tom Mann did have some influence in 1910 to 1918 and played a role in major strikes, particularly through the powerful shop stewards' movement of the time. Although British syndicalism was fairly localized, for a brief period it gained an audience among some trade union leaders who began to see striking as a way of changing government policies. But there was no real support for the syndicalist strategy of overthrowing the government. The 1926 General Strike, for example, was not syndicalist-inspired: it was effectively a large 'sympathy strike' with the miners, union leaders being at pains to declare that they were not seeking to overthrow the government.

Advocates of strikes as vehicles for political change have not been typical of British trade unionists, who have tended to see strikes as weapons of 'last resort' and have shown a marked reluctance to see their role in anything other than strictly 'industrial' terms.

· UNION AMBIGUITY ·

Indeed, the British trade union consensus has been ambiguous about striking at all, let alone doing so for political reasons. The 'new model' leaders of the mid nineteenth century were generally hostile to strikes. The engineers' leader, William Allen, spoke of the unions' desire to be 'respected and respectful',[27] and in 1867 he told a Royal Commission, 'we believe that strikes are a complete waste of money . . . We endeavour at all times to prevent strikes. It is the very last thing we would think of encouraging.'[28] Even the later, more radical, 'new unions' were by no means always enthusiastic. As Will Thorne, General Secretary of the Gas-workers and General Labourers' Union, told his members in 1893: 'Strikes, through whatever causes, should be avoided wherever possible. Some employers think that many of us live and thrive upon strikes. What can any leader gain through a strike? Look at the worry, anxiety and responsibility they have to contend with during a strike.'[29]

During what may be regarded as the 'classic' strike of British trade union history – the General Strike – the General Council of the Trades Union Congress (TUC) stated in its official strike news bulletins: 'The General Council does not challenge the Constitution. It is not seeking to substitute unconstitutional government. Nor is it desirous of undermining our parliamentary institutions. The sole aim of the Council is to secure for the miners a decent standard of life. The Council is engaged in an industrial dispute. In any settlement, the only issue to be decided will be an industrial issue, not political, not constitutional. There is no constitutional crisis.' A key TUC figure, the railway workers' leader J. H. Thomas, said during the strike: 'In a challenge to the constitution God help us unless the government won.' The unions' willingness to embark upon the General Strike should not be misinterpreted, for the General Council 'reluctantly authorized the struggle. And they drew back from it as soon as they understood its full implications.'[30]

Such views would not be out of place in the trade union world today. On the contrary, they would be echoed by the 'new realism' which dominated the 1983 TUC conference. This was advocated by union leaders on the right who felt it was necessary for the movement to change its strategy. They were concerned about the way in which the Tory election victory the previous June might lead to a further erosion of traditional forms of union power. They did put their finger on a problem ducked by many on the left – the gap between rank-and-file members and union officials, from national leaders down to shop stewards. But they posed the question to union organizations: 'Can you deliver your members to strike?' in such a way as virtually to rule out militancy as a serious option. Their 'new realism' was tantamount to 'new defeatism'.

The 'new realists' did lose credibility for their advocacy of an accommodation with the Tories after the government's uncompromising stand in banning unions at GCHQ in January 1984, and later during its aggressive treatment of the striking miners. But their views remained widespread in the movement. This was confirmed by the unwillingness of most union leaders to advocate solidarity industrial action in support of the miners, and the inability of even those who wanted to do so to 'deliver their members'. Another indication was the 'no-strike' offer made by some civil service union leaders in return for having recognition rights reinstated at GCHQ. 'No-strike' deals were actually agreed by the Electrical, Electronic, Telecommunication and Plumbing Union at mostly foreign-owned electronics factories; by June 1985, the union had signed fourteen such agreements covering over 10,000 employees. During the teachers' pay dispute in 1985, the President of the National Association of Head Teachers suggested that teachers should give up the right to strike in return for new pay review machinery. The same year, David Warburton, a senior TUC figure and national officer of the General, Municipal, Boilermakers and Allied Trades Union described as 'short-sighted and obsolete' the view that strikes were an effective weapon against employers.

Union ambiguity is also due to the fact that stoppages occur within a culture that is fundamentally antagonistic to strikes. The evidence shows that the media consistently present strikes unfavourably, as 'disruptive' and 'unreasonable' actions.[31] Strikes, as one study noted,

take place within a hostile environment ... They are conventionally described as industrially subversive, irresponsible, unfair, against the interests of the community, contrary to the workers' best interests, wasteful of resources, crudely aggressive, inconsistent with democracy and, in any event, unnecessary ... Union officials are particularly prone to the anti-strike environmental influences because they are frequently made out to be responsible for the behaviour of their members ... Once they are committed to a strike call, union officials tend to become defensive, apologetic and concerned about taking avoiding action. When they are actually engaged in a strike, they are frequently motivated by a desire to end it quickly irrespective of the merits of the issue.[32]

·'POLITICAL' AND 'INDUSTRIAL'·

It is usual to argue that explicitly political strikes remain a relatively rare phenomenon in Britain.[33] And, taking a 'political strike' to be one which seeks overtly to change a government policy or some other political decision (in other words using a definition comparable to the Department of Employment's concept of a 'political stoppage'), this argument is hard to deny. However, viewing it on a broader canvas the picture is less clear-cut.

All industrial action is 'political' in the sense that it involves struggle, conflict and power relations. But there are different levels or types of workplace action and politics. Some strikes are manifestly 'political' in the highest sense, such as those called to protest against anti-union laws in the early 1970s, or those organized by health workers in 1975 to press the Labour government to implement its election manifesto commitment to phase out private pay-beds from public hospitals. Even strikes over wages, production levels or job distribution can have a wider political impact. It depends both upon their *objectives* and the way they are *perceived* and *reacted* to.[34]

Consequently there is very little to be gained by attempting to formulate an abstract definition of something called 'a political strike', especially since the traditional trade union division between 'industrial' and 'political' activities has become less clear. Important trade union struggles over wages or conditions increasingly impinge directly on government economic strategy and thereby attain a political dimension.[35]

Intervention in industrial relations by government and agencies of the state – the legal system, the police and the military – has been the *decisive factor* in transforming strikes into major political conflicts, rather than the stance of the unions. Although this has been the case historically, it has been far more so in the post-war era as control of labour and wages has been seen by successive

Labour and Conservative governments to form the lynchpin of their economic policies.

The post-war expansion of the public sector meant that the state was thrust into the front line by virtue of its own position as an employer. With a third of all British employees (and a majority of trade unionists) in central and local government, the public services and nationalized industries, industrial relations in the public sector became more critical. This was especially so as economic crisis started to bite in the 1960s and the pressure followed to control and then reduce public expenditure. As has been pointed out:

The problem, therefore, is to distinguish between strikes which constitute a political challenge and strikes which are purely industrial protests by government workers ... The difficulty arises because strikes involving the government never appear at the outset as uncomplicated industrial issues, even if they are ... the public is likely to get an impression that the issue is political and it will place itself firmly on the side of the government.[36]

The problem identified here is accentuated by developments from the 1970s onwards:

Government ministers, the courts and various statutory agencies have become far more actively and overtly implicated in the field of labour relations than ever before in peacetime. The distinction between 'industrial' and 'political' issues, always artificial and misleading, has in the process become increasingly unconvincing; and strikers themselves have on occasion viewed their actions in a far more directly 'political' light than in the past.[37]

· STALEMATE ·

This period was also characterized by high levels of public expenditure and welfare provision, stronger state powers and greater centralization – all part of a social democratic consensus, in turn based on what some socialist writers have described as a 'stalemate' between capital and labour.[38] Trade unions, through their defensive strength, managed to protect the living standards and working practices of their members. But decisions over production and investment remained the prerogative of capital. The resulting stalemate prevented a resolution of Britain's growing economic crisis.

Labour and Tory administrations shared a common commitment to the social democratic consensus. As will be shown, however, Labour's much closer relationship with the unions meant that its leaders treated strikers rather differently from the way in which the Tories treated them. On the one hand, Labour Cabinets were more able to win voluntary union agreement for far-reaching restrictions on strike action in moments of crisis: examples include the maintenance of Second World War strike prohibitions for six years into peacetime, and the three years of successful pay restraint from 1975 to 1978. On the other hand, pressure from the unions forced the Wilson Cabinet to back off from its 1969 proposals, contained in *In Place of Strife*, to introduce new legal curbs on strikers; whereas two years later the Tory government of Edward Heath brought in the Industrial Relations Act containing similar, though even tougher, curbs.

These events were occurring under the shadow of a growing economic crisis. The period since the Second World War can be divided in two: the boom between 1950 and 1973, and the recession which followed the oil crisis of 1973–4. Even during the boom years, Britain's performance was 40 per cent below the average growth rate for industrial countries and 50 per cent below in 1973–9.[39] This was superimposed on a long-term decline in the British economy relative to its industrial competitors since the late nineteenth century. Since 1880, the rate of growth of Britain's national income has often been less than half that of its main competitors, and so has its growth rate in productivity. For a long time, people in Britain were cushioned from the reality of this decline by the country's large share of world trade and its ability to expand as its markets grew within that share. But this became increasingly difficult as Britain's share of world trade in manufactures fell from about 40 per cent in 1880 to under 7 per cent in the 1980s.[40]

This economic climate had an accelerating impact on British politics and industrial relations as labour and capital struggled to compete for increasingly scarce resources. As the post-war political consensus started to crack after the oil crisis of 1973–4, differences became clearer. When Labour was re-elected in 1974 it brought in legislation giving workers greater protection than ever before, much to the dismay of the right, which was becoming increasingly assertive in the Conservative Party, in the judiciary and in the police. After 1979 the Thatcherites tried to abandon the previous consensus and replace it with a new rightist one. This involved breaking from the stalemate by undermining working-class strength through creating a permanent pool of unemployed, and through a systematic assault on union rights and specifically on strikers.

·THE NEW STATE·

Consequently, while it is legitimate to point to the similarities which have characterized both parties in government, it is a mistake to underestimate the evident differences. For example, although the Callaghan government did not attempt to prevent the police and the judiciary from breaking the Grunwick strike in 1977, it is inconceivable that a Labour government would have let the full weight of state power be deployed against the miners as the Conservatives did in 1984–5 – if only because there would have been a revolt within the party and the whole trade union movement.

Therefore when we speak of 'the state' it is important to recognize that this does not imply an entity with a fixed policy stance. The British state is a more subtle animal. While broadly reflecting the aims of those interests dominant in capitalist society, it exercises a mixture of 'reform' and 'repression' in relation to strikes and unions.[41] Sometimes concessions are won by strikers, sometimes their rights are attacked. The precise outcome at any one time is determined by the economic situation, the balance of class forces, the strength and ideology of the labour movement, and which party is in office.

Nor is the state monolithic. It may be better considered as a 'state system', consisting of the government, the administration, Parliament, the military, police, judicial structure and local authorities, with the people who occupy leading positions in each institution wielding effective power and constituting what may be described as a 'state elite'.[42] These various agencies have traditionally acted with a certain autonomy. But in the 'new state' their role has been evolving in a way which, though generally in line with the interests of private capital, more and more reflects *their own* bureaucratic and political objectives.

These are not necessarily identical to the objectives of the government of the day. Although it is widely believed that the police, the courts and the armed forces are 'independent of politics', the experience of modern strikes shows rather that they are becoming independent from channels of democratic accountability. An accelerating trend in the 1970s and 1980s, this was only brought into greater harmony with the objectives of the government when Mrs Thatcher was elected in 1979. Had Labour remained in power, it could well have found itself drawn towards conflict with the judiciary, the police and elements in the armed forces who had become increasingly hostile to the labour movement.

· STATE 'NEUTRALITY' ·

The government and these agencies often invoke the 'national interest' to justify their intervention in strikes, denying that they are strike-breaking as such and claiming a mandate on behalf of the 'whole nation'. The double-edged use of the term 'national interest' was evident in the spectacle of Thatcherite ministers applauding the opposition Solidarity movement in Poland for taking forms of strike action in the early 1980s which their own new laws had made illegal in Britain. Ironically, the Polish regime's attack on Solidarity was defended in the familiar language of *its* particular 'national interest'. The usual rebuttal to such a comparison involves the proposition that strikes in 'undemocratic' countries are justifiable acts of resistance. But more often than not, double standards tend to cloud the real issues. For example, few Conservatives can be found backing strikes by black workers in South Africa, and some on the left are hostile to strikes within the Soviet bloc.[43]

Underlying public debate in Britain is the widely-held belief that the state in Britain is 'neutral' and will therefore pursue the 'national interest' rather than a politically partisan one during industrial conflict; its institutions – the government of the day, judiciary, police, military and civil servants – will act in the interests of the 'whole country'.

However, as will be confirmed in later chapters, this popular belief does not stand close scrutiny. In practice, defending the 'national interest' has involved adopting a strike-breaking role.[44] As one study of strikes in Britain shows,

The idea that the state is 'above sectional conflicts' and plays a 'neutral' role in industrial relations is therefore mistaken; but it is of great ideological importance. When the government intervenes in a dispute, on the side of the employer, any attempt by the union concerned to stand firm can be presented as 'undemocratic' and 'a challenge to the constitution'. Where trade unionists themselves regard the state as 'neutral', their resolve is likely to crumble before such an ideological offensive.[45]

State 'neutrality' is associated with the denial of conflict and class division as central to the way a capitalist society such as Britain's operates. On this view, the *structure* of industry is seen as essentially harmonious and therefore conflict must be the result of 'ignorance or subversion'.[46]

Popular perception of the issues at stake is often in terms of the *right* of 'government to govern' and of 'management to manage': strikes are seen as threatening this 'right' and therefore challenging the 'natural order of things'. But underpinning this popular characterization are the twin notions of state neutrality and denial of class conflict. These play a key role in determining whether a strike is *seen* as 'political' or not: if they are popularly accepted, then various parts of the state including the government will be viewed almost as impartial referees, representing an over-arching national consensus. And any challenge by trade unions to that consensus will be seen as disruptive and probably 'politically motivated' as well. In contrast, unless they are especially obdurate or incompetent the position of employers and mangement will generally be viewed as *part* of the consensus. This is because capitalist interests and the 'national interest' are assumed to be identical.[47]

But a modern capitalist society like Britain's has a 'dominant class' and a 'subordinate class', the division being determined mainly by the persistent division of ownership.[48] And when this fundamental truth is accepted, it follows that in a conflict of interest between these classes the state cannot remain 'neutral': by the way that the government, the police or other state agencies act, they will be forced to take sides in class conflicts.

But the state's role is not a simplistic one of outright opposition to workers. Since they have been unable to *resolve* the fundamental conflict in a capitalist society between workers and employers, between labour and capital, governments have also sought to *manage* it.[49] This has involved containing pressure and regulating industrial conflict by a dual strategy. On the one hand, efforts are made to curb strikes or to minimize their effects; on the other, attempts are made to 'co-opt' unions in order to reduce their disruptive potential.

A picture emerges, therefore, of strikes operating within a deeply political environment. Strikers are *limited* by legal and political constraints; they are *regulated* by employer and government intervention; and they are *controlled* by state agencies. They are also *affected* by a British union ideology which, though willing to sanction strikes, has been historically inhibited about militancy, especially that which can result in overt political conflict. In a society where workers have to sell their labour, strike action is the ultimate way for workers to exert their veto and therefore their power. But only on very rare occasions have British workers *initiated* industrial action for overtly political reasons. It is principally the response of employers and the state which has determined whether strikes become 'political' in the sense of threatening the power of dominant interests.

LIMITS ON 'THE RIGHT TO STRIKE'

In 1978, the head of the Appeal Court, Lord Denning, criticized those who saw 'the right to strike' as a fundamental right of humankind. In a lecture at Birmingham University, he said: 'I would declare at once that there is no such right known to the law, not at any rate when it is used so as to inflict harm on innocent bystanders, or disrupt essential services or to bring the country to a halt. So far as the law is concerned, those who do such things are exercising not a right but a great power, the power to strike.' [1]

In the absence of a written constitution or a Bill of Rights, it is difficult to claim that *any* human rights as such exist under British law. British constitutional practice relies not simply on specific parliamentary laws, but on historic precedents accumulated since feudal times which are interpreted by judges to make up the common law; it also includes the exercise of the royal prerogative by ministers who can act on behalf of the monarch and issue what are termed 'orders-in-council'. Britains 'unwritten constitution', as it is called, produces a constitutional fuzziness, especially in areas of social conflict. On the whole, this has suited the dominant class in Britain, although it was significant that Lord Hailsham, Conservative Lord Chancellor from 1970 to 1974 (and also from 1979), called for a written constitution in 1976, because he felt that the constitution was 'wearing out' due partly to the power enjoyed by trade unions at that time. [2]

Effectively, there are no constitutional limits to government action to break strikes. As one study of the use of the armed forces in strikes put it, 'constitutional rules reflect what politicians can get away with'.[3] In the event of a strike leading to an 'emergency', the government can also rely on constitutional practice stating that, 'In times of grave emergency, normal constitutional principles may have to give way to the overriding need to deal with the emergency.'[4] All this gives senior civil servants, judges, the police and Cabinet ministers wide scope for *discretion* in their handling of strikes.

Furthermore, claims that some sort of absolute right to strike exists on the one hand, or can be undermined on the other, are based on a fundamental misunderstanding. The fact is that workers through a process of class struggle have only won *concessions* from the state as part of settlements at particular points in British history. Typically, these concessions result from political pressure and equally, therefore, they are vulnerable to being withdrawn under political pressure from the opposite direction.

Certainly, claims about a specific right to strike are misplaced: there is no such positive right. Since 1871, unions have only enjoyed 'negative' rights: they have simply been granted immunities from action through the courts to prevent certain strikes:

the distinctive feature of the British experience . . . is that for most of our modern industrial history trade union independence has been brought about by carving areas of immunity away from the common law. It is not so much a question of saying 'you have a right to form a union or to go on strike' as, rather, saying 'if you do these things you will not be taken to court for doing them'.[5]

From the earliest days of trade unionism the immunities won for strikers have been repeatedly attacked by judges and by hostile governments. Recently, the 1980 and 1982 Employment Acts and the 1984 Trade Union Act have imposed a series of constraints legalizing strikes under very narrowly defined circumstances. To avoid court action, a strike must be strictly limited to a 'trade dispute' with the employer; it must not involve large-scale or 'secondary' picketing; and it must have been authorized by an individual membership ballot which itself meets stringent requirements.

·WORKERS SPECIFICALLY PREVENTED FROM STRIKING·

Some workers are denied even such limited rights to strike. The best-known examples are the police and the armed forces. Aliens (i.e. workers who are not British citizens) commit a criminal offence if they 'promote industrial unrest', unless they have worked in the industry for at least two years. Merchant seafarers are guilty of a criminal offence if they disobey orders at sea or take industrial action to stop a ship sailing. Under the 1970 Merchant Shipping Act they can go on strike if their ship is safely berthed in a British port – but then only if they have given forty-eight hours' notice of an intention to terminate their contracts. Apprenticeship terms sometimes bar or restrict strike action which can be undertaken by adult workers in the same trade, and various professional and vocational bodies are prevented under their own rules or codes of conduct from striking. Within the nursing profession, the General Nursing Council's decree that to strike was inconsistent with a nurse's duties was deliberately aimed at promoting nurses' representation through 'professional bodies' rather than bona fide trade unions. There has also been growing pressure to impose extra restrictions upon workers in essential services.

In practice, however, those rights which do exist are determined more by *political* than by legal criteria. Even the most theoretically legal strike is still vulnerable to a hostile court action. Transparently illegal strikes can go unchallenged if court action is considered to be either ineffectual or counter-productive. As one guide to rights at work shows: 'The extent to which employers launch legal offensives depends on their financial strength, the availability of substitute labour, the political climate, public feeling and the solidarity of strikers and their supporters.'[6]

·BANS IN THE FIRST WORLD WAR·

The most clear-cut government prohibitions have appeared in wartime, and these are interesting not least because they shed further light on the political circumstances in which strike bans can be implemented.

Shortly after the First World War started in August 1914, the TUC issued a statement jointly with the Labour Party calling for the immediate termination of all strikes and urging 'amicable settlements' to disputes. But this conciliatory spirit was soon undermined. The government wanted to step up production for the war effort and increasingly challenged protective industrial practices built up by unions after years of struggle.

Workers' hostility to ministers with whom they had been locked in battle during turbulent strikes only just before the war resurfaced, despite the desire of union leaders to cooperate with the government. Much rank-and-file resistance was channelled through the powerful shop stewards' movement of that period, its strength being shown first in a strike by 8,000 engineers on Clydeside in February 1915 over a wages grievance. It lasted three weeks and, though denounced by their union's national leadership, the workers made some gains from an arbitration hearing established after a government ultimatum.

Meanwhile the government had appointed a committee to determine how to achieve better industrial output and, four days after the Clyde strike had ended, it issued its first report on 'Avoidance of Stoppages of Work', arguing:

Whatever may be the rights of the parties in normal times, and whatever may be the methods considered necessary for the maintenance and enforcement of those rights, we think there can be no justification whatever for a resort to strikes or lock-outs under present conditions, when the resulting cessation of work would prevent the production of ships, guns, equipment, stores, or other commodities required by the Government for the purposes of War.[7]

Although the report justified restrictions on strikes specifically affecting *war production*, it provided an opening for restrictions across the board, because it could be argued that almost all industrial output assisted the successful prosecution of the war effort. Subsequently, the report's thinking was put into effect in a fresh agreement signed with major unions.

But there was criticism from the trade unions when the government moved to take statutory powers to tackle the escalating problem of unofficial strikes (i.e. strikes not authorized by union executives and usually locally inspired). A Bill was introduced into Parliament enforcing compulsory arbitration and making strikes illegal. Miners' leaders argued that it would 'seriously interfere with the individual rights of trade unionists, and with the fundamental principles of trade unionism itself'. The Miners' Federation president, Robert Smillie, said:

There is one clause in the Bill which makes it a criminal offence to incite workers to strike . . . if that clause goes through, and the miners are included in this Act, there will not be sufficient prisons in the country for the accommodation of the miners' leaders who will incite to strike . . . The miners are willing to continue giving full service to the country during the present crisis, but they are not prepared to come under the coercion . . . in this Bill.[8]

Nevertheless, the government proceeded to implement the 1915 Munitions of War Act. It defined munitions work very widely indeed to cover virtually all manufacturing production and repair, and made it compulsory for disputes to be referred to the minister for binding arbitration; unless there was a delay by the minister in processing this, it would be illegal for workers to strike.

But when 200,000 South Wales miners went on strike in July 1915, the government did not enforce the Act as it certainly could have done. Instead, it decided that prosecuting such a formidable force would be counter-productive and conceded a settlement on the miners' terms a week into the strike: 'the first indication of the fact that if a large enough number of workers in a vital industry ignored anti-strike legislation there was nothing the government could do about it except behave as if no such legislation existed. Experience in the Second World War supported this view.'[9]

The 1915 Munitions of War Act even proved ineffective against smaller groups of strikers. Action against them was taken under military regulations. For instance, in March 1916, six members of the Clyde workers' committee were 'deported' from the Clyde to other parts of the country. They had helped organize strikes by engineers against rent increases and against government seizure of their militant paper, *The Worker*. Another strike against the government occurred in 1917, when engineering workers protested at the abrogation of agreements with unions exempting skilled workers from being conscripted into the army; the men won some concessions after a three-week strike, but eight of their leaders were arrested under Defence of the Realm regulations. Thus it became clear that strike bans linked to compulsory arbitration could not be enforced on large bodies of strikers, especially if they had local community support.*

·BANS IN THE SECOND WORLD WAR·

The Munitions Act was repealed in 1918. But, after Churchill had formed his coalition government during the Second World War in May 1940, similar bars on strikes in favour of arbitration were introduced with the agreement of trade union leaders under a Defence Regulation known as Order 1305. This was extended in 1944 to make it an offence to incite workers in *essential services* to strike. Order 1305 was not generally used against strikers, however, the government seeing it more as a declaration of intent to which the unions were party, but it acted as a threat to dissuade workers from striking.

The only major case of strikers being prosecuted was when 1,600 miners at the Betteshanger colliery in Kent went on strike for three weeks in January 1942 after a dispute with management over compensation for working on difficult coal faces. 1,050 coal-face workers were prosecuted and although most were given small fines, three local union branch officers were imprisoned. This provoked a real dilemma for the authorities. There were negotiations in prison until finally an agreement was signed which effectively conceded the miners' claim. But they still refused to go back to work until their officials were released. The inter-

* In both World Wars only a small proportion of strikers were prosecuted for offences they had committed under such laws.[10]

vention of the Home Secretary was required to achieve this after they had served just eleven days of sentences of up to two months. In addition, only nine of a total of over 1,000 men paid their fines. The rest never did so, the government being forced to advise local justices not to enforce warrants committing them all to prison because it recognized that this could provoke a bigger strike.

Nevertheless, Order 1305 remained in force after the end of the war until it was eventually withdrawn in 1951. This extension into peacetime of stringent restrictions developed under wartime conditions shows how political expediency can undermine the ability of workers to strike.

·THE ARMED FORCES·

No distinction between times of war and peace is made for members of the armed forces. They are not allowed to be represented by a trade union with any negotiating rights. Although membership of a union on an individual basis is legal, in practice only two groups join: either those about to leave the force for jobs which require union membership, or bandsmen who sometimes become members of the Musicians' Union in order to perform off-duty. Anybody attempting to organize the military into a union, or inciting industrial action, is committing a criminal offence (and members of the forces cannot strike because to do so would leave them in breach of their duty to obey a higher command).

In July 1969, Roy Hattersley, then Labour Defence Minister, told the Transport and General Workers' Union that trade unionism in the armed forces would be 'unacceptable', because it would 'imply the recognition of the union principles of collective bargaining and the right to withdraw labour . . . A serviceman who withdrew his labour could be charged with failure to obey a lawful command. A group of men who took strike action might be charged with mutiny.'[11]

In addition, the armed forces are excluded from employment

protection and health and safety legislation, and there are no effective channels for their members to pursue grievances, either individually or collectively: 'They are entirely at the whim and mercy of their officers with no practical means of redressing abuses.'[12]

Not surprisingly, therefore, outbursts of unrest have occurred from time to time, in which unionization has been raised as an issue. As recently as 1977–8, the work carried out by soldiers in the fire brigades strike focused attention on their own pay which compared unfavourably with fire brigades workers. There was some discussion in the media and in Parliament about the need for members of the forces to have their own negotiating body. At one point the Defence Minister, Fred Mulley, said he had no objection to the armed forces, 'if they are so minded', seeking such representation – though he subsequently made it clear that he personally did not favour trade unions in the forces.[13]

There have been other instances of elements in the armed forces veering towards the labour movement. During the late 1830s and early 1840s, army leaders were very concerned about evidence of Chartist sympathies among the troops. During the early 1900s, there were some rebellions in the ranks over pay and poor conditions. After the Russian revolution, some British soldiers attempted to form 'Councils of Workers and Soldiers', and in 1917, 1918 and 1919 there were a number of military strikes and mutinies. There were some demands for wider unionization and even for affiliation to the TUC. A small Soldiers', Sailors', and Airmen's Union was formed in 1919, provoking accusations from the Metropolitan Police Special Branch that the union had 'wholeheartedly accepted the Soviet idea and was in touch with the more revolutionary members of the London Trades Council . . .'.[14] During the Second World War there was widespread support in the ranks for radical ideas and when it ended a number of strikes occurred over grievances.

Attempts to dissuade soldiers from intervening in strikes have been firmly dealt with. For example, in 1912 a number of syndicalists were arrested during a period of intense industrial unrest. In their newspaper, *The Syndicalist*, they had published an 'Open

Letter to British Soldiers' urging them not to shoot strikers if ordered to do so, and their leading activists, including Tom Mann, were prosecuted and jailed under the Incitement to Mutiny Act 1797. In July 1924, John Campbell, the acting editor of the Communist Party newspaper, *Workers' Weekly*, published an article encouraging soldiers to align themselves with the working classes of the world: 'let it be known that neither in the class war nor in a military war, will you turn your guns on your fellow workers', it said. He was eventually prosecuted with other leading communists, and imprisoned for a year on a conspiracy charge linking sedition and incitement to mutiny. In 1933, four South Wales miners (also members of the Communist Party) were prosecuted for inciting soldiers to defect. Then in 1934 the government brought in the Incitement to Disaffection Act, strengthening its powers to deal with such agitation.

More recently, however, the main concern of military leaders has been to avoid their members being influenced by dissident forces and ideas in the wider community. But this presents a problem, because two-thirds of the army is based in the United Kingdom and daily life brings many soldiers into contact with the issues of controversy in the civilian population. As has also been pointed out: 'The British army is a volunteer army and thus is necessarily involved in attracting its members from society and returning them to that society. It is thus bound to be engaged in a process of interaction with that wider society and its competition for labour resources.'[15]

Certainly, soldiers are actively discouraged from having sympathies or connections with any groups on the left.[16] In 1984 the government introduced amendments to the Queen's Regulations, making it an offence for members of the armed forces to take an active part, not only in political parties, as had previously been the case, but also in pressure groups such as the Campaign for Nuclear Disarmament, the environmental group Greenpeace and Animal Aid.

Efforts are also made to dissuade soldiers from any attraction they might have to the labour movement. A former soldier who was put in a military prison for refusing to participate in breaking the 1975 Glasgow refuse collectors' strike explained: 'There is a constant barrage of propaganda, through film shows and officers' talks about greedy workers, communists and trade unions having too much power.'[17] Clearly, even stringent legal bars on trade unionism and strike action in the armed forces are not sufficient: they need buttressing with an ideological attack as well.

The argument that members of the forces cannot enjoy union or strike rights without jeopardizing the nation's security is widely accepted. But in Germany, for example, trade union membership is permitted, and about 100,000 soldiers are members of the Public Services and Transport Workers Union which negotiates on their behalf with the military authorities.[18] And, while a strong case can be made for denying strike rights during wartime, it is doubtful whether a strike by soldiers in peacetime would jeopardize daily life as much as a strike by civilians in an essential service.

· THE POLICE ·

Police officers are prohibited from joining a bona fide union under the 1964 Police Act, Section 53 of which also makes it illegal to induce them to strike, to withhold any other form of service or to commit a breach of discipline.

However, these restrictions have not always applied. There were police strikes in London in 1872 and 1890 for higher pay and better conditions, and rank-and-file police officers were among the first public servants to form their own union. The emergence of an independent Police Union during the First World War had been preceded by other initiatives to promote police unionism, most of these being as much a reaction to the tyrannical powers of senior officers as to discontent over living standards.[19] Grievances built up until the police were driven to their first national strike in August 1918. It lasted just two days, the government being forced to make substantial concessions to achieve a settlement, the terms of which were a major victory for the Police Union.

Nevertheless, its claims for official recognition were resisted.

Ministers were anxious about what they saw as the political threat contained in the 1918 strike. They felt that it might escalate into a general strike, the Prime Minister, Lloyd George, believing that the country had then been 'nearer to Bolshevism . . . than at any time since'.[20] The government was especially worried about the close links which existed between the Police Union and the labour movement at the time. The union was even affiliated at one stage to the Labour Party, the TUC and many local trades councils.

As a result the Government introduced a Bill in Parliament to outlaw police trade unionism and strikes. A new Metropolitan Commissioner of Police, General Sir Nevil Macready, was appointed with a brief to oppose the Police Union. He had a reputation as a strike-breaker, having commanded troops at Tonypandy in 1910. And the union's strike in 1919 to protest at the new legislation was forcefully put down. Troops were brought in and 2,364 strikers dismissed immediately, never to be reinstated. Shortly afterwards, the 1919 Police Act came into effect, making illegal both police membership of a trade union and attempts to induce officers to strike or disobey orders.

A new Police Federation was formed under the Act expressly as a substitute for the now banned Police Union. The Federation could not act as a fully-fledged trade union. Besides being denied the ability to take industrial action, it had no proper negotiating rights. The government's determination to prevent the police undertaking political activities was also evident in the Act's bar on the Federation having any links with outside bodies. In 1932, Wal Hannington, leader of the National Unemployed Workers' Movement, was arrested and later convicted under the Act. In a speech to a rally of 150,000 in Trafalgar Square, he said: 'We ask the police to understand that what we are marching for is in their interests as well as the interests of the unemployed . . . Let the working class in uniform and out of uniform stand together.'[21]

Unlike the position in other liberal-democratic countries,* opposition to the very notion of police trade unionism or strikes is

---

* Police trade unionism is quite legitimate in France, West Germany and Scandinavia, for example, and there have also been periodic police strikes in the United States of America.

now so deeply ingrained in British culture that it is easy to forget the real issues at stake. In truth, strikes by members of the fire brigades, by ambulance crews, electricity supply workers, water workers, or doctors could have even more serious consequences for life and property than police strikes. As one study points out:

Nonetheless, no other civilian occupation has been subject to so complete an outlawing of union activity. It seems that the opposition to police unionism derives more from a military model of the appropriate form of police organization than concern about public safety.[22]

The motivation behind the restrictions was specifically to deny the police the opportunity to exert *political* power in alliance with the labour movement, and to ensure that the force was capable of taking over from the military as the state's main strike-breaking agency. Police militancy subsided partly because of the curbs contained in the 1919 Act and partly because of new pay links giving them above-average rises.

However, after the Second World War, when pay grievances and recruitment problems had provoked a fresh crisis, a Home Office committee under Lord Oaksey recommended that the Police Federation be given new bargaining rights. The *quid pro quo* for this was the committee's reaffirmation of the case against trade union and strike rights for workers engaged in maintaining law and order.

There was relative stability until fresh unrest broke out in the 1970s. The real value of police pay was being eroded by high inflation, and police officers also became more militant as a result of the front-line political role they were increasingly required to perform in major political conflicts, whether these were strikes or public protests. Motions demanding the right to strike were debated at the 1970 and 1975 Police Federation annual conferences and, although they were rejected, the fact that the issue was raised at all was significant. In 1976, rank-and-file officers demanded the right to strike at a series of meetings throughout the country, their militant mood persisting in the face of opposition from Federation leaders. Then in May 1977, during a bitter battle with the Labour government over pay, the Federation's annual conference voted overwhelmingly for the right to strike. But such radicalism was born out of 'economic' grievances; over 'non-economic' grievances, the Federation remained deeply conservative, as evidenced by the same conference's rejection of affiliation to the TUC and the more openly right-wing stance adopted on social policies.[23]

This militancy subsided after an official committee under Lord Edmund Davies had recommended a new formula giving the police above-average pay rises each year. From 1979 onwards the Thatcher government ensured that they were treated more favourably than any other major group of public-sector workers, though by May 1985 there were renewed signs of discontent over pay, pensions and allowances when the Conservative Home Secretary, Leon Brittan, was barracked by delegates at the Federation's annual conference.

Preferential treatment on pay was justified in terms of the position of the police as guardians of public order. But it can also be interpreted as being in exchange for accepting a ban on strike action. Fire brigades workers are comparable with the police in the public safety role they perform, and they were also granted a preferential pay formula on the understanding that it would avoid repetition of a strike like their first-ever national one in 1977–8. This highlighted the drift in government thinking towards 'no-strike' agreements in essential services.

·ESSENTIAL SERVICES·

During the nineteenth century governments gradually accepted that one of their functions was to provide essential services, and they were anxious to protect these from industrial disruption. Under Section 4 of the Conspiracy and Protection of Property Act 1875 it was made illegal for gas or water workers to deprive people of their supply by going on strike, and this restriction was later extended to electricity workers under Section 31 of the Electricity (Supply) Act 1919. In September 1919, the National Union of Manufacturers had attempted to persuade the government to extend the provisions of the Police Act of that year. At a meeting, it resolved:

In order to make good government and administration of this country more secure, the government be requested to extend the provisions of the Police Act to all nationalized public services, including the telegraph, telephone, postal and excise services, together with the mines and railways if and when nationalized . . .[24]

This move was unsuccessful, but similar arguments resurfaced in the 1970s and 1980s, following the growth of industrial action in the public sector. Between 1960 and 1979, 47 per cent of the total days lost through strikes, involving 200,000 or more working days, were in the public sector.[25] Although under Schedule IX of the 1971 Industrial Relations Act the ban imposed on electricity, gas and water workers had been lifted, this was more in the way of a tidying-up measure than any sudden affirmation of the right to strike of these key workers. The understanding between government, management and unions that there would be no strikes in the nuclear power industry illustrates the way in which the vulnerability of modern technological and industrial processes may be used to deprive workers of strike rights. Similar environmental, safety or national security reasons could be advanced to impose restrictions upon workers in defence, aerospace, power generation, nuclear fuels and research, petro-chemicals or off-shore oil installations.

By the late 1970s, leading Conservative Party members were advocating strike bans on workers in essential services. The proposal was canvassed in a consultative Green Paper issued by the Thatcher government in 1981. However, it pointed to the difficulties of enforcing the law if strikes by key groups of workers were made illegal and argued that voluntary 'no-strike' agreements might be preferable, while still leaving open the possibility of new legislation.[26] In 1985 the Tory Secretary of State for Employment, Tom King, said he was considering a strike ban in essential services and he won the public support of the leader of the Social Democratic Party, David Owen.

·POSTAL AND
TELECOMMUNICATIONS WORKERS·

The vulnerability of workers in essential services to having their ability to strike undermined was revealed in 1976–7. Some 200,000 members of the Union of Post Office Workers (UPW)* had always assumed that they did have the right to strike. Indeed they had exercised it during a one-day national stoppage in 1964 and again during the seven-week national strike over pay in 1971. The union also took 'secondary action' by boycotting mail and telephone operator calls to France for one week in 1973 in protest against French nuclear tests in the Pacific. There were no legal repercussions on any of those occasions, nor during numerous work-to-rules, overtime bans and local stoppages which occurred in the Post Office. In 1921 the union had taken part in a trade union boycott of Hungary in protest against the 'white terror' that followed the overthrow of the left-wing government there; but the Postmaster-General did not suggest that the union's ban on mail to Hungary was illegal.[27]

It was only in November 1976 when the UPW boycotted mail to Grunwick that doubt arose as to whether postal workers could withdraw their labour legally. Attempting to stop the boycott, the ultra-right-wing National Association for Freedom (NAFF) sought an injunction on the grounds that the union was committing a criminal offence by being in breach of the 1953 Post Office Act. However, in the belief that the Grunwick dispute would go to arbitration, the UPW suspended its action. The legal issue was not tested until three months later, in January 1977, when NAFF asked the Attorney-General for an injunction against the UPW over its plan for a one-week boycott of mail and telecommunications to South Africa as part of an international trade union protest against apartheid.

The Attorney-General refused, but NAFF obtained the backing of the Appeal Court, presided over by Lord Denning. The issue became clouded by a celebrated clash between Lord

* Re-named the Union of Communication Workers when British Telecom was split off from the old Post Office in 1981.

Denning and the Attorney-General, Sam Silkin, over their respective powers and duties – a conflict eventually resolved in Mr Silkin's favour by the House of Lords in July 1977.

However, posts and telecommunications workers were still saddled with a major new problem resulting from these proceedings and those over the Grunwick case. The judges in the Appeal Court and the Lords had reinterpreted historic sections of Post Office legislation, making it a criminal offence to interfere with mail or telecommunications, and applied these to modern forms of industrial action. The relevant clauses in the 1953 Post Office Act can be traced back to 1710, when the General Post Office was established during the reign of Queen Anne. At that time the mail service was regularly attacked by footpads and highwaymen, and it was made an offence wilfully to detain or delay any postal letter or packet. The same wording, 'wilfully detains or delays', was maintained in later legislation and is found in Section 58 of the 1953 Act and Section 45 of the 1863 Telegraph Act.

These sections were never intended to apply to trade unionists. They were devised to stop criminal interference with communications from inside or outside the services. A trade union official planning industrial action is plainly different from a robber pilfering the mails or a company bribing a postman to delay an urgent communication to a rival. Yet Lord Denning argued in his judgment, 'Many statutes are not at all clear but those are clear beyond doubt', while Lord Justice Ormrod stated that the unions were planning 'the plainest breach of the criminal law which it is possible to imagine'.

The judiciary chose to interpret the law in a particular way, with Lord Denning giving an almost metaphysical authority to this choice when he reaffirmed the classic view of the 'common-law' role of judges:

Whenever a new situation arises which has not been considered before, the Judges have to say what the law is. In doing so, we do not change the law. We declare it. We consider it on principle: and then pronounce upon it. As the old writers quaintly put it, the law lies 'in the breast of the Judges'.

The decisions of the Appeal Court and House of Lords meant that all forms of industrial action by postal or telecommunications workers were now potentially illegal, including stoppages, work-to-rules, overtime bans and a refusal to cross a picket line in a trade dispute, with serious doubt being thrown over a complete close-down of the services because of an all-out strike.[28] In effect, they were political judgments. The courts gave a political interpretation which altered the law without parliamentary approval, leaving postal and telecommunications workers suddenly in an anomalous position more akin to that of police officers than electricians.

· CIVIL SERVANTS ·

Civil servants are another group placed in a sensitive position over strikes. Recruitment to the civil service was only made on a basis of open competition from 1870, and it was not until some years later that the effects of the old system of patronage had declined. Workers in the Post Office (a civil service department until 1969) formed the vast majority of civil servants then and they were the first to establish unions. Despite strong opposition from the Postmaster-General, postal unions were formed from the early 1880s. In the 1890s, the first steps were taken to set up associations in other parts of the service. But it took the radicalizing effect of the First World War both to intensify support for unionism among civil servants and to force the government to recognize their right to bargain; from 1919 proper negotiations were conducted through the Whitley system.

The civil service unions showed no real interest in striking, and during the 1926 General Strike the Civil Service Clerical Association (CSCA) confined its solidarity with fellow trade unionists to donations and a voluntary levy of members. Even this proved controversial and there was dissent within the union. The government was concerned at the threat of new links between its own employees and the labour movement, and decided to impose firm restrictions on the rights of civil service unions. In May 1927, the Attorney-General told Parliament:

The situation [in the General Strike] was that organizations of civil servants, whose undivided allegiance the state has a right to claim, were, in fact, through their officials, actively engaged in fomenting a rebellion against the state. That, in the judgment of the government, is an intolerable situation in which to find the established civil servant.[29]

Under the 1927 Trade Disputes and Trade Unions Act it was made illegal for civil service unions to remain affiliated to the TUC or the Labour Party (as both the CSCA and UPW had been). This ruling remained until Labour repealed these provisions in 1946, and meanwhile the internal bargaining procedures within the civil service had been strengthened. However, Labour's 1946 Trade Disputes and Trade Unions Act should not be interpreted as affirming a right of civil servants to strike. Labour's Attorney-General made it clear in Parliament that nothing the government was doing made it 'more legal' for civil servants to strike than it had been in 1927: 'this government, like any government as an employer, would feel perfectly free to take any disciplinary action that any strike situation that might develop demanded'.[30]

The first time the CSCA decided to take limited industrial action was in 1962; significantly, this unusual step was provoked by government pay restraint. The union's newspaper argued in an editorial that civil servants were effectively being taken advantage of by their unwillingness to strike: 'It is grossly unfair. Civil Service pay is rigorously frozen. Pay increases are gained by other workers whose unions have used or threatened to use the strike weapon.'[31]

As pay controls, especially in the public sector, became more central to the policy of successive governments, so civil service unions became more militant. Finally, the largest union, the CSCA (later renamed CPSA), enthusiastically adopted a strike policy at its 1969 annual conference. The decision was taken specifically because of a government White Paper pay ceiling of 3.5 per cent, against a background of earlier restraint which had hit clerical staff in the service particularly badly. The report adopted at the conference made clear the essentially political dilemma facing civil servants as a group:

The problems are related to the strong position which the government as employer occupies and the functional difficulties with any action which affects the machinery of government and can be interpreted as a significant challenge to the authority of government or to policies which the government pursues from time to time which it is alleged are intended to apply to the community as a whole.[32]

During the late 1970s and early 1980s, strikes by groups of civil servants became commonplace, their militancy being in direct proportion to government pay squeezes. In turn, this encouraged periodic demands from some Conservatives for a strike ban to be imposed, and from others, including members of the Social Democratic and Liberal Parties, for 'no-strike' agreements. In December 1983 the government issued guidelines imposing new restrictions on the rights of civil servants to participate in political activity. The guidelines also limited the rights of leaders of civil service unions to engage in public controversy over 'political issues' which did not relate strictly to matters affecting their members' pay and conditions; the definition of these matters remained a moot point.[33]

By 1984 there were regular instances of civil servants being disciplined for supporting other workers on strike. One case concerned a miner's wife who took part in a Scottish TUC 'Day of Action' in support of the miners' strike. She died a few days after receiving a letter threatening disciplinary measures for her action; her family and union colleagues believed the two events were directly connected.[34] Other civil servants were disciplined for the same 'offence', one union official commenting: 'This is sheer political victimization. They are totally politicizing our terms and conditions of service and making a blanket denial of civil liberties.'[35] Following a nine-month strike by computer operators at the social security centre in Newcastle upon Tyne, a high-level civil service report criticized 'politically motivated' strikers and proposed decentralizing the government's computer network to reduce its vulnerability to industrial action.[36]

·GCHQ·

The pressure on civil servants was starkly revealed by the unilateral decision of the Thatcher administration to ban trade unions from the surveillance and monitoring centre, Government Communications Headquarters (GCHQ). Without any warning, let alone prior consultation with the unions concerned, the ban was announced on 25 January 1984.

The ostensible reason for this was government concern that strikes could disrupt the national security function of GCHQ. Yet there was no evidence that the unions organizing the 7,000 staff there had ever contemplated industrial action capable of seriously damaging security. Industrial action at GCHQ taken as part of wider civil service pay campaigns in 1979 and 1981 did not affect the centre's operations: union members went out of their way to stand in for colleagues who only took action in non-essential areas; and there were more people at work during these periods than on public holidays.[37]

The shocked reaction of staff to the ban confirmed that they would not have endangered security interests. Furthermore, the government announced no plans to cancel the trade union rights of staff engaged on equally, and in many cases much more, sensitive intelligence work elsewhere in the civil service. The real motive seems to have been the authorities' wish to install lie-detectors under pressure from the American government which relied on GCHQ for some of its intelligence. The unions had opposed government proposals for introducing lie-detectors, principally because of serious doubts about their reliability.

However, despite widespread protests – including a ruling from the International Labour Organization that the ban was in breach of its Convention 87 governing freedom of association – the Court of Appeal and later the House of Lords upheld it. The result was that a government decision to deprive civil servants of their right to national trade union membership could not be questioned by the courts if, in the view of the ministers concerned, such action was necessary in 'the interests of national security'. Since the judges declared that the sole arbiters of what was 'national security' would be the government, and specifically the Prime Minister, the implications of the decision went well beyond GCHQ. It means that civil servants may find their ability to organize and to strike threatened any time 'national security' can be invoked.

·POLITICAL RESTRICTIONS·

It is clear that the rights of trade unions to strike have over the years been subject to the ebb and flow of forces which are highly political. Public-sector workers (especially those in essential services) are especially vulnerable because the case for restricting or abolishing their rights ultimately rests upon arguments rather similar to those used to impose bans on trade union or strike action by members of the armed forces and the police.

Therefore it is important to view any denial of 'the right to strike' within an overall framework of the state's stance towards trade unions, rather than according to special pleading to justify limits on specific groups of workers in 'sensitive areas'. It is also important to acknowledge the immense scope in the British system of government for *political discretion* to impose such limits.

AN HISTORIC CONFLICT

Whenever a serious industrial confrontation arises there is a tendency for public debate to assume that 'this sort of behaviour' did not occur in 'the good old days'. Partly a product of popular nostalgia and partly of popular amnesia, such an assumption also reflects a sense in which strikes always do seem *immediately* and somehow more uniquely threatening of the status quo than at any previous time. But British social history shows that from the time workers first began to combine to advance their interests, they found themselves periodically in conflict with dominant interests in general and governments in particular.

Because the distribution of resources and of income is basic to the character of society, and because the share claimed by workers is such a determining factor in that distribution, governments have persistently tried to control the power of labour. However, this has not only involved attempts to influence labour's *share*. Anxious to improve national productivity, governments have also been interested in the whole labour *process*, in order to influence workers' *performance*.

As early as the fourteenth century wages were regulated under parliamentary legislation, through local justices of the peace. Under the 1563 Statute of Artificers these justices were given powers both to fix wages and to enforce penalties for breaches of contract. Such official regulation met with a degree of broad consent since, in the gild system of those pre-capitalist times, hierarchical relationships were not subject to frequent challenge.*

These arrangements continued until the eighteenth century, when the system of production altered radically. Rapid growth of

---

* Most books on labour history speak of 'masters and *men*' in the gild system, but women workers were involved too.

commerce and communications, industrialization (with the introduction of machinery proving a key factor), the accumulation of
capital by a few owners – all these sharpened the divide between
masters and workers. Where they had previously shared common
craft interests, now these were supplanted by sharper class differences. A consensual basis for government regulation of wages
between the two groups disappeared, and the system fell into
disuse.

· WORKPEOPLE BEGIN TO COMBINE ·

Workers were therefore forced to consider combining as a separate
entity with distinct interests increasingly in conflict with those of
employers. But Parliament was less interested in protecting their
craft interests in the traditional way, because the new employment
relations meant that this could undermine the increasingly differentiated interests of their masters. As Adam Smith wrote in
1776 in his classic text, *The Wealth of Nations*: 'Whenever the
legislature attempts to regulate the differences between masters
and their workmen, its counsellors are always the masters.'[1]
Thus workers were forced to organize to place pressure directly
on their employers. Where Parliament refused to respond to their
petitions, they had to turn to direct sanctions known as 'go-slows'
or 'turn-outs'. 'The use of the word "strike" in the sense of "a
stoppage of work" is apparently an innovation of the early nineteenth century. But the phrase "to strike work" was used in the
eighteenth century, presumably on the analogy of a ship striking
sail.'[2]

By the late eighteenth century, unions were beginning to take
root in the form of local trade clubs meeting in public houses.
They were usually craft-based, comprising mostly skilled
handworkers not yet subsumed by the industrial revolution:
compositors, carpenters, joiners, cabinet-makers, shipwrights and
so on.

Parliament meanwhile adopted a *laissez-faire* stance towards
wage regulation, to the advantage of the new business classes

who wanted a freer labour market which they hoped to control. But this non-interventionist policy on wages was coupled with a highly interventionist attitude towards workers' organizations. Tough legal curbs were enforced to suppress combinations by workers.

However, these curbs did not fully achieve their political objective. Workers were able to evade regulation or to establish welfare organizations known as 'friendly societies', which in practice served to defend their wider interests. These began to spread during the eighteenth century, to the extent that 'the dividing line between friendly societies and wage bargaining remained in doubt, especially as workers combining for wage-bargaining purposes, which were of doubtful legality, could use the organization of a friendly society as a legal mask for their activities'.[3]

Incipient trade unionism of this type was thought to pose a major challenge to the authorities who became increasingly concerned in the latter part of the eighteenth century. Public order was seen as a real problem, especially in the rapidly growing towns of the industrial North. The government was also nervous about the implications of disturbances abroad, notably the French Revolution of 1789. Fears grew in the governing classes that organized workers would not only compel employers to improve their conditions, but might also merge with revolutionary movements to threaten the established order.

· THE COMBINATION ACTS ·

At the turn of the century the ability of workers to undertake industrial action was limited by the Combination Acts of 1799 and 1800: they reinforced existing common law and made almost all trade unionism illegal. The significance of this legislation lay less in its 'industrial' than its 'political' objectives. Although the Acts did allow for summary trials, thereby making prosecutions of workers easier, existing common and statute law already made almost all trade unionism and certainly all strikes illegal. Their real purpose was a *political* one, because the government saw industrial unrest as a political threat.

This was evident, for example, in the reaction of the government to the spread of associations of weavers in Lancashire at the time. The Home Secretary could not have expressed more clearly the government's motives in a letter he wrote in 1799 to a magistrate in Bolton about the problem: 'If nothing injurious to the safety of the government is actually in contemplation, Associations so formed contain within themselves the means of being converted at any time into a most dangerous instrument to disturb the public tranquillity.'[4] It is significant that the Combination Acts were introduced alongside other repressive measures, including imprisonment without trial and attacks on press freedom.

If anything, however, the Acts had the opposite effect to that intended. They did not stem the tide of industrial unrest. On the contrary, workers began to organize with even greater vigour, the Acts merely forcing them into more clandestine forms of action. The activities of women workers in this deserve more recognition than is usually accorded. For example, protests and riots by Lancashire cotton weavers caused *The Times* to remark in June 1808:

The women are, if possible, more turbulent and mischievous than the men. Their insolence to the soldiers and special constables is intolerable and they seem to be confident of deriving immunity from their sex.[5]

The early nineteenth century was a period of huge change from merchant and agricultural capitalism to industrial capitalism, and this produced massive unrest. There were demonstrations against food shortages and low wages, and the replacement of people by machinery led in some cases to what has been termed 'collective bargaining by riot',[6] with the sabotage of new machinery being part of this process. Between 1811 and 1817, the 'Luddites' – followers of the mythical General Ned Ludd – destroyed new textile machinery that was displacing their traditional craft skills and jobs. So seriously did the authorities take this that at one stage in 1812 there were 12,000 troops stationed in Lancashire, the West Riding and Nottinghamshire – more than Wellington commanded in the Peninsular War.[7] Meanwhile, political agitation was widespread – and was frequently suppressed with even more force than workers experienced: the Peterloo massacre in 1819, where eleven peaceful demonstrators were killed by Yeomanry in Manchester, being perhaps the most notorious example.

However, if the perception of a wider political threat produced a repressive stance towards strikes, this stance had to be reassessed in the light of experience. It became clear that the Combination Acts had 'served only to bring illegal Jacobin and trade union strands closer together', wrote E. P. Thompson,[8] and the Webbs described how this amounted to 'veiled insurrection'.[9] As one labour historian recorded:

The Combination Acts did not kill trade unions. They either went underground as secret societies operating to regulate work customs and practices, or disguised themselves in ill-fitting clothes as friendly societies for the provision of sickness and burial benefits, etc. Artisans persisted with their traditional combinations which in a number of cases could trace descent to the early decades of the eighteenth century, and the habit spread to newer workers in the newer trades of cotton, textiles, engineering and mining where they often operated quite openly.[10]

In 1824 a House of Commons committee, set up to investigate the problem, reported that the Acts had helped to produce circumstances 'highly dangerous to the peace of the community'.[11] Thus when the Acts were repealed the same year, this was out of political expediency. The government simply recognized that it had chosen the wrong tools and looked for more efficient ones to secure the same objective: reducing the power of organized workers by inhibiting or preventing them from striking.

This was in an environment in which, as the Webbs described it,

From the very beginning of the century the employers had persistently asserted their right to make any kind of bargain with the individual workman . . . They had . . . to perfect freedom of contract and complete competition between both workers and employers. In order to secure absolute freedom of competition of individuals it was necessary to penalise any attempt on the part of the workman to regulate, by combination, the conditions of the bargain.[12]

So when it came to replacing the Combination Acts, this was done within the framework of lifting restrictions on businessmen, giving them the maximum freedom to accumulate capital, while also controlling a more assertive working class. All the Tudor statutes giving workers rights to seek protection from Parliament had been repealed in 1813. Now the 1824 Act repealed previous statutes on combinations and permitted specifically 'peaceful' combinations.

Soon afterwards, however, the economy experienced a sudden boom of which workers took advantage by demanding better conditions, and there was a spate of strikes, including some violence. This engendered considerable alarm in governing circles and a new Act was rushed through in 1825. Although it reaffirmed the previous year's repeal of the laws on combinations, it tightened up considerably on the scope for strike action. 'Molesting' or 'obstructing' persons at work were made sufficient grounds for combinations to be rendered illegal. The vagueness of these offences gave considerable scope for employers and the authorities to act against strikers.

· THE TOLPUDDLE MARTYRS ·

The case of the Tolpuddle Martyrs, six farm labourers from the Dorset village of Tolpuddle who were prosecuted in 1834, has become the classic example of the authorities making a target of a group of workers for avowedly political reasons. Their case followed long years of growing rural poverty, aggravated by enclosure legislation under which farm workers lost to landowners and big farmers their historic rights to use common land. The subsequent exploitation of agriculture by large landowners provoked farm workers to organize more effectively.

A minority supported the quasi-insurrectionary activity identified in 1830 with another mythical figure, 'Captain Swing'. Operating mainly in southern and eastern England, they rioted and destroyed farm buildings and equipment (especially new machinery that was beginning to replace their jobs). These were years of militant working-class agitation. There was pressure on Parliament for a Reform Bill. There were strikes in the new factory towns: for example, the county of Durham was in turmoil in 1831–2, with marines and cavalry called in to break strikes. Troops also intervened in Wales to confront striking miners and ironworkers in 1831. The same year over a thousand soldiers were called in after a strike against wage cuts by spinners in Manchester had erupted into violence, which included the murder of the son of a leading mill-owner.

Taken in isolation, the activities of the Tolpuddle labourers themselves could hardly be construed as a serious threat. While they had discussed wages issues within their friendly society, its purpose was primarily one of protecting the welfare of sick or unemployed members. But, in the context of wider social developments, they provided a convenient vehicle for making an example to others.

The Home Secretary at the time, Lord Melbourne, had become personally alarmed at the growth of agricultural trade unionism throughout the country. Having family connections in Dorset, he became engaged in correspondence with the Presiding Magistrate there, James Frampton, and the Lord-Lieutenant of the County, Lord Digby, over reports of local labourers organizing. The three of them used their positions of power to give effect to their strident anti-unionism and resolved to make a test case of the unfortunate Tolpuddle Six.

However, it was not obvious how to proceed against them, because their actions in organizing a welfare fund did not contravene any specific law. And the way in which the authorities overcame this obstacle gives some insight into the methods which could be used to control workers' activities.

First, Lord Melbourne suggested to Magistrate Frampton that he try an Act of 1817 which prevented 'Seditious meetings and Assemblies'. Under it, any group whose members took oaths not specifically required or authorized by law could be deemed to constitute an unlawful combination. Thus, even though trade unions had ceased to be illegal by virtue of the 1824 repeal of the

Combination Acts, the wording of the 1817 law – brought in for the quite different purpose of clamping down on revolutionary plots – was manipulated to catch the Tolpuddle farm workers who were arrested under it one February morning in 1834.

Still greater ingenuity was required, however, when it was discovered that there might after all be a loophole in the 1817 Act. To overcome this Lord Melbourne and his advisers used the device, often found in political trials, of linking one Act to another in a fresh charge. By happy coincidence the 1797 Mutiny Act contained ambiguous wording that enabled it to be used against groups other than the armed forces for whom it had been enacted. It also had the advantage of permitting a much heavier sentence – up to seven years' transportation – and Lord Melbourne was determined to see such an exemplary punishment. Despite the absence of any evidence of sedition, the labourers were indicted under the 1797 Act for 'administering or taking unlawful oaths' for seditious purposes.

They were duly convicted and deported to Australia, their trial being something of a charade. The foreman of the Grand Jury which decided to allow the case to go for trial was Lord Melbourne's brother-in-law; the other Grand Jurors included James Frampton, his son, his stepbrother, and other magistrates who had signed the warrant for the men's arrests. The 'petty jury' in the trial itself consisted of farmers 'specially selected . . . to reach the desired verdict'.[13] And the judge revealed his own prejudices when he said that if trade unions were allowed to continue, 'they would ruin masters, cause a stagnation in trade and destroy property'.[14]

Defence counsel argued that the indictment could not possibly apply to poor labouring men who had been members of the Tolpuddle Friendly Society whose purpose was to act as a co-operative savings group to help the men should they fall ill or be unemployed. How, he asked, could a society whose objective was to 'provide against seasons of scarcity and obviate starvation' be considered an illegal combination for 'seditious or mutinous confederacy'? But his plea was ignored:

It was a beautifully spun web – it was foolproof and it was legal. For as the *Law Magazine* later said, 'It is not with administering an oath not required or authorized by the law, that the Dorsetshire Labourers stood charged, as still seems to be imagined by the leaders of the Unions . . . but with administering an oath not to reveal a combination which administers such oaths.' You may need to read this subtle distinction a few times, but once absorbed, it explains how the indictment was strictly within the letter of the law. Whether it was within the spirit is another matter, as are the reasons which motivated the indictment.[15]

The case provoked widespread anger and protests. The outcry was such that the martyrs were eventually released. Even *The Times* declared: 'The crimes which called for punishment were not proved – the crime brought home to the prisoners did not justify the sentence.'[16] However, it was unusual mainly for being such a *blatant* example of the bending of the law for political purposes. There were many other attacks on working-class organizations where they appeared to threaten the interests of those who monopolized power and wealth. Certain strikes caused particular anxiety, and it was the overt use of political power against them which turned them into 'political strikes'.

That unions should have emerged at all during this period was a considerable achievement, because they still had no specific legal legitimacy. One factor helping to strengthen trade union organization was structural change in the economy. The expansion of industry and markets spawned larger employers with larger workforces who were better able to organize. The improvement of transport and communications assisted the organization of labour, as well as of capital. From local, craft-based societies, national groupings began to evolve which formed the basis of the trade union movement as we know it today. Some of these were akin to 'friendly societies' which largely avoided confrontation. Others found themselves in an almost constant running battle with employers and agencies of the state.

·EARLY WOMEN TRADE UNIONISTS·

Being mainly confined to craft and skilled workers, these early unions excluded semi-skilled and unskilled workers. This led them to bar women from membership. With the exception of textiles and 'traditional' women's jobs such as needlework, women were excluded from skilled work and therefore from the unions seeking to protect it.[17] (This practice seems to have begun in the eighteenth century; in earlier times, women had not been excluded from skilled work and some of the highest-paid workers 'might as well be women as men'.)[18]

The dominant attitude in these early days of trade unionism was that women threatened men's jobs – an attitude which persisted for at least the first three-quarters of the nineteenth century and which was expressed by a leading trade unionist who argued that their objective was to 'bring about a condition . . . where their wives and daughters would be in their proper sphere at home, instead of being dragged into competition for livelihood against the great and strong men of the world'.[19]

Thus women were driven to organize their own form of trade unionism and to take strike action. Notable strikes by women included a successful one for higher wages by Kensington washerwomen in 1834. There were outbreaks of militancy by women textile workers, some of them being broken by the police or by the absence of effective trade union organization. But, outside the textile industry, women's strikes had little effect in terms of improving their wages or dreadful conditions of work. Although 'the exploitation of women was second only to child labour',[20] the 'official' male trade union movement gave them no real support. This encouraged tension and sometimes conflict between male and female workers, which weakened the strength of the trade unions.

It is also important to note both how small a force trade unionism was for most of the nineteenth century and how union membership fluctuated according to economic conditions. In 1815, only a minute proportion of workers were union members; by 1834, there were still fewer than 20 per cent in membership; in

1842, a bare 1.5 per cent. In 1888, just 5 per cent of the labour force (or 10 per cent of all adult male workers) were organized, being outnumbered three to one by domestic servants. Not until the end of the century did really large proportions of workers start joining unions.[21]

Yet there seemed at times to be an 'incredible frequency' of strikes: 'No week passes, scarcely a day, indeed, in which there is not a strike in some direction, now against a reduction, then against a refusal to raise the rate of wages . . . sometimes against new machinery, or for a hundred other reasons.'[22] These could also take a serious turn, as happened in 1843 when striking Manchester brickmakers stormed one brickworks armed with guns and fought a battle with armed guards of the employer, smashing up the works.

· 'NEW MODEL' UNIONS ·

By the middle of the nineteenth century, what came to be known as the 'new model' unions were establishing themselves. But they were highly fragmented, small, and concentrated in relatively few urban areas. Sectionalism was rife, particularly between skilled craftsmen and newer manual workers, and there was no uniform attitude towards strikes, the state or politics. In the years to 1850,

Solid practical lessons in the matter of organization and tactics, in the true anti-intellectual tradition of British 'common sense', were the main components . . . What was found to work on a limited scale – at least as far as skilled workers were concerned – was control of entry to local labour markets, and the provision of welfare benefits. Other workers, such as the miners and cotton-spinners, learned that strikes, provided they were launched when markets were buoyant, could be an effective weapon. The lessons learned related more with how to cope with capitalism, and less with how to overthrow it.[23]

'New model' leaders wanted trade unionism to be 'respectable', able to appeal for public sympathy, rather than to rely on the industrial muscle of strike action to secure improvements. At the time there was considerable ambiguity in the attitude of unions towards strikes. For example, the Portsmouth lodge of the Ironfounders even proposed in 1849 'not only the cessation of strikes, but the abolition of the word "strike" '![24] Perhaps more typical was the attitude of one of the major unions, the Amalgamated Society of Engineers, where, 'Since the main attraction of the union was its friendly society function, strikes were frowned upon because they consumed valuable assets.'[25]

Consequently, although almost all strikes had the potential for challenging the authority of the government, and although some trade unionists saw industrial action partly as a means of altering the balance of power in favour of the working class, the general thrust of trade unionism was much more pragmatic and defensive. There is no evidence of the emerging trade union movement seeking to pursue a policy of political confrontation through strikes: a movement reluctant to strike even on bread-and-butter issues was hardly likely to do so on political questions.

There were still outbreaks of militancy, such as those around the 'Nine Hours Movement' which organized strikes for a shorter working day (nine instead of ten hours) in the 1860s. There were also instances of violence, such as when the Sheffield Grinders blew up the house of a blackleg in 1866. But by then systems of arbitration and conciliation found much more favour among trade unions than industrial action. Union leaders felt that strikes in themselves had achieved only limited improvements. Furthermore,

Insofar as conciliation avoided strikes, it involved a minimal drain on union funds ... Basically though, the liking for conciliation was a function of the ideology of the union leader. He did not cast himself in the role of a revolutionary, either actual or potential. He was not out to change the world but to make it slightly more bearable. In this respect there is no good reason for believing that he differed markedly from the outlook of his members.[26]

In general the unions accepted the legitimacy of the parliamentary system as it existed then, and directed their political energies towards obtaining the vote. Indeed the 1867 Reform Act gave the vote to most of those organized in unions, since they were almost all artisans who constituted what amounted to a 'labour aristocracy'.[27] The launch of the Trades Union Congress in 1868 encouraged such a 'respectable' view of how change might be secured, for it started to serve as a mediating body between unions and the government. Union leaders then as now were more likely to be found in the corridors of power than on the picket line. There were still major industrial confrontations, however. In 1869, four were killed and twenty-six wounded when troops fired on a crowd of demonstrating miners in North Wales. And in 1871 engineers in the North-east went on strike for five months and won a reduction in their working day, though without the backing of their national executive.

· GOVERNMENTS AND STRIKES ·

Meanwhile governments continued to cast a wary eye on the growth of trade unionism, sometimes strengthening workers' rights, sometimes reducing them, according to the balance of class forces at any particular period. For example, the 1859 Molestation of Workmen Act specifically exempted peaceful picketing in trade disputes over wages and hours from the penalties for 'molesting' or 'obstructing' contained in the 1825 Act. But terms such as 'threats' and 'intimidation' could still be loosely interpreted at the authorities' discretion, and many strikes could still be caught by common-law offences such as conspiracy or restraint of trade.

Furthermore, as will be seen in Chapter 8, the judiciary remained hostile to trade unionism and judges found ways of penalizing strikers when they wanted to. In the *Hornby v. Close* case in 1867 the Boilermakers Society was even prevented by the courts from suing the Treasurer of its Bradford branch for embezzling union funds. Union officials believed that the 1855 Friendly Societies Act had given protection to union funds. But the Lord Chief Justice stated that unions were not covered by the Act: although unions were not criminal any more, they were still outside the law, he maintained, arguing pointedly that unions acted 'in restraint of trade'.

This judgment was later reversed in the 1871 Trade Union Act, which also gave unions certain *immunities* from aspects of the common law. But it is important to understand that the 1871 Act did not give unions any *positive legal rights*. They were merely granted immunity from the civil or criminal consequences of their actions in 'restraining trade'. A large loophole remained through which employers could seek the assistance of judges to curb trade union power, particularly since in the same year a Criminal Law Amendment Act was passed which significantly narrowed the scope for legal picketing and strike organizing.

Attitudes had gradually been changing. The view of employers who saw some advantage in encouraging 'responsible' trade union-ism was reflected in an editorial switch of policy by *The Times* which had declared in July 1869 that unions should be given 'free scope for legitimate development'. This period was indeed one in which the government made some concessions concerning the ability of unions to establish viable *organizations* while sim-ultaneously trying to maintain the maximum possible freedom to regulate and control their ability to win any *strikes*. Not that this dual strategy was necessarily a premeditated one; more likely it was the product of the conflicting forces of labour and capital on the state itself. As Roy Lewis explains,

major developments in labour law have occurred at times of economic and social conflict. The nature and extent of legal regulation has been determined not by some abstract rule-making force, but by the interplay of judicial innovations, public policy controversy, the relative power of management and labour interests, and party politics with a view to electoral advantage. Labour law past and present is explicable only within a firm historical framework which takes account of all these factors.[28]

A similar story applies to the 1875 Conspiracy and Protection of Property Act. It represented an advance for the unions in that it gave strikers immunity from the simple crime of conspiracy if they were involved in a trade dispute; it also gave greater protection to peaceful picketing. On the other hand 'political' strikes remained illegal, and the Act specifically debarred strikes in the essential services of gas and water supply.

These latter restrictions were of special significance in that they revealed the government's concern to ensure that its own authority was safeguarded even if labour law was liberalized in the private sector. The era of the 'nightwatchman state' was drawing to a close, as the government began improving certain central services and creating an infrastructure more conducive to the efficient accumulation of private capital. But to perform this emerging new role efficiently, the government needed to buttress its own powers. This was a time when policing became better organized (including the establishment of the Criminal Investigation Department (CID) of Scotland Yard in 1878 and the force's original Special Branch in 1883). Local government was reorganized. However, this steady encroachment of government into different areas of social activity and organization meant that it was also increasingly vulnerable to any challenge to its authority through strikes, whether or not that was specifically intended by the workers involved.

· NEW UNIONISM ·

In the late 1880s, a fresh stage in the development of unions began, marking a 'new unionism', as it was called. The main change was caused by the rapid unionization of unskilled workers, operating often through 'general' unions that encouraged a break with the craft-based, skilled unionism previously dominant. They were both more belligerent and more open to socialist ideas, as indicated by a change in the attitude of the TUC, whose President declared in his address to the 1887 Congress, 'socialism has lost its terrors for us. We recognize our most serious evils in the unrestrained, unscrupulous and remorseless forces of capitalism.'[29]

The influence of Marx was beginning to spread in Europe, and socialist groups started to grow in Britain. When one of these, the newly-formed Social Democratic Federation, organized a demonstration against unemployment in London in 1886, it turned into the most serious riot the capital had seen for decades. Unemployment was high at the time, wages had remained stagnant for years and unskilled labourers were in a mood to revolt. In July 1888 there was a socialist-led strike of women at Bryant and May's match factory in London's East End, known as the 'matchgirls' strike'. It made a huge impact on the popular mood, and afterwards there were successful major strikes by gas workers and water workers.

Although conflict between men and women workers continued, mechanization meant fewer skilled jobs and the increasing absorption of women on to the production line, causing even the craft unions to review their exclusion of women from membership.[30] Male trade unionists continued to strike occasionally over the employment of women as cheap labour, and at least some employers may have sympathized with the Post Office manager who favoured the recruitment of women because he thought they were 'less disposed than men to combine for the purpose of extorting higher wages'.[31] But the new unions started actively to recruit women and in 1892 there was an historic instance of unity between striking women employed by Sanders confectionery company in Bristol and striking dockers, cooperation between the two continuing after the strike.[32] During the 1890s women stepped up the pressure for full recognition and equality within the trade union movement, often voicing their demands through their pressure group, the Women's Trade Union League.

The militancy of the time was seen as a direct threat, with one labour historian recording:

Through all the decade of the nineties and well into the new century, a hostility developed toward trade unionism in general and new unionism in particular that bordered at times on the hysterical ... This whole period after 1889 is one of a developing counter-attack by the propertied classes against the industrial organizations of the working people.[33]

Greater force was deployed against strikers than at any time since that directed at the Luddites some eighty years before. In April 1893 shipping employers moved in a thousand blacklegs from London to break a strike by dockers and seamen in Hull. During the consequent anger and unrest, the government drafted in three companies of Dragoons and also dispatched two gunboats to the river Humber in case any of the strikers tried to disrupt local shipping; the public disturbances soon subsided.

In September 1893 troops were used at Featherstone in Yorkshire during a lock-out of miners. This time they fired on a crowd, killing two men and wounding sixteen others after a riotous incident in which loaded coal wagons had been overturned by some miners. More troops and police were brought in to other areas during the same lock-out, provoking a protest from the Miners' Federation that had echoes in the 1984–5 miners' strike:

While we strongly denounce all who take part in rioting as the worst enemies of the miners' cause, yet we cannot help believing that the pressure of imported police and military in such large numbers acts as a forcible incentive to rioting and disorder, and hereby urge on the government to withdraw at once all newly imported soldiers and police.[34]

Not all trade union activity was this turbulent, however: most of it was relatively mundane, concerned with negotiation and conciliation rather than confrontation.

Meanwhile the traditional stance of the government had been altering. This change was expressed by a Permanent Secretary at the Home Office who turned down a request to establish an inquiry into the ribbon weavers' strike of 1860, saying, 'What right has the government to interfere in this matter, except to keep the peace?'[35] By setting up the Labour Department of the Board of Trade in 1893, 'the government abandoned the doctrine of non-interference to try to avoid the damage and distress caused by great strikes and lock-outs.'[36] Other moves were made to improve the capacity for government intervention, such as the 1896 Conciliation Act which promoted the settlement of disputes by consent.

However, this strengthening of the government's hand did not necessarily mean a diminution of the power of private capital. Employers reacted with bitter hostility to the new arbitration arrangements and tried to defy the Conciliation Act, *The Times* declaring in 1897: 'There is no room for the namby-pamby methods of the arbitrator.'[37] Furthermore, the courts continued to give hostile judgments against strikers by upholding *civil* actions brought against them, in circumstances where Parliament had legislated to prevent *criminal* prosecutions from being brought.

·TAFF VALE·

This trend was highlighted by the famous Taff Vale case. There had been a strike on the Taff Vale railway in South Wales in August 1900 after a dispute over pay. Although it was settled within eleven days, the company sued the Amalgamated Society of Railway Servants for organizing picketing against blackleg labour. The case went right up to the House of Lords, which gave its historic judgment in 1901 making unions liable for a claim for damages resulting from strikes. It effectively undermined rights to strike and picket which workers understood Parliament had expressly granted. Even if it was still permissible to strike or to picket in principle, in practice to do so invited serious consequences in the form of heavy damages granted by the courts; the Railway Servants had to pay £42,000 in fines and damages following the Taff Vale judgment.

Trade unionism was also under attack in other quarters. Using language and arguments that might well have appeared in its editorials eighty years later, *The Times* ran a series of articles in 1902 on 'The Crisis of British Industry', arguing that 'trade unionism and the restrictive practices it encouraged were responsible for the weakened competitive position of British industry compared with American and German'.[38] (In reality, this confused cause and effect. After the mid-Victorian boom, occasioned by the fact that Britain had been the first country to industrialize, came competition from nations such as America and Germany which had industrialized later and more efficiently. Trade union growth did not weaken Britain's competitiveness. Rather, in its weakened competitive position, British industry's attempts to maintain profit levels by squeezing workers harder provoked more effective resistance from workers through new unions, in turn provoking attacks from employers and their allies.)

In this climate, unions were spurred on to campaign publicly to advance their rights. Affiliations to the newly formed Labour Representation Committee – the precursor to the Labour Party – jumped from 353,070 in 1900 to 847,315 by early 1903. Taff Vale effectively forced the unions to 'go political' and take seriously their need for an independent party of labour.

Eventually, following the election of a Liberal government and twenty-nine Labour MPs, the government brought in the 1906 Trade Disputes Act. This removed the scope for the kind of civil action allowed by the Taff Vale judgment, making both peaceful picketing and persuasion to strike more obviously lawful activities. It entrenched in Britain what is known as an 'abstentionist' legal structure for trade unionism. That is to say, unions were given almost blanket immunity from civil actions, adding to the rights they had won not to incur sanctions under the criminal law in certain circumstances, but still not granting them any positive legal rights as such. Collective bargaining, rather than statutory rights, remained the main instrument of workers' protection and advancement.

This was also a period in which trade unionism began to transform itself once more. Whenever the economy swung from expansion to depression, the balance of class forces altered and trade unionism grew stronger or weaker accordingly. For instance, in the late 1880s to early 1890s, when the economy boomed, the 'new unions' had grown in parallel: union power was more able to assert itself in conditions where there was no reserve pool of unemployed for company owners to draw upon and where their need to expand made them more vulnerable to demands from their workers. But from 1891, there was a period of economic downturn, the 'new unions' fell back (some of them crumbling completely), and workers' wages and conditions were depressed.

Then came the trade upturn in 1910. Trade unionism enjoyed a new lease of life: a total union membership of 2.5 million in 1910 was sustained through the war and grew to a peak of 8.3 million in 1920. The onset of depression in 1920–21 marked another turning-point, with membership slipping back to 5.3 million by 1926. However, although the fortunes of unions ebbed and flowed, the fluctuations in membership masked what was still a steady consolidation of working-class strength over this period: in 1892, there was no working-class political party and just 1.5 million workers were unionized; by 1926, there were 151 Labour MPs, the party had already formed a government and union membership stood at 5.3 million.

The character of trade unions also changed in tandem with the restructuring of the economy. This was a period in which 'factory capitalism' came of age. There were mergers, concentrating production and leading to monopolies or near-monopolies in some key sectors. And these changes affected unions in two major respects. First, union organization and energy could be more concentrated and therefore often more effective. Second, skilled workers who had formed a traditional 'labour aristocracy', somewhat remote from their unskilled colleagues and certainly less militant, experienced a sharp deterioration in their position, this in turn affecting their outlook. The labour historian Eric Hobsbawm described what happened:

As production concentrated and the owner–manager gave place to the joint-stock corporation ... a whole set of novel managerial, technical, and white-collar grades wedged themselves between the 'skilled man' and his 'master' ... Step by step the labour aristocrat found himself forced into the ranks of the working class; and, on the whole, he moved to the left.[39]

The prominent socialist activist and trade union militant, Tom Mann, a skilled engineer, is perhaps the best-known example of a 'labour aristocrat' moving to the left.

· GOVERNMENT INTERVENTION ·

Meanwhile, government intervention in industrial relations had been increasing significantly, accelerating in the first two decades of the twentieth century. A number of factors encouraged this.

The centralization of capital made even private-sector industrial confrontations take on a more 'national' character. There was an accompanying growth of national union organizations which, for the first time, could call national strikes. Governments could not stand aside from the implications of these developments: miners' strikes, for instance, could have an enormous impact, as in 1912 when all industrial earnings were reduced by 12 per cent and 60 per cent of iron and steel workers became unemployed within three weeks.[40] And because the state itself was becoming a larger employer of labour (mainly through local authorities at this point), it had a greater interest in shaping the pattern of trade unionism. Also, governments were increasingly aware of the relative vulnerability of the British economy to foreign competition. As Hobsbawm argues, 'British labour and industrial relations began to be seen as a relevant aspect of British "national efficiency".'[41]

A new spirit of interventionism was apparent elsewhere too. The Liberals were anxious to retain their working-class support which was slipping away to the emerging Labour Party, and they embarked upon a wide-ranging programme of social reform. For the first time workers were able to claim compensation for industrial diseases, and there were new regulations covering school meals, school clinics and child medical inspection. In 1908 a non-contributory old-age pension scheme was introduced. In 1909 the first Trade Boards – nowadays called Wages Councils – were set up, giving some protection to the ill-organized and the lowest-paid. A 'People's Budget' was introduced by Lloyd George in 1909 to 'wage implacable warfare against poverty and squalidness', as he put it. In 1911 the Liberals, still under pressure from the labour movement, introduced sickness and unemployment insurance schemes which, though limited, effectively laid the foundations for the post-1945 welfare state.

Similarly, the reversal of the Taff Vale judgment in the 1906 Act, together with the later 1913 Act legalizing union financial support for the Labour Party, resulted from labour movement pressure. But these reforms also reflected a new consensus in which unions had obtained greater social legitimacy. Speaking during a House of Commons debate on the 1906 Bill, the Liberal Prime Minister, Sir Henry Campbell-Bannerman, argued: 'The great mass of opinion in the country recognize fully now the beneficial nature of trade union organizations, and recognize also the great services that those organizations have done in the prevention of conflict and the promotion of harmony between labour and capital.' Echoing this, the Tory Opposition leader, A. J. Balfour, observed that 'there is no party ... who does not recognize to the full all that trade unions have done, the gap they have filled in the social organization'.

But this was only one side of the coin of growing government intervention. The other was a determination to regulate or defeat the growth of strikes. In 1907 there were long disputes on the north-east coast against wage cuts: one by engineers lasted seven months, another by shipwrights and joiners nearly five months. The same year, there was a major dock strike in Belfast. At one stage the strikers and their sympathizers were openly attacked when 10,000 troops were drafted in. Cavalry charges and infantry fire in working-class districts of the city resulted in some deaths and many injuries. Nevertheless, the government showed itself equally willing to negotiate when circumstances demanded, such as in response to the first threatened national railway strike in November 1907, when it intervened directly and proposed a new conciliation system for the industry.

· 1910–14: THE FORWARD MARCH ·

From 1910 there followed four years of intense and widespread labour unrest. One factor responsible appears to have been the upward movement of prices after a period in which stationary wage levels had been masked by a progressive decline of prices. In the resulting militancy, strikes were seen as a major threat to the established order. The government used troops against strikers more regularly than at any other period: ostensibly this was to protect the public; in practice, as one labour historian put it, 'they protected blacklegs and the property of employers'.[42]

In a famous incident, troops and police were used against striking miners at the Welsh village of Tonypandy in 1911. Thirty thousand striking miners had been involved in violent clashes with police and troops across South Wales, and at Tonypandy one striker was killed in a running battle lasting over ten days. The same year, seamen and dockers went on strike all over the country. The port of London was closed down, and the Port of London Authority, with the blessing of the government, refused to negotiate. A senior civil servant reported 'strike fever and madness in the ports, with fires and looting'; the city of Hull, he found, was 'near revolution'.[43] Winston Churchill, then Home Secretary, threatened to send in 25,000 troops to break the strike, but mass demonstrations of workers in the area eventually forced the authorities to back down, and most of the men's demands were conceded by an arbitration award. In Liverpool the dock strike escalated into a general transport strike, embracing tramway and railway workers as well. There was an outcry after police had attacked demonstrating strikers, and troops were drafted in. They shot and killed two men during one clash, and warships were moored in the river Mersey, their guns trained on the city. Troops were also used to try and break the national railway strike of 1911, killing two strikers in Llanelli. But once more the government was forced to retreat from its repressive stance and it instructed the railway companies to negotiate an agreement acceptable to the unions.

In 1913 official figures reported more strikes than ever previously recorded, with government anxiety being reflected in a typical newspaper comment at the time:

Perhaps the most salient feature of this turmoil at the moment is the general spirit of revolt, not only against employers of all kinds, but also against leaders and majorities, and parliamentary or any kind of constitutional and orderly action.[44]

These fears were enhanced by reaction to the general strike in Dublin in August and September 1913. Police brutality, resulting in the killing of two workers and the wounding of 400 others, provoked outrage on the British mainland, with trade unionists openly discussing the arming of workers and a general strike.

Syndicalist ideas of revolutionary trade unionism – of sympathy strikes leading to a cataclysmic general strike – were widely advocated by Tom Mann and others. The President of the miners' union told the Trades Union Congress, meeting in Manchester:

If revolution is going to be forced upon my people by such action as has been taken in Dublin and elsewhere I say it is our duty, legal or illegal, to train our people to defend themselves ... It is the duty of the greater trade union movement, when a question of this gravity arises, to discuss seriously the idea of a strike of all the workers.[45]

·TENSIONS WITHIN UNIONS·

During all this ferment, however, there remained a tension within the trade union movement between the leadership and rank-and-file militants. Often union leaders tried to restrain militancy. Many of the strikes at the time started spontaneously, with socialists and syndicalists playing a leading role, and they were denounced by union leaders as 'a disruptive influence out to undermine properly constituted authority for ulterior political ends'.[46] At one stage, the government's chief industrial conciliator wrote: 'Official leaders could not maintain their authority. Often there was more difference between the men and their leaders than between the latter and their employers.'[47]

This was also a period in which the demands of women workers made a greater impact. Between 1906 and 1914, female membership of unions doubled, from 166,803 to 357,956, and there were regular strikes, often coordinated by the Women's Trade Union League and the National Federation of Women Workers. Still largely excluded from craft unions, some women had separate unions of their own, while others were recruited by the 'general' unions.

But although the trend was away from craft unionism towards 'general' or 'industrial' unionism, sectionalism remained widespread (divisions between men and women were only part of the problem). This sectionalism, so basic to the character of British trade unionism, inhibited solidarity activity between unions and undermined any impetus there might have been to undertake 'political' strikes. Most strikes were settled quickly after wage increases were conceded or union recognition granted: a pragmatic and conciliatory stance, rather than a revolutionary one, remained the dominant characteristic of the movement.

· WARTIME LEGITIMACY ·

Nevertheless, by the summer of 1914 British trade unionism 'was working up for an almost revolutionary outburst of gigantic industrial disputes', wrote the Webbs, and Lloyd George spoke of the threat of 'insurrection'.[48] Only the outbreak of the First World War prevented a further escalation of working-class militancy which might even have attained revolutionary proportions.[49]

In fact the war endowed the unions with greater legitimacy. From the start, the government tried to obtain support from national union officials to prevent industrial unrest and secure production targets. A joint declaration between the unions and the Labour Party urged that existing disputes should be terminated and strikes avoided for the duration of the war. Some union leaders were even given ministerial office. Locally, shop stewards also won greater acceptance because their cooperation over war production was needed. Partly under pressure from the unions, the government agreed to set up a new Ministry of Labour in January 1917; its responsibilities included arbitration and conciliation in disputes.

As Middlemas explains, 'In reacting against the threat of revolution . . . Britain developed its own distinctive form of triangular collaboration in the industrial sphere, between government, trade unions and the business class.'[50] This tendency towards corporatism gradually replaced the nineteenth-century political system, which had broken down under the weight of class and interest group conflict.

Consequently, although the war deflected any radical objectives trade unionists might have had, it ended with working-class power and influence considerably strengthened. This picture was not so clear-cut for women, however. Over 1.5 million women joined the labour force during the war, their membership of unions jumping by 750,000 – an increase of about 160 per cent compared with one of about 45 per cent in male membership; by 1918, 383 unions had women members, 347 of these being mixed and 36 women-only.[51]

Initially, the influx of women workers met with some resistance from men seeking to protect their skilled jobs and there were a number of disputes. But pressure from employers and new powers taken by the government to aid the war effort undermined much of this resistance, and women workers gained new strength. They were also prepared to be militant, as in August 1918 when 3,000 women tramway workers won a strike against an unequal war bonus. Their victory came after the London trams had been halted and the strike had spread to other English towns.[52]

The wartime role of women enabled them to win greater recognition inside the trade union movement (for example, the Women's Trade Union League was absorbed into the TUC in 1921). But their main gains outside came in the form of increased legal and political rights. Within months of the war ending, nearly 600,000 women workers lost their jobs, and by 1923 much of their wartime progress as *workers* had been lost.[53]

·POST-WAR CONFLICT·

After the war, workers who came home to promises of 'a land fit for heroes' soon had their hopes dashed, and they reacted by resorting to industrial militancy. In the two post-war years of 1919 and 1920 industrial disputes shot up. There was also a greater willingness to threaten strikes for political or economic objectives. Many shop stewards were influenced by socialist and syndicalist ideas. Yet the official union leadership frequently acted to neutralize such militancy and direct it away from political issues to more legitimate industrial territory.

The role played by national union officials prompted Bonar

Law to remark that unions were the only thing standing between his class and the breakdown of the established order. 'The lesson of this period ... was that trade unionism could amount to a considerable weapon of social control.'[54] Employers, too, came to accept that it was necessary to recognize unions and even shop stewards.[55] The government seemed to be pursuing a course of encouraging responsible unionism while repressing rank-and-file militancy, Churchill arguing in Cabinet that:

Trade union organization was very important, and the more moderate its officials were, the less representative it was; but it was the only organization with which the government could deal. The curse of trade unionism was that *there was not enough of it*, and it was not highly enough developed to make its branch secretaries fall into line with the head office. With a powerful trade union, either peace or war could be made.[56]

The government thus benefited from allowing trade unions to operate legally – as long as they did not use their extra-parliamentary power to act politically. On that strict understanding, their legitimacy was also enhanced by the co-option of union leaders into the machinery of government – for example, they were given places on various statutory committees – with Tory leaders recognizing that many of them 'could be bought, argued or charmed into conformity'.[57]

But the government remained absolutely determined to act against strikes which challenged its authority. In 1919 the miners went on strike, followed by engineers, and then railway workers threatened to do so as well. Although the miners were placated with a Royal Commission to examine their demands and a settlement was secured on the railways, the government was deeply alarmed at the cumulative effect of this unrest, particularly the role played by militant shop stewards.

The Cabinet had established an Industrial Unrest Committee to make contingency arrangements during strikes in February 1919, and the same month the Prime Minister, Lloyd George, complained of 'those men who were seeking to destroy not merely trade unionism but the state'. Other members of the government added their voices, the Leader of the Commons, Bonar Law, arguing that 'both miners and railwaymen are servants not of employers but of the state: that a strike would be against the state and that the state must win and must use all its power for that purpose, otherwise it would be the end of government in this country'.[58] As one labour historian commented, the government's reactions 'were based on the fear that a widespread dispute would take place which would be directed towards political ends'.[59] In fact this fear proved to be groundless. The union's leadership did not seek sympathy action from other unions; it went to considerable lengths to distance itself from any idea of confronting the government, and finally negotiated a settlement with the government.

· MODERNIZING STATE POWERS ·

For their part, government officials felt their organization during the railway strike, coordinated by the Industrial Unrest Committee, had 'fairly knocked the strikers sideways', and they resolved to make it more permanent and more comprehensive.[60] In October 1919 the government established a Supply and Transport Committee (STC) to maintain essential supplies and services during strikes. (It was also known as the National Emergency Committee.) Two principal factors determined the official thinking behind this new initiative: concern at pre-war labour militancy and experience of the central apparatus used in wartime to control industrial relations. There was also

the lurking fear that industrial unrest was simply the precursor of political revolution ... The unprecedented strength of trade unionism after the war revived pre-war syndicalist ideas, and in particular the notion of concerted nation-wide action in a general strike. Since the development of wartime collectivism had to a very great extent placed the government, rather than the owners, in control of industry, labour ambitions readily resolved into direct confrontation between unions and government. In these circumstances the line between industrial and political power was fine indeed.[61]

Membership of the STC included several Cabinet ministers who supervised the activities of civil servants in the Supply and Transport Organization (STO). By March 1920 eleven regional commissioners had been appointed, who were answerable to the STO. It appears that the decision to by-pass local councils in this way was taken partly because of the Labour Party's success in the municipal elections four months earlier, when it won a number of boroughs.[62]

Then in October 1920 an Emergency Powers Act was brought in, enabling the government to declare a state of emergency and to take over and run essential services if the community was deprived of 'the essentials of life'. Effectively an anti-strike measure, it was first used in the 1921 miners' strike: army leave was cancelled, reservists were called up and troops were moved in. Civil service machinery was also revamped to increase the government's capacity to deal with the consequences of national strikes.

Meanwhile, a Police Act had been introduced in 1919 to quell dissent within the police and prevent any form of independent trade unionism or a recurrence of strikes in the force, of which there had been two within the previous year. From now on, police rather than troops would be the main agency for dealing with breakdowns in public order during strikes.

· A SHOWDOWN NEARS ·

During 1920, however, union militancy began to ebb. It had grown in the economic boom which occurred during and immediately following the war, but in 1920 this collapsed into a recession which lasted into the 1930s. The world market for coal was overstocked and international commodity prices fell, provoking a crisis in British industry. Unions became preoccupied with fighting against wage cuts rather than for wage increases.

However, the unions did show themselves willing to countenance an overtly political strike in 1920, when Russia was threatened with invasion by Poland – an act in which many in the labour movement felt Britain might become implicated. When the

Poles were driven back out of Russia, the Soviet army pursued them into their own country, and the British government indicated that it felt obliged to assist the Poles. After London dockers refused to load a ship bound for Poland because they suspected it was carrying arms, and railwaymen resolved to 'black' any munitions bound for Poland, a joint union–Labour Party Council of Action was formed. The Council of Action spoke of 'direct action' against any British intervention and set up local organizations in preparation. Even normally moderate union leaders declared that this was necessary to prevent an escalation into a new European war. Eventually the threat of war subsided after the Russians had been pushed back out of Poland. But the fact that a general strike failed to materialize should not obscure the importance of it being threatened in the first place by trade union leaders who had previously shown little appetite for political strikes.

For their part the miners were invariably 'suspected by the government of having political motives, irrespective of the actual content of the miners' grievances'.[63] This was partly because of their strategic role in the economy, and partly because they were waging a public campaign for nationalization of the mines. In any event the government responded to the miners in highly political terms – sometimes using troops, sometimes intervening in an unprecedented way to secure a negotiated settlement – while giving every impression, by its responses to the 1920 and 1921 miners' strikes, that a day of reckoning was near.

The minority Labour government elected in 1924 was able to secure TUC support in settling a railway strike soon after coming into office. But the STO continued to operate, being run by civil servants with little direct control by Labour ministers.[64] It recommended a state of emergency over a bus and underground strike in London and the government proclaimed this on 28 March, revoking it three days later after securing a settlement. But the emergency was fiercely criticized by the TUC and the Labour Party's National Executive Committee, and for the remaining seven months of Labour's short period of office the STC was not convened. When the Tories came into power in

November, they soon revived the STC and updated its emergency plans.

This showed how a different government could bring a change of *policy* towards strikes. But it was unable to alter the *general direction* of the state which seemed set on a collision course with strikers.

· THE GENERAL STRIKE OF 1926 ·

It was not long in coming. In the next few years the government and the unions sparred with each other until a point of catharsis was reached which effectively resolved the conflict between state and workers for a generation: the General Strike of 1926. Both the preceding events and the strike itself effectively illustrate the basic themes of this book.

The miners had won a favourable national wages agreement in 1924 from a court of inquiry, and the employers were determined to get this altered. Having initiated talks with the miners' union which did not achieve any agreement, the employers then gave notice of their intention to terminate the wages agreement as from July 1925. In its place they proposed new arrangements, including longer working hours and wage cuts. Not surprisingly, the miners rejected these proposals and began to rally support from the rest of the trade union movement. With the threat of wage reductions being such a potent issue, other unions were more willing to offer practical solidarity than in the past. The TUC General Council was given the authority to call national strike action, but, within hours of this being acted upon, the government backed down. Baldwin, the Prime Minister, announced that the government would subsidize the coal industry until May 1926 and the employers suspended their ultimatum while an inquiry was launched into the industry.

The day on which all this happened – 31 July 1925 – came to be known as 'Red Friday', and there was jubilation throughout the labour movement at an apparent victory. However, as Baldwin later confided, the government was simply not ready to take on the unions at that point: instead it was 'buying time to prepare the national defences against the possible recurrence of this threat'.[65]

In the subsequent parliamentary debate to ratify the coal subsidy, the issues were spelt out clearly.[66] Baldwin spoke of the menace to democracy posed by 'a great alliance of trade unions who had the power and the will to inflict enormous and irreparable damage on their country'. Winston Churchill noted

a growing disposition among the great trade union authorities of the country to use the exceptional immunities which trade unions possess under the law, not for the purpose of ordinary trade objects, but in the pursuit of far-reaching political and economic aims . . . We have heard in this Debate of an attempt to hold up the whole community, of the threat of cutting off the vital supply services. The use of such a threat as a political weapon, which has been more and more apparent in recent years, is a grave fact which will require the profound and continuous attention of the House of Commons.

However, trade union leaders refused to accept this allegation of ulterior political motives. A typical reaction came from J. R. Clynes, the General and Municipal Workers' leader. He insisted that the unions' behaviour was that of a movement 'wholly and solely . . . in defence of wage standards . . . indicating a deep sense of responsibility . . . in this instance the workers were not the attacking party. They simply put their backs to the wall, as men who were called upon to act on the defensive.'[67]

These differing interpretations were to figure prominently in subsequent public argument around the General Strike. Meanwhile, the government was busy preparing for a showdown. The Supply and Transport Committee met and drew up detailed contingency plans to maintain essential services, to use volunteer labour, to deploy the police and armed forces as required and to conduct a propaganda campaign to persuade the public to support the government. Through the STO, the regional commissioner system was activated in readiness.

Ten members of the Communist Party's Central Committee were also prosecuted in an overtly political trial in 1925. A charge of conspiracy was linked to sedition and incitement to mutiny, and they were jailed for a year. The evidence against them was extremely flimsy, being drawn from party documents, most of them published. The prosecution made great play of an article in the party's paper, *Workers' Weekly*, which had urged troops to refrain from acting against workers if there were a general strike. The prosecution also argued that British communism itself was a doctrine that amounted to a seditious conspiracy – and the judge supported this view in his direction to the jury. As one writer commented: 'Perhaps the trial may best be understood by its results, which were most useful for the government: the leadership of the Communist Party was removed from the political and industrial scene by means of the common law, at a time which was crucial for the preparation of . . . the general strike.'[68]

The public subsidy for the coal industry was due to expire on 30 April 1926 and, as this date neared, the government effectively forced the trade unions to choose between humiliating retreat and outright confrontation. With the government's acquiescence, the employers issued the miners with an ultimatum: unless they accepted wage cuts, an increase in their working day and district-based rather than national agreements, they would be locked out.

In subsequent negotiations, both the government and the TUC's General Council played a major part. There was a breakdown on the day the subsidy ran out and both sides withdrew to prepare their forces. The government issued a Royal Proclamation under the Emergency Powers Act on 1 May and began to activate its anti-strike machinery. The miners relinquished control of the strike to the General Council which dispatched strike notices to certain unions. Eleventh-hour negotiations were staged between the Prime Minister, Stanley Baldwin, and the TUC. But the question of wage reductions remained the main obstacle. Although the TUC was anxious to find a compromise, at one stage summoning the miners' leaders to accept a deal, the talks eventually collapsed when the Cabinet decided that, in the face of a threatened general strike, it could not 'surrender to coercion'.[69]

The next day, 3 May, government ministers addressed the House of Commons, presenting the issue as a threat to the country's constitution.[70] The government, Baldwin argued, found itself challenged with an alternative government ... when you extend an ordinary trade dispute in this way, from one industry into a score of the most vital industries in the country, you change its character ... they were threatening the basis of ordered government, and going nearer to proclaiming civil war than we have been for centuries past ... it is not wages that are imperilled; it is the freedom of our very Constitution ...

Churchill said he saw no difference whatever 'between a general strike to force a Parliament to pass one Bill which the country does not wish for, and a general strike to force Parliament to pay a subsidy ... it is a conflict which, if it is fought out to a conclusion, can only end in the overthrow of parliamentary government or in its decisive victory'. A Labour spokesman retorted that it was 'merely a plain, economic, industrial dispute', and the TUC tried all it could to deny that it was trying to provoke a constitutional crisis. On the contrary, the TUC was a reluctant participant, reflecting the widespread desire among union leaders to be 'non-political'.

Thus the two squared up to each other, the government choosing the ground over which the battle would be fought. To the surprise of most, the unions' response was massive. Some 3 million workers were involved and, despite the government's pre-planning, only minimal services were operating. Men and women workers united on class lines, their traditional disunity being overcome. Women played a more active role than is usually acknowledged and their contribution was specifically praised by some unions.[71] The TUC was nevertheless on the defensive from the outset. Its preparations had been pathetic compared with the ten months of planning on the government's side. Rather than seeking to mobilize political support to force the government to back down, the TUC wanted a way out. It behaved almost as if it were running a large trade dispute when in reality the government had deliberately turned it into a political strike.

But the government's approach fell short of the outright suppression which ministers like Churchill wanted. Instead, Baldwin got his way. The armed forces were mobilized but kept in the background, with volunteers being recruited to try to run essential services. In the provinces 200,000 'special constables' were recruited and in London 40,000 were on duty by the end of the first week; most were young upper- and middle-class volunteers.[72] A body known as the Organization for the Maintenance of Supplies was established unofficially by leading upper-class figures to mobilize like-minded citizens in the government's aid.

Under the Emergency Powers Act, the government could close down newspapers which *it* determined were publishing 'seditious' or 'false' news and these powers were widely used against people found producing, distributing or even possessing literature that might encourage sedition or disaffection. There were 3,149 prosecutions arising from the strike and of these 1,760 were due to offences of 'incitement' under the Act.[73] Victims included a Lambeth tram-cleaner who was fined more than a week's wages for shouting 'We want the revolution', and a striker who was imprisoned for a month for tearing down a government poster in Lancashire. The BBC did not allow union leaders to make broadcasts and even stopped the transmission of a conciliatory sermon by the Archbishop of Canterbury; although there was apparently no specific instruction from the government, the BBC's Managing Director, John Reith, knew that any broadcasts sympathetic to the strike would invite further restrictions on the Corporation's freedom.[74]

As had been envisaged, the STC took up its duties backed by regulations made under the 1920 Emergency Powers Act. One of these regulations, made on 11 May but never actually implemented, even prohibited banks from paying out money to anyone 'acting in opposition to the national interest'.[75] (Ten years later government law officers found that, in depending upon local councils for distribution of coal and food, the STO had actually acted illegally since this particular use of local authorities was not authorized under the Act.)[76]

Compared with the tactics adopted by police and troops in the big strikes immediately before and after the war, public order was maintained with minimum force. Nevertheless, police clashed frequently with crowds of strikers and broke up demonstrations, and the Special Branch infiltrated local strike committees.[77] There were also calls for union leaders to be prosecuted, and at one stage a High Court judge even declared the strike to be illegal. But government prudence ruled out any dramatic court action. The Cabinet did prepare a secret 'Illegal Strikes Bill' which prohibited 'any strike which has any other objective than the maintenance or improvement of conditions of labour in the industry or branch of the industry in which the strikers are engaged', and plans were made to rush it through Parliament.[78] However, these were overtaken by events.

After pressing in vain for the government to negotiate, the TUC eventually moved over the heads of the miners to offer Baldwin, on 12 May, a settlement that amounted to unconditional surrender. As one labour historian explained: 'The end did not come because the strike was weakening, or because the union leaders feared arrest or were frightened by the statement that the strike was illegal. It came because the General Council had entered a strike it was afraid of winning.'[79] The miners tried to prolong the dispute, but theirs was by then a lost cause. The government moved to increase their hours, as the employers had originally wanted, and by November all the miners had drifted back to work, defeated and demoralized, their union bankrupted and its industrial strength shattered.

· THE CORPORATIST DRIFT ·

The consequences of this defeat were immense. The government brought in the 1927 Trade Disputes and Trade Unions Act. This made illegal both sympathy strikes and strikes intended to pressure the government or which imposed hardships on the community. 'General' or 'national' strikes were thereby made unlawful. The Act's provisions were so tightly drawn that almost any strike was potentially illegal if it could be shown that it had 'political' consequences. Public servants joined gas, electricity and water workers in having restraints placed on their rights to take industrial action. The Act completed its political attack on the labour movement by changing the system of 'contracting-out' of paying the political levy to one of 'contracting-in'. It also prevented civil servants' unions from affiliating to the Labour Party or the TUC.

The government continued to pursue its objective of a 'moderate' and 'responsible' trade union movement. The outcome of the General Strike had widened the gap between union leaders and shopfloor militants, and the 1927 Act was designed to do likewise. It effectively boosted moderate trade unionism by attacking workers' rights to engage in strikes and political action, and drove unions towards an accommodation with government. Thus the foundations were laid for a steady drift towards joint government, industry and union cooperation within a system where 'corporate bias' predominated.[80]

An early vehicle for this drift was the 'Mond–Turner talks' which got under way in early 1928 with the government's blessing. These were discussions between top industrialists and TUC leaders aimed at securing industrial reconciliation and a consensus on broad economic policies. (Sir Alfred Mond was the head of Imperial Chemical Industries and Ben Turner the Chairperson of the TUC.) Left-wingers, such as A. J. Cook of the miners, attacked these talks as acts of 'class collaboration'. But in reply the Transport and General Workers' leader, Ernest Bevin, expressed the dilemma of most union leaders: 'It is all very well,' he told Cook, 'for people to talk as if the working class of Great Britain are cracking their shins for a fight and a revolution, and we are holding them back. Are they? There are not many as fast as we are ourselves.'[81]

A period of industrial conciliation followed in which the 1929–31 Labour government under Ramsay MacDonald did not use the emergency planning apparatus coordinated by the STO. It preferred to promote negotiated outcomes to major disputes. Settlements were in any case easier to secure against a background of rising unemployment (reaching 3 million by the end of 1931). In a switch of roles during a strike against wage cuts in January 1931, the South Wales miners asked for the Emergency Powers Act to be used against the coal-owners, but the government confined its intervention to one of conciliation to achieve an agreement. After

MacDonald's break with Labour and the election of the National Government in 1931, the civil servants who had kept the STO ticking over felt less vulnerable to accusations they had faced from the labour movement of playing a provocative role, and their emergency planning machinery was overhauled.

Despite the efforts of the National Minority Movement – a group launched by communists to promote a broad left campaign for socialist policies in the unions – and later the National Unemployed Workers' Movement, there was a low level of labour militancy in the 1930s. The unions became gradually more institutionalized:

More and more, as the thirties unfolded, the trade union leaders assumed the status of an official Industrial Opposition, as closely involved in playing the game in the industrial field as their parliamentary colleagues were in the political field. More and more the trade union leaders spoke and acted as responsible heads of vast, highly centralized concerns, engaged by means of well-tested and routinized processes of bargaining and compromise, in the hiring out of their members' labour, and deeply concerned to avoid any disturbance of industrial discipline.[82]

'The trade union movement has become an integral part of the state,' Bevin told the 1937 TUC conference, and he was rebuked by the Labour left-winger, Harold Laski, for 'collaboration with Capitalism'.[83] Union leaders justified their role in terms of preventing their members' position from being further undermined during the world-wide recession. It is also important to note that after 1931 unemployment fell from 3 million to 1 million and that real wages for those in work continued to rise. A combination of these factors made the majority of trade unionists who did have jobs reluctant to jeopardize them by strikes and distanced them from the poverty-stricken unemployed: unfavourable conditions for working-class militancy.

A certain equilibrium was reached in which the government did not question the legitimacy of unions and indeed encouraged their institutionalization on the basis of a relationship in which the government was dominant and which strengthened the grip of moderation in the labour movement. The balance within that relationship only began to alter during the run-up to the Second World War when union cooperation was needed in the rearmament programme. After the Nazis marched into Austria in March 1938, the government struck a private agreement with TUC leaders to assist with the movement of skilled workers into defence industries. By 1940 the escalation of the war made the government even more dependent on union support, and there was a shift back towards enhanced union power within the 'corporate triangle' between government, unions and industry.[84]

The settlement this represented between capital and labour undoubtedly meant that the unions had come a long way towards becoming legitimate, influential and in a sense 'governing' institutions in British society. Nevertheless, the historic conflict between unions and the capitalist state remained unresolved, for unions and their interests were accommodated only to the extent that they avoided a strike-based strategy and confined their political activities strictly to parliamentary channels. Looked at in this way, the settlement amounted to a more concrete expression of an objective which had been pursued by successive governments over many decades as they sought to come to terms with growing working-class strength.

4
MODERN GOVERNMENTS
AND STRIKES

'The most powerful man in Britain' – more powerful even than the Prime Minister. According to opinion polls in the mid 1970s, that was the way the public regarded Jack Jones, leader of the giant Transport and General Workers' Union. In September 1978, MORI found that 82 per cent of the electorate felt unions were 'too powerful' (this figure had stood at around three-quarters for most of the decade).* By the early 1980s, however, the pendulum had swung back, with the Thatcher government successfully attacking union rights; after the 1983 general election, the proportion of people feeling unions were 'too powerful' fell to 68 per cent.

The key factor overshadowing that change has been the role of the state in industrial relations since the Second World War. Government intervention in strikes occurred on an unprecedented scale, performing a 'peacemaker' role through conciliation, arbitration and inquiry; attempting to regulate wages through incomes policies; and initiating new industrial relations legislation.[1] The courts and the police acted frequently against strikers, and the armed forces were used periodically. As the government became locked in its most testing battles with unions since the 1926 General Strike, more states of emergency were declared than ever before: of the twelve declared under the Emergency Powers Act since it was passed in 1920, nine were post-war, five of them between 1970 and 1974.

All this was because control or regulation of labour came to

* MORI found that even 73 per cent of *trade unionists* said their unions had too much power in September 1978; by February 1985, this had fallen to 40 per cent.

play a more central role in the economic policies of successive governments. The methods used may have been very different. They ranged from fastidious regulation of collective bargaining immediately after the war, through the 'beer and sandwiches' negotiations in 10 Downing Street conducted by Prime Ministers in the 1960s and 1970s, to a more aloof dependence on the courts and the police by the Thatcher regime. But the purpose was very similar.

The state interposed itself between the two sides of industry, not 'as a neutral but as a partisan . . . One of the most notable features in the recent evolution of advanced capitalism is the degree to which governments have sought to place new and further inhibitions upon organized labour in order to prevent it from exercising what pressures it can on employers (and on the state as a major employer) in the matter of wage claims.'[2] Furthermore,

Wage earners have always had to reckon with a hostile state in their encounter with employers. But now more than ever they have to reckon with its antagonism, in practice, as a direct, pervasive and constant fact of economic life. Their immediate and daily opponent remains the employer; but governments and the state are now much more closely involved in the encounter than in the past.[3]

· THE WAR LEGACY ·

When the phenomenon of ever-enlarging government activity in post-war Britain is explained, attention is usually focused on the immense and urgent task of reconstruction that required public-sector action and planning. Less emphasis is placed on the continuity into peacetime of the interventionist and collectivist consensus about government policy established during the war.

Winning the war had required not simply military planning, but social and economic planning on a huge scale. This also resulted in millions of people suddenly finding themselves better off. Between 1938 and 1945, prices rose by 48 per cent, while average wages jumped by 80 per cent – a real increase in income for working-class people who also benefited from more progressive taxation policies.[4] And the reward for sustaining their wartime efforts and sacrifices was the promise that the government would ensure conditions were better in the future as well. The effect was to 'legitimize' state intervention as never before in Britain. From above, the machinery of Whitehall was geared to it. From below, there was pressure for it from 'a new popular radicalism, more widespread than at any time in the previous hundred years'.[5]

This affected the pattern of industrial relations for many years. Indeed, there is evidence that some thought had been given to post-war industrial policy well before the war had ended. First, there was a certain anxiety among the more perceptive in the Conservative ranks, such as Quintin Hogg, then a young MP, who told the House of Commons in 1943,

if you do not give the people social reform, they are going to give you social revolution . . . Let anyone consider the possibility of a series of dangerous industrial strikes following the present hostilities, and the effect that it would have on our industrial recovery.[6]

Second, union leaders involved in wartime government, including the influential Ernest Bevin, were looking to their position in peacetime. Like many people at the time, they thought Churchill's immense prestige as a war leader would carry the Tories to an inevitable election victory. So they began to explore informally the basis for subsequent trade union cooperation with the Conservatives, including the possibility of participation in a coalition government of reconstruction. Labour Party leaders such as Dalton and Morrison seemed well disposed towards this when it was mooted in 1943. So was Churchill, who even indicated his agreement to amend the 1927 Trade Disputes and Trade Union Act which had so restricted union rights.[7]

· PEACETIME INTERVENTION ·

Cooperation in the war effort had created a degree of political consensus over industrial policy, 'in which party political power was diminished' and even extensions of public ownership were not particularly controversial.[8] So far as labour relations were concerned, the objectives in war and peace turned out to be similar: to obtain the maximum output from the workforce without seriously challenging the ownership of capital. And the solutions were similar, too: complicated legal regulation of wage bargaining; complex systems of arbitration; and regular exhortations to make sacrifices 'in the national interest'.

Labour's resounding 1945 election landslide was followed by the immediate repeal of the 1927 Trade Disputes and Trade Unions Act. However, these advances in working-class strength did not produce a commensurate rise in industrial militancy. On the contrary, the period from 1946 to 1952 'was marked not only by a historically low level of strike activity but also by a downward trend'.[9]

There were several reasons for this. Working-class support for the reforming Labour government of Clement Attlee contributed to relative industrial peace. Workers benefited from a re-distribution of income boosted by an increased 'social wage' from new welfare benefits. The cooperative stance of the unions was also influenced by the intense loyalty to the government displayed by their leaders.

The latter's loyalty had grown out of wartime involvement in government. Bevin had become a Labour Cabinet minister and Walter Citrine retired from being TUC General Secretary to take key positions in the nationalized industries, first as a member of the National Coal Board and then as Chairperson of the Central Electricity Authority. In their place, three strong union leaders emerged, Arthur Deakin of the Transport and General Workers' Union, Thomas Williamson of the General and Municipal Workers' Union and William Lawther of the miners – 'a triumvirate ... moderate in policy and together commanding, with the support of one or two smaller unions, enough votes to control the policy of the Trades Union Congress'.[10] They were able to deliver a significant degree of industrial discipline.

The consent of the unions became crucial to achieve the urgent aims of reconstruction. Economic conditions were very difficult. The population was war-weary, there was a shortage of investment and industry was run down. Raw materials were scarce and there was a severe labour shortage. As a result, a range of government controls, including rationing and planned subsidies, were instituted.

But with more jobs going than there were workers available, and with workers themselves looking to better their conditions after years of austerity, control of wages became an important objective of industrial policy, dependent on union support. To a very large extent the trade union leadership was co-opted and provided a channel for the government to achieve that objective. In effect a 'new social contract' evolved around the economic power of unions.[11]

·UNION GROWTH AND WOMEN·

The end of the war saw the trade union movement organizationally much stronger. Membership had grown by 29 per cent, from 6,053,000 in 1938 (including 4,669,000 affiliated to the TUC) to 7,803,000 in 1945 (including 6,671,000 affiliated).[12] Women accounted for a high proportion of this growth, their numbers rising by about 800,000 in 1938 to 1,340,729 in 1945.[13]

Government conscription of women for war work and the services had been a radical innovation, and it placed women on an equal footing in a new way. With some 2 million entering industry and over half a million joining the forces, economic necessity 'once again caused the concept of "women's role" to be turned on its head'.[14] Although the Ministry of Health stated in 1941 that women should find their own child-minders privately, the government took on part of the burden of women's traditional home responsibilities by improving maternity facilities and by establishing publicly funded nurseries.*

But by the end of the 1940s the war 'might never have happened for women workers'.[16] Restrictive practices emerged again and women found themselves excluded, with union connivance, from skilled employment. Unions made no effort to press for equal pay, and seemed content for women to be directed back into the home as before.

·WAGES, STRIKES AND WORKERS·

When the war ended, agreement had been obtained from unions and employers to the most far-reaching system of compulsory arbitration introduced in peacetime. Strikes and lock-outs were banned through machinery established during the war. The Conditions of Employment and National Arbitration Order No. 1305, which had operated from July 1940, remained in force until August 1951. It enabled collective bargaining to continue, but in the event of a breakdown the dispute had to be referred to the Minister of Labour. The latter could either attempt to settle it by direct conciliation or refer it to the National Arbitration Tribunal, whose decisions were binding. Other emergency powers to deal with possible industrial conflict were extended beyond the war under the Supplies and Services (Transitional Powers) Act 1945. Meanwhile, senior civil servants in the Home Office were pressing the Labour Cabinet to anticipate possible industrial unrest by reviving the Supply and Transport Organization.

The government's strategy for regulating labour evolved into a multi-pronged one. First, there were the wage controls mentioned above. Second, there were public appeals to workers not to inflict hardship on the country. Third, with most strikes in this period

* Before the war there were about 100 nurseries throughout the country, most of them funded by charities; by 1943, the peak of women's contribution to the war effort, there were 1,182 (912 day nurseries and 270 nursery schools) – all government funded – though still only a quarter of the young children of women war workers had nursery places.[15]

being *unofficial*, ministers tried to isolate them by blaming 'political extremists'. Fourth, troops were used when strikes broke out. (Civil servants had in fact authorized the first such use of the military while Attlee was still choosing his Cabinet: between three and four hundred soldiers were deployed to unload ships caught by a dispute in the London docks.)

As Labour settled into office, the dock strike spread throughout the country and by early October 1945 over 6,000 troops had been deployed. The TGWU leader, Arthur Deakin, asserted that the stoppage was being orchestrated by Trotskyists, though the evidence for this was scanty indeed.[17] In reality it was an outbreak of rank-and-file unofficial militancy fairly typical of those years. By late October it had escalated, eventually involving a total of 43,000 dockers and 21,000 strike-breaking troops.

Concerned that the strike might jeopardize the prospects of national recovery, Attlee agreed to set up a Cabinet committee 'to authorize such emergency action as may be necessary, by reason of industrial disputes, to maintain supplies and services essential to the life of the community'.[18] It came to be known as the Industrial Emergencies Committee, though in fact it met for the first time only in 1947 and played no role in this dock strike which ended with a voluntary return to work soon afterwards. The new Labour government had 'won' its first industrial confrontation by taking a firm stand which included the use of troops to do strikers' work.

However, by 1947 the strains imposed by tight wage controls were reaching breaking-point, and the government published White Papers that year and the next, threatening further controls unless wage settlements were moderated. In 1949, with the government's economic problems persisting, such controls were in fact imposed.

· INDUSTRIAL EMERGENCIES ·

Meanwhile the Industrial Emergencies Committee (IEC) met for the first time in January 1947. On its agenda was another unofficial dock strike, and growing shortages of food and other supplies. It agreed a detailed programme of emergency measures, including mobilizing the armed forces and arranging special transport. But the strikers agreed to end the dispute before a formal state of emergency was declared. The experience provoked a reassessment of the IEC's role which was extended to cover emergencies other than industrial ones, partly in order to deflect any criticism that it was nothing but a strike-breaking agency. The Emergencies Committee, as it was known later, became a permanent standing committee of the Cabinet: effectively, 'With its name changed and its scope widened, the STO was back in business.'[19]

The following year, 1948, came another unofficial strike in the docks, and the Emergencies Committee was convened again. The previous winter the committee's regional machinery had been strengthened, and now it began preparations to use troops to move goods. The dispute arose from a claim by London dockers for extra payments to handle dangerous substances, and spread throughout June. Although the Emergencies Committee planned to use some 12,000 troops and 3,000 vehicles to operate the docks, it became apparent that this would be insufficient. Recruitment of a volunteer labour force was considered. But it was resolved instead to rely on the Emergency Powers Act, in order to put 'the government on the offensive against the unofficial strikers', as an official briefing paper explained.[20]

A formal state of emergency was declared under a proclamation issued on 28 June 1948 – the first one since 1926 – and this, coupled with appeals from the government and from union leaders, prompted the dockers to reconsider their position. Within a few days they had voted to return to work, and the state of emergency lapsed in late July.

Outbursts of unofficial strike action continued to plague the government and union leaders alike. In the summer of 1949, the Emergencies Committee decided to recommend a state of emergency over another dispute in the docks, and this was proclaimed on 11 July. The Cabinet's strategy was influenced by the Attorney-General, Sir Hartley Shawcross. He proposed the appointment of a special 'Port Emergency Committee' with executive powers to run the docks and impose discipline. Such powers, he admitted candidly in a paper to the Cabinet, were probably not legally enforceable. Nevertheless, he argued, a legal challenge was unlikely:

I have advised that this risk should be taken and that the Regulations should cover matters on which action is required without undue regard to the niceties of the law. In an emergency the government may have, in matters admitting of legal doubt, to act first and argue about the doubts later, if necessary obtaining an indemnification Act.[21]

In other words, the government were employing strike-breaking tactics with a cavalier attitude to their legality. As it happened, the proclamation inflamed the situation, more dockers went on strike, troops were mobilized and other emergency measures adopted. Within a fortnight, however, the dockers decided to return to work.

This 1949 dock strike resulted in a more intensive search for comprehensive emergency measures to deal with industrial unrest. Subsequent internal Whitehall discussion raised a number of possibilities, including consideration of restrictions on workers in essential industries.

Between January 1945 and autumn 1950 there were about 10,000 stoppages, nearly all of them unofficial.[22] Although virtually all were also illegal, not one striker involved was prosecuted under Order 1305, the government preferring to rely on its emergency measures. Then, in a switch of tactics, the government prosecuted ten leaders of 1,700 gas workers who went on strike against a pay settlement. They were sentenced to a month's imprisonment (reduced on appeal to a £50 fine each) and this provoked an outcry in the trade union movement. The government's new line was maintained when seven dockers were arrested in February 1951 and charged with conspiracy to incite fellow dockers to strike in contravention of Order 1305.

After pressure from the TUC, Order 1305 was finally withdrawn in August 1951. It was replaced by the Industrial Disputes Order No. 1376, based on the same Defence Regulation and containing compulsory arbitration powers but with no prohibition on strikes.

·POLITICS AND UNOFFICIAL STRIKES·

Throughout Attlee's time in office, controversy persisted over the extent to which strikes were 'politically inspired', and government ministers made regular allegations to that effect. Such allegations had been made before, of course, but the novel feature of this period was the extent to which union leaders joined in with attacks on 'political strikes' too. Most of the strikes were unofficial and initiated against the express wishes of union leaders. They therefore challenged the corporatist consensus of which unions were institutionally part, and union leaders saw this as a threat to the maintenance of that consensus.

Sometimes the government, the TUC and union leaders seemed to be acting in concert to oppose unofficial strikes. For example, in the 1949 docks dispute where troops were used, the Transport and General Workers' Union subsequently expelled three members of the dockers' unofficial committee and disciplined five others. That caused a fresh strike in the spring of 1950, in which troops were deployed once again.

In the 1948 dock strike Attlee broadcast an appeal to the rank-and-file over the heads of the unofficial strike leaders, alleging the latter were 'just a small nucleus who have been instructed for political reasons to take advantage of every little disturbance that takes place to cause the disruption of the British economy, British trade, and to undermine the government and destroy Britain's position'.[23] The TGWU leader, Arthur Deakin, also said that it was a political strike; but the police could find no evidence to support his allegations of manipulation by members of the Communist Party.[24]

In reality, the government was using the epithet 'political' as a way of discrediting *unofficial* strikes. Bevin made clear the government's main concern during a special meeting of Cabinet ministers reviewing the same dock dispute, when he demanded that the government break the strike. Minutes of the meeting record his argument that: 'If the strikers got their way, the government would be at the mercy of unofficial strikes for many years to come.'[25]

The government also felt political militancy was at the root of unofficial 'lightning strikes' in the electricity services. In 1949 the Cabinet agreed to inform the Electricity Authority that 'the government would support them in resisting unauthorized strikes threatening public supplies of electricity, which appeared to be fomented for political reasons or without adequate justification'.[26]

The atmosphere around the heightening 'Cold War' contributed to a particular government paranoia about the role of 'communist agitators'.* But the real problem was not this, as the Chairperson of the Port of London Authority, Sir John Anderson, told the Prime Minister in May 1950. While it was 'fashionable' to blame communists for the persistent pattern of strikes in the docks,

It seemed to him that the real trouble was that the rank-and-file of the dock labourers did not trust their leaders. They were under the impression that their official leaders were too closely associated with the employers and to some extent the government and did not really stand up for the interests of the men. That was why the unofficial leaders commanded confidence.[27]

His opinion summed up the situation. The government's co-option of a willing union leadership may have helped to quell any *official* strikes, and indeed contributed to a low level of strikes overall, with the number of working days lost by strikes falling from 3.7 million in 1944 to 1.4 million in 1950.[28] But this very process opened up a gap between the leadership and the union rank-and-file which was filled by *unofficial* action. Much of it centred on the docks, which were strategically still crucial to the economy in that post-war period, which had a record of bad industrial relations, and in which rank-and-file workers had developed a reputation for militancy. (In that sense the dockers during the 1950s were in a similar position to that of the miners in the 1970s and early 1980s.)

In his last speech as General Secretary of the TUC, Walter

* The 'communist bogey' was regularly wheeled out, with scant regard for the truth, to suggest that strikes were illegitimate, later examples including the 1966 seamen's strike and the 1984–5 miners' strike.

Citrine told its conference in 1946 that the trade union movement had 'passed from the era of propaganda to one of responsibility'.[29] If true then, that statement was still true by the end of the Attlee administration and the Tory victory in 1951. Unions had gradually become 'governing institutions, existing thereafter as estates of the realm, committed to cooperation with the state, even if they retained the customary habit of opposition to specific party governments'.[30]

But in an environment where capital and managerial power remained concentrated in a few hands, that change in role encouraged a degree of polarization between leaders and led, as one study confirms:

At the national level trade union leaders became an established part of the political process: government economic strategies required the co-operation of the unions ... At the local level workers were finding that their strength lay on the shopfloor ... Thus where the leaders were trying to help governments introduce an ordered capitalism, the rank-and-file were following traditional *laissez-faire* policies of taking the market for all it could bear.[31]

· FROM CONCILIATION TO CONFRONTATION ·

This was the background against which Churchill came to power again in 1951, any suggestion that the election of the Tories might herald a more confrontational relationship between the government and the union leadership being quickly dispelled. The new Minister of Labour, Sir Walter Monckton, was chosen for his skills as a pragmatist and a conciliator (though Churchill told him upon his appointment: 'I have the worst job in the Cabinet for you'). The Tories made it clear they wanted industrial peace: 'I am a firm believer in government by consultation and consent,' said Monckton.

The TUC was similarly conciliatory, warning its members not to resist government measures by industrial action and announcing: 'It is our longstanding practice to work with whatever government is in power and through consultation with ministers and with the other side of industry to find practical solutions to the social and economic problems facing the country.'[32]

Living standards continued to rise and major strikes were avoided through government intervention and conciliation. But increasingly the government's attitude began to change. It became more difficult for the government to intervene successfully because of the almost wholly local nature of most disputes; its machinery was geared to dealing with national disputes. One of the issues with which it became preoccupied was the phenomenon of 'wage drift'. The practice of topping-up national agreed wage settlements through local bargaining became more widespread. Partly this was because shortages of skilled labour increased the bargaining strength of local trade union representatives; partly it was the continuing momentum towards workplace bargaining as national unions were drawn into cooperation with the government (the number of government committees on which the TUC was represented rose from sixty in 1949 to eighty-one in 1954).

Since 1945 wages had been running steadily ahead of productivity while Britain's share of world trade was steadily declining, and by 1955 Tory economic policy was becoming dependent on wage restraint, especially in its role as employer in the public sector. Once more, the unions became a major political problem. Within the Tory ranks, traditional hostility to trade unionism resurfaced, one MP stating in the House of Commons:

A new entity has emerged in the body politic, the power of trade unions to intervene in an organized fashion in our lives, either to promote or to bring to a dead stop the intricate processes upon which a modern state depends . . . Are we not witnessing the emergence of a new Estate of the Realm?[33]

He was speaking against the background of the 1955 rail strike, when 60,000 footplatemen went on strike to protect their traditional position as skilled workers running the trains. At the same time a dock strike started. On 31 May the government declared a state of emergency, putting into effect the measures which had evolved in the late 1940s. Both disputes were settled some weeks later by Monckton, the Minister of Labour.

The pattern of growing confrontation continued as the government's determination to control wages grew. In 1956 right-wing domination of the TUC was broken with the death of Arthur Deakin. The succession of Frank Cousins as General Secretary of the TGWU marked a leftward shift in the union. He persuaded the 1956 TUC conference to accept a motion rejecting the government's policy of controlling the economy 'by wage restraint and by using the nationalized industries as a drag-anchor'. In a memorable phrase, Cousins argued: 'In a period of freedom for all, we are part of the all.' [34]

In 1957 there were more days lost through strikes than in any year since 1926. With shipping employers complaining publicly that the government had pressured them to compromise over a strike when they had been prepared to fight it out with the unions, the Prime Minister (now Harold Macmillan) circulated a White-hall memorandum saying: 'We should try to correct the view which has recently gained ground among the public and the press that it is the government's duty in the interests of the national economy to prevent strikes at almost any cost.' [35] Economic problems were undermining the industrial consensus established over the war period and 'union power' came back on to the political agenda as a contentious issue.

·INCOMES POLICIES AND STRIKES·

Also in 1957, the steady move towards a formal incomes policy was given further impetus by the setting-up of the Council on Productivity, Prices and Incomes. Confined to a role which was mainly exhortatory, it had little influence beyond creating a public climate more conducive to incomes restraint. It made great play of being independent and impartial, though its first report in early 1958 was denounced by the TUC for being 'partisan' and 'one-sided' in its support for government policy.

The strains in the government's economic programme were

certainly forcing it to become more explicitly 'one-sided', *The Times* commenting on the shift from conciliation to wage restraint:

The system of government conciliation grew up on the assumption that the government were not involved and could hold the ring impartially. It may be difficult for it to survive in its present form now that governments habitually have policies of their own on wages.[36]

This was vividly illustrated in the 1958 London bus strike, which ministers were determined to defeat. First, they isolated the bus workers by securing a conciliatory settlement of a simultaneous dispute on the railways. Second, they held out over the seven weeks, despite inconvenience to the public, before the strikers finally returned to work having settled for rather less than they had wished. Third, ministers exploited the TUC General Council's refusal to agree to a request from the workers' union, the TGWU, to extend the strike by calling out other groups of workers in solidarity. The TUC was worried about being dragged into a political strike, despite the government being the party responsible for making it one. Even the very act of submitting the bus workers' claim had 'appeared as a challenge to the government'.[37] This was because the government had ultimate financial responsibility for their nationalized employer, London Transport. Furthermore, a successful strike could have led to a leapfrogging process with bus workers outside London, so endangering the Tories' counter-inflation policy which rested on public-sector curbs.

· WAGE RESTRAINT IN THE 1960s ·

Between 1950 and 1960 the annual number of strikes had doubled, with over 90 per cent of them being unofficial. In the new decade wage restraint became the lynchpin of government economic strategy. The Chancellor announced a 'pay pause' in 1961, followed in spring 1962 by a 'guiding light' of 2.5 per cent together with a government White Paper, *Incomes Policy: the Next Step*, giving guidance for employers and arbitrators to use in settlements. But resistance by various groups of workers to the 2.5 per cent policy quickly undermined it. The dockers' threat to strike produced a settlement of 9 per cent, with Macmillan conceding: 'This is a great blow to our incomes policy and makes it difficult to see where we go now.'[38]

The next step was to establish a National Incomes Commission. With no statutory powers, Macmillan admitted that it relied on 'public castigation'. The NIC participated alongside a new National Economic Development Council (NEDC) – which involved government, employers and union leaders – in 'tripartite' discussions to produce a consensus around key economic objectives. Ineffectual though these institutions were, they signalled the government's attempt to grope towards a method of regulating wages which ran alongside the free collective bargaining system cherished by the unions, while leaving unchallenged the power of private capital.

When Labour came to power in 1964, they went even further towards wage control, establishing the Prices and Incomes Board in 1965, followed by a series of wage restraint policies, including a pay freeze during the 1966 economic crisis. Indeed incomes policy came to dominate labour relations in the 1960s, and this had major repercussions which included 'politicizing' almost all serious strikes. As was argued during this period,

the relations between 'political' and 'economic' struggle have changed. The emergence of a state drive to impose a centralized incomes policy is one of the defining characteristics of contemporary capitalism. The effect of this is to make possible an aggregation of local issues and disputes into a *national struggle* over the distribution of the economic surplus. An incomes policy makes capitalism as a system transparent in a sense that it never was previously.[39]

In practice the unions reaffirmed their traditional reluctance to adopt such a strategy of extending and generalizing disputes: they reacted defensively to government pay curbs, only breaching them on an individual, sectional basis. Invariably they were also prepared to go along with a government-encouraged 'special case ideology' (i.e. one which treated each claim on its merits and which only conceded demands on the basis of the workers concerned being considered a special case). That made unified action and common demands between unions difficult to achieve.

· THE 1966 SEAMEN'S STRIKE ·

The seamen's dispute in 1966 was, then, the longest and most bitter strike since the war, lasting six weeks over May and June. The National Union of Seamen claimed a pay increase and a reduction in the working week to forty hours without loss of pay. On 23 May, a week after the strike had begun, a state of emergency under the 1920 Act was declared by Harold Wilson's government. It also set up a Committee of Inquiry and appealed to the union, but to no avail. Finally a revised offer was accepted and the dispute ended on 30 June.

The government's response was notable for the open attempt Labour's leaders made to characterize the strike as a political one. In a fireside chat on television, Harold Wilson asserted that it was 'a strike against the state, against the community', adding,

what is at issue here is our national prices and incomes policy. To accept the demand would be to breach the dykes of our prices and incomes policy . . . Our determination to insist on these principles when the cost is great will be taken by everyone at home and abroad as a proof of our determination to make that policy effective.[40]

Coming as it did against a background of economic crisis, the strike was seen as a test of the government's resolve to impose deflationary policies by taming union power. Media comment hostile to the unions was quite clear about the political issues at stake. Four months earlier the voice of the business world, the *Economist*, asserted: 'The only way to achieve an incomes policy in 1966 is going to be by outfacing the trade unions in some big national wage struggle.' In the middle of the strike, one Fleet Street financial editor wrote from a meeting of bankers in Basle:

The Central bankers thoroughly approve the government's stand against the seamen. They have always urged Mr Wilson to have a showdown with the unions ... If the Prime Minister had failed to meet the challenge, the atmosphere at the Basle meeting would have been very different. As it is, it seems that we can still count on a certain amount of goodwill.[41]

But although it increased the pressure on them, exhortation did not shake the resolve of the strikers. So Harold Wilson adopted a different tactic – to smear them. After another fall in the value of the pound, he told the House of Commons on 20 June that the strike was inspired by a 'tightly-knit group of politically motivated men ... who are ... endangering the security of the industry and the economic welfare of the nation'. Wilson was relying on raw intelligence information from M I5. In fact it revealed more about the political prejudices of the security service than it did about the nature of the strike, the reality of which was completely misrepresented by his attack. However, it undoubtedly weakened the resolve of the strikers, and the union's executive accepted a revised offer just a few days afterwards.

· LABOUR AND STRIKES ·

Partly because of the strike, Labour's economic strategy now lay in ruins. It adopted the first statutory incomes policy in peacetime on 20 July: prices and wages were frozen for the rest of the year, to be followed by another six months of severe restraint. Effectively the government allowed itself to be blown off course as its National Plan, introduced only a year before, was abandoned. Further confrontations with unions contributed to the government's economic problems. The 1967 dock strike, for instance, was a major factor in the damaging devaluation of the pound in November 1967. But strikes like this occurred out of frustration with continuing wage controls. The unions did not have undermining the government's authority as their main objective.

The wider pattern of industrial strife during the late 1960s was also a product of the contradictions between the national and local levels of collective bargaining. The trend towards shopfloor power had been increasing and the authorities were preoccupied with the problem of 'unofficial' strikes again. A Royal Commission on Trade Unions chaired by Lord Donovan was set up in 1964, and its findings, published in 1968, focused heavily on unofficial strikes. In evidence to the Commission, the General Secretary of the National Union of Railwaymen, Sidney Greene, indicated the frustration of union leaders:

. . . . when the management puts up some forward-looking proposals, the difficulty is to get them accepted by our members. I do not instruct them . . . I may not be opposed to these new ideas in any way, but the difficulty is trying to get the members to swallow all these things at once.[42]

The problems created by this local–national tension were compounded by the way wage restraint produced anomalies within pay structures. And the fact that local productivity deals were not restricted by incomes policy guidelines led to another major anomaly. Workers outside the manufacturing sector were not as able to vary their output and take advantage of local productivity schemes, and their union leaders were forced into strikes to maintain their position in the wages league. Often these were white-collar or public-sector workers – such as bank employees and teachers – not previously noted for their militancy. Between 1967 and 1969 the number of days lost in strikes more than doubled, from 2.8 million to 6.8 million (rising still further to 11 million in 1970); meanwhile profits and exports declined, investment stagnated and so did consumption.[43]

Against this background, the Labour government brought out a White Paper, *In Place of Strife*, in January 1969. The minister responsible, Barbara Castle, saw it mainly as a mechanism for tackling the unofficial strike issue, which had preoccupied Donovan, more quickly than the recommendations of the report itself could be implemented. She also had 'party political' motives. Curbing strikes, she argued, would be 'spiking the Tory guns' in the run-up to the coming general election.[44]

The most contentious parts of the White Paper were its proposals to give the government the power to order unions to ballot their members over strikes which would have a serious impact on the economy or the national interest, and to order a 28-day 'cooling-off' period in unofficial strikes. Failure to obey such government orders would render unions liable to fines. Not surprisingly, there was uproar in the labour movement. Eventually the government had to back down.

The 1964–70 Labour government made a virtue of its willingness to intervene in strikes, Harold Wilson using his authority as Prime Minister to settle disputes personally on five separate occasions. Later Wilson set out some principles which guided him. A prime minister, he wrote,

should intervene only as a last resort and no party to a dispute should be encouraged to believe that he will intervene at all. In no circumstances should he be regarded as a court of appeal ready to reverse or amend what the ministers responsible have urged on the parties. In the main – there can be exceptions – he should be prepared to intervene only when there is a procedural deadlock which cannot be resolved without his intervention. One exception is a strike which could inflict severe damage on the economy . . . Another is . . . to make clear . . . what his ministerial colleagues have told the unions and employers is the last word. A rare case is where someone's face needs to be saved . . .[45]

However, Labour had enjoyed mixed relations with the unions. While there was general support for the Wilson government among trade unionists, the confrontations over wages, culminating in the White Paper, undoubtedly strained the link between the Labour leadership and the labour movement, and were seen as a major contribution to the government's subsequent defeat by the Tories in June 1970. The post-war system of 'corporate bias' involving cooperation between government, industry and unions was already under strain by the time Labour came to power in 1964. But from 1966 it was increasingly de-stabilized (a process which was to continue in the 1970s), one result being to undermine the broad political consensus which had existed between the major political parties since 1940.[46]

·WOMEN ADVANCE·

Meanwhile women were gradually emerging as a major force on the labour market and in the unions. Most of the gains women made during the war had been taken away from them afterwards, though this in itself made women trade unionists even more determined to fight for equality, their opponents as likely to be local and national trade union establishments as employers. During the 1950s, lip-service was paid to equal pay in the form of resolutions carried each year at TUC and union conferences. But there was no determination to give these any priority and equality seemed as far away as ever.[47] The only major gain was the achievement of equal pay in the civil service.

However, by the 1960s things had begun to change. More married women were working, and their increasing dissatisfaction at having to do two jobs without proper support meant that demands for child-care facilities started to grow. Labour's election victory on a manifesto which included the promise of equal pay for equal work also helped to change the climate. The recruitment of women into the expanding area of white-collar and public-sector employment led to a big jump in the number of women in unions: between 1964 and 1970, over 70 per cent of TUC membership growth was accounted for by women.[48]

Although the headlines were captured by what were to all intents and purposes *male* strikes for higher pay, 'there went on almost separately the struggle of women for parity in unions and for economic equality'.[49] Little by little, concessions were gained. Women shop workers started to win strikes for union recognition. Trade unions started paying more attention to insistent demands from their growing force of women members.

Then in 1968 came the strike of women machinists at Ford's. It was over management's refusal to recognize their status as skilled workers and their demand for parity with men on the appropriate skilled grade. After three weeks they won a partial victory, settling for 92 per cent of the skilled rate. But to women workers elsewhere it seemed more like a total victory and became a key event. Being a strike over women's right to have full recognition for skilled work, it went beyond the issue of equal pay and linked into the rise of the women's movement and the rapid spread of feminist ideas at the time. Pressure grew on Labour to implement its manifesto pledge, and the Equal Pay Act 1970 followed. Pressure also grew within the trade union movement to take women's rights seriously for the first time. Consequently the struggle of the Ford women was a good example of how a strike can act as a catalyst for much wider political and social reform.[50]

· CONFRONTING STRIKERS IN THE 1970s ·

The right-wing platform on which Edward Heath's Tory government was elected in June 1970 was a further sign of the break-up of the post-war consensus. Heath plunged almost immediately into a series of confrontations with the unions. In this first period of office, from June 1970 to November 1972, the Tories pursued what could be described as a 'premature Thatcherite' programme. They were determined to resist public-sector wage claims and to undermine union power through a new Industrial Relations Act.

The Act, introduced in 1971, in many respects reflected the aims of the ill-fated *In Place of Strife* – for example, in its requirement for a 'cooling-off' period before strike action could commence. Various forms of industrial action were defined as 'unfair industrial practices', and if unions did not comply with the new law they could be brought before a special court – the National Industrial Relations Court (NIRC). By making national unions legally responsible for the activities of their local officials, the Act specifically intended to curb unofficial strikes. Indeed, Heath had earlier seemed to reflect much of the Wilson government's frustration with shopfloor militancy when he said:

The trouble in Britain today is not that the trade unions are too strong but that they are too weak in this important sense: that compared with other countries it is getting more and more difficult for employers to make firm agreements with trade unions which they will keep, because well over 90 per cent of all the strikes that take place in Britain start as unofficial strikes and then subsequently are blessed by the unions.[51]

The 1971 Act embodied a whole new approach to industrial relations. It abolished the structure of trade union and labour law which had been built upon statutes from 1871 to 1906. It aimed to curb strikes by means of legal penalties. It also aimed to regulate trade union organizations by requiring them to apply for acceptance on to an official register, and by vetting their rule books.

The labour movement reacted angrily to what was the most serious legislative assault on its rights since 1927. In February 1971, about 140,000 trade unionists joined a TUC demonstration against the new law while it was still proceeding through Parliament. And, although the TUC rejected demands from the left for a series of strikes against the Bill, Congress House was unable to prevent 'unofficial' militancy. This was organized through shop stewards' committees, mostly coordinated by the Liaison Committee for the Defence of Trade Unions, a group launched by the Communist Party which included sections of the Labour left. There were a number of one-day protest strikes against the legislation: on 8 December 1970, 350,000 workers were involved; on 12 January 1971, 180,000; and well over a million successively on 1 March and 18 March.

After a certain amount of to-ing and fro-ing, the TUC adopted a hard line of resistance to the Act, instructing its affiliates not to register as required and refusing to recognize the law. The engineers' leader, Hugh Scanlon, told the 1972 TUC conference that the 'courts which are active under the Act are brazenly political'.

During the period from 1969 to 1973, an unusually high number of days (over 6 million) were lost from strikes in the category described as 'political stoppages' by the Department of

Employment.* The confrontationist stance of the Tories provoked a militant response from rank-and-file union activists in particular. The powerful, left-led shop stewards' movement of the time was quite willing to take on the government by organizing strikes. Contrary to the traditional pattern in which governments were mainly responsible for upping the stakes and turning major strikes into political confrontations, these protest strikes *were* explicitly aimed at undermining the ability of the Tories to enforce their anti-union policies. And, unlike the early 1980s, the unions gained support from their members because the whole labour movement was confident and assertive; because the economic climate was healthier; and because the Heath Tories were not so politically determined to confront trade unionism as the Thatcher ones.

· TRIALS OF STRENGTH ·

The first major confrontation had occurred within a month of Heath taking office, when 42,000 dockers came out on strike throughout the country. The government declared a state of emergency on 16 July, though the dispute ended soon afterwards when a Court of Inquiry conceded a pay rise.

But the real battleground was in the public sector. In the autumn of 1970 there were a series of strikes by local government workers, and at one point soldiers were used in the London Borough of Tower Hamlets to replace striking refuse collectors. Then came industrial action for higher wages by electricity workers. They imposed a work-to-rule and an overtime ban from 7 December. Five days later the Heath government declared its second state of emergency, enabling the Electricity Council to regulate its supplies and to impose power cuts. But within a week

* The Department records in its official strike statistics only those stoppages arising from industrial disputes concerning terms and conditions of employment. Stoppages in protest against government policies it considers to be 'political', though this can be confusing because strikes against public expenditure cuts would be regarded as 'political' whereas strikes against redundancies resulting from those same cuts would not.[52]

the government decided it could not break the strike (partly because the troops were not felt to be capable of running the power stations), and conceded a relatively generous settlement to end the dispute.

That concession was more a reflection of the power workers' strength than any lack of government resolve – as Post Office workers soon discovered in their first-ever long strike. It lasted from 20 January to 8 March 1971 and resulted in the loss of over 6,250,000 working days – then the largest number in any dispute since the 1920s. But the union achieved only a marginal increase on management's original offer, its members being forced back to work in the face of government intransigence.

However, the atmosphere of conflict continued and in January 1972 the miners started their first national strike since 1926. Initially the government seemed determined to resist the strike and on 9 February declared its third state of emergency. But the very next day came a turning-point in the dispute. It was also to prove a watershed in the state's response to strikes.

After skirmishes spreading over six days, Saltley coke depot in Birmingham – containing the country's main supply of coke for gas and power stations – was closed: 15,000 pickets, including 'flying pickets' of miners from other parts of Britain, proved too much for the police. It now became clear that industry was threatened with a complete shutdown, and the government switched its tactics, allowing the miners to be treated as a special case.

· RESISTANCE TO THE 1971 ACT ·

Shortly afterwards the government had to back down again, this time over a railway dispute. It highlighted the shortcomings of the Industrial Relations Act. The government first applied to the NIRC for a 'cooling-off' period under provisions in the Act covering national emergencies. The court granted one of fourteen days, and the unions complied with this. After it had expired, however, the unions reimposed their overtime ban and work-to-rule. The government then applied to the NIRC to order a compulsory ballot of members to determine whether the industrial action should continue. In the event, this manoeuvre came badly unstuck because over 80 per cent of the railway workers voted to maintain their action. The result was a double blow to the government: the Act was discredited and a settlement was conceded against its policy of wage restraint.

By the summer of 1972, the Act had been reduced to a state of farce over industrial action by dockers whose traditional work was being replaced by the use of containers. On 14 June 1972 the NIRC ordered three dockers, members of the TGWU, to be imprisoned for contempt of court. They had defied a court order prohibiting them from indulging in 'unfair industrial practice' by blacking certain haulage firms which handled containers. With warrants for their arrest due on 16 June, there were threats of widespread strikes by dockers and others, and a major crisis grew. Then came an extraordinary development: the appearance on the scene of the Official Solicitor – a previously obscure figure described as an 'officer of the court'. Because the unions did not recognize the NIRC, the men were not legally represented and the Official Solicitor intervened on the basis that he was looking after their interests. He requested the Appeal Court to review the sentence of imprisonment imposed on the dockers. It did, the sentence was lifted and, conveniently, the moment of crisis passed.

But the blacking continued and there were further legal proceedings. On 21 July the NIRC again made an order, this time against five shop stewards: they were taken to Pentonville prison and became known as the 'Pentonville Five'. Unofficial strikes in the docks broke out immediately, spreading to other industries as well. Amid protests to the government from the TUC, events began to escalate towards a one-day general strike. On 26 July the House of Lords considered a related legal case and delivered a judgment 'with unprecedented speed', as one legal expert described it.[53] (Normally it would have taken another two months.) The law lords ruled that the union's *leadership* and not the imprisoned shop stewards should be held responsible for the picketing that had occurred at the container depots. Once more the Official Solicitor intervened, formally drawing the attention of the NIRC to the House of Lords' ruling. This gave a pretext for the President of the Court, Sir John Donaldson, to release the dockers.

Yet he had said only a month before, of the Pentonville Five: 'By their conduct these men are saying they are above the rule of law. No court should ignore such a challenge. To do so would imperil all law and order.' And just a few days before, he had said: 'The issue is whether these men are to be allowed to opt out of the rule of law . . . It is a very simple issue but vastly important, for our whole way of life is based upon acceptance of the rule of law.'

That he was able to swallow these strong words and release them suggested 'a strong suspicion of judicial compliance with political expediency'.[54] Effectively, the government, with the assistance of the courts, had manipulated the procedures of the law in order to ward off a national crisis provoked by its own legislation. Under the threat of widespread strikes, the protection of 'our whole way of life' had, within the space of a few weeks, been turned on its head.

· A SWITCH IN APPROACH ·

With its economic problems mounting, the government was by now operating an increasingly formal incomes policy. In the spring of 1972 Heath had offered a more cooperative relationship with the unions in return for voluntary wage restraint. But this was rejected and, in November 1972, he introduced a statutory incomes policy. Early the following year his Counter Inflation Act gave the government powers to control pay and prices for three years, with a new Pay Board and Price Commission to regulate the policy.

Initially there was strong opposition to this: for example, early in 1973 the civil service unions called their first-ever one-day national strike, followed by overtime bans and a work-to-rule, and there were selective strikes by hospital ancillary workers. On 1 May the TUC organized a national stoppage involving 1,600,000 workers. But gradually the resistance diminished, and the number of working days lost through strikes fell compared with figures for the first two years of the Heath administration.

By this time incomes policy, rather than the Industrial Relations Act, had become the prime instrument for controlling organized labour. The Act's impotence in the face of determined union opposition was underlined by a confrontation with the engineering union, the AUEW, in 1973. After it had directly challenged the Act's authority, the union's assets were sequestered by the courts. In response it threatened a national engineering strike which was only averted when an anonymous group of businessmen stepped in and paid a fine imposed on the union, thereby purging its contempt. Employers were clearly unhappy with the Act, the Director-General of the Confederation of British Industry, Campbell Adamson, stating later that it has 'sullied every relationship at national level between unions and employers'.

In November 1973 came a series of events which were to culminate in the downfall of the government. The first was an international oil crisis, causing a shortage of fuel and a massive price rise. At the same time there was industrial action by the miners and by electrical power engineers. Unpredictable power cuts soon followed, and on 13 November Heath declared a state of emergency; a month later he ordered manufacturing industry to switch to a three-day week to conserve energy.

The government managed to secure a settlement with the power engineers, but not with the miners. As the crisis deepened, there was pressure within the Conservative Party for a general election on the theme 'Who governs the country?'. The miners balloted their members and obtained an 81 per cent vote for a strike. Soon afterwards, amid accusations of a 'political strike against a constitutional government', Heath did call an election.

The Tories fought it on a 'Who rules the country?' platform, Heath asking in his opening broadcast: 'Do you want Parliament and the elected government to continue fighting strenuously against inflation? Or do you want them to abandon the struggle against rising prices under pressure from one particularly powerful group of workers?'[55] The electorate gave a mixed answer: they rejected the Tories, gave the Liberals their biggest post-war vote, and allowed Labour in to form a minority government.

But the conventional wisdom that the unions had brought down the government should be qualified. Heath *chose* to call an election – and he lost it. The fact that Britain seemed almost ungovernable at the time had more to do with the Tories' *policies* than any desire by the unions to overthrow a constitutionally elected *government*. With the trade unions ascendant and the right on the defensive, the political and industrial climate was also very different from the one which the miners were to face in their next big strike in 1984–5.

· LABOUR BACK IN ·

Although a 'social contract' was negotiated between the new government and the unions under which they would behave 're-sponsibly' in return for repeal of the 1971 Act and new pro-union laws, there was an outbreak of strikes, mostly from workers in the public sector demanding favourable treatment. Pressure for wage increases mounted, though in accordance with the social contract the TUC agreed to guidelines limiting settlements to compensate only for rises in the cost of living.

The two years after 1974 were probably the height of union influence over government. A detailed programme of legislation was enacted, giving unions and individual workers new rights. The 1974–6 Trade Union and Labour Relations Acts restored to unions the legal immunities that had been swept aside by the 1971 Act. The 1975 Employment Protection Act secured new collective bargaining and job security rights. The 1974 Health and Safety at Work Act and the 1975 Sex Discrimination Act instituted much-needed reforms in traditionally neglected areas of workers' rights.

Public perception of the extent of the unions' power was echoed by a senior Tory Shadow Cabinet minister, Reginald Maudling, who argued in 1976 that Britain's unions now possessed 'the power to bring any capitalistic economy to a halt'. He was especially concerned with what he termed union 'monopoly power' in key public services, the disruption of which by strikes could almost paralyse an increasingly interdependent society.[56]

In reality, British trade unions have been 'powerful' only at certain points in history. The pre- and post-First World War periods of labour militancy were examples. Another was undoubtedly in the 1960s and early 1970s. But even in this recent period, unions normally had power only in the negative sense of being able to veto changes, maintain some control over their immediate working conditions, or refuse offers of wage increases until management improved them. Relatively few unions possessed sufficient industrial muscle to win strikes and fewer still to challenge government policies. The truth is that 'workers go on strike not because they have power but because they lack it, and are driven with great reluctance and at considerable financial cost to themselves to withdraw their labour in sheer frustration'.[57] Despite public perception of all-powerful unions in the 1970s, it is significant that wages in Britain remained the lowest in Western Europe.

The public tends to have an exaggerated impression of the influence of unions partly because, to exercise any leverage, unions have to act in a *highly visible* manner. They have to go on strike, to picket, to demonstrate, to make their presence felt. In contrast, a financier can wield enormous power simply by making a telephone call, such behaviour being publicly invisible.

Television has been a major factor behind the widespread misconception of union power. Because TV is geared to reporting *visible action*, it tends to concentrate on what trade unions are doing. A picket-line clash or a union mass meeting in the company car park makes 'better TV' and therefore more impact than a closed meeting during which management might decide to switch its investment policy – despite the fact that the latter event will invariably have far more significance in the development of a dispute. Inevitably people come to confuse the regular intrusion of unions into the public arena with power.

Even during the mid 1970s there were major constraints on union power:

What trade union leaders enjoyed under the Labour government was not so much the power to determine the substantive drift of policy as the ability to participate in a new set of procedural rights which created the impression of influence that the resulting drift of policy so often belied.[58]

· THE GRUNWICK STRIKE ·

The limitations of these procedural rights were cruelly exposed in the Grunwick strike of 1976–7. Although it had modest beginnings it was to become a major strike – and one made overtly political by the company's management, the police and the courts. Grunwick centred on the right of workers to join and be represented by a union of their choice. It began during the August heatwave of 1976 when workers, fed up with bad conditions, walked out from the company's film-processing laboratory in north-west London. Repeated attempts to establish recognition for the union of their choice, APEX, failed: normal procedures led nowhere against an obdurate employer.

Within months, Post Office workers seeking to support the strikers by refusing to handle the firm's lifeblood – its mail – found themselves constrained by the courts. Picketing of the firm escalated into bitter confrontations between trade unionists and the police. The aggressive tactics of the elite police Special Patrol Group inflamed the atmosphere and provoked many trade unionists involved to wonder about the tangible benefit of the laws passed by Labour. The small firm of Grunwick quickly became both the centre of a national controversy and a symbol of the failure of even pro-union laws to protect the interests of workers.

They resorted to the new arbitration machinery established under the Employment Protection Act, and requested the Advisory, Conciliation, and Arbitration Service (ACAS) to intervene. It polled the strikers and found them overwhelmingly in favour of joining APEX. The management, however, had refused ACAS permission to consult those still working inside the company. And when ACAS recommended that APEX be granted recognition and negotiating rights, Grunwick refused to accept the recommendation.

The whole ethos of the new arbitration procedure – which depended on both parties accepting the outcome – had been rejected by a management which made no bones about its right-wing views and was advised throughout by right-wing members of the Conservative Party. The company now went to court to get ACAS's recommendation for union recognition declared void. It failed in the High Court which ruled in favour of ACAS. But this was overturned in Lord Denning's Appeal Court on 29 July 1977.

Meanwhile another official avenue had been pursued. Partly in order to cool an inflamed situation which it found distinctly embarrassing, the Labour Cabinet appointed a court of inquiry under Lord Scarman which sat for two months, investigating all aspects of the dispute, and came out broadly in favour of union recognition and in support of APEX.[59] But again the company remained unmoved, also defying government attempts to persuade it to reach an agreement with APEX.

By the time Scarman had reported and ACAS had become bogged down in the Court of Appeal, the strike's momentum had run out. Repeatedly urged (by, among others, Labour and union leaders) not to indulge in mass picketing, not to request blacking of mail by postal workers, and instead to rely on the due processes of the law and of official arbitration through both ACAS and the Scarman inquiry, the strike committee found itself deflected and squeezed into sullen submission. It was little wonder that, when she was asked about the lessons of the affair, Mrs Jayaben Desai, the most prominent of the strikers, remarked bitterly: 'Do not put faith in law and procedure. Rely on your own strength.'[60]

The labour movement had erected a legal infrastructure based upon consensus, which when challenged by a recalcitrant employer was found sorely wanting, and dependence upon which actually deflected the strikers from pursuing a strategy of direct action and sympathy action which might well have secured them victory. The power of capital, of the police and the judges, was ultimately more decisive than formal arbitration procedures that rested on the willingness of employers and employees to arrive at a consensus. A *Financial Times* journalist wrote that, at Grunwick, 'The gulf remained unbridgeable . . . [because] Britain is still two nations. The class conflict continues.'[61]

·FROM COOPERATION TO CONFRONTATION·

A year after defeating Heath in the election, Labour had started to drift away from the programme on which it had been elected towards a conventional and later quasi-monetarist economic policy. Once more it became totally preoccupied with wage restraint. Partly because of inflationary pressures built in when Labour took power, prices surged upwards. Partly because of catching up after the Heath wage curbs, the guidelines agreed with the TUC in 1974 were repeatedly breached. By June 1975 prices were 26 per cent higher than a year earlier and wages 33 per cent higher.[62]

Union leaders (Jack Jones in particular) became alarmed that the economy might collapse, and with it the government. So they agreed to a voluntary system of wage restraint, during the first year of which (1975-6) increases would be limited to a flat rate of £6 weekly. By 1976 strikes and working days lost were both at their lowest levels for a decade.[63] A second year of restraint followed, with the TUC's full agreement. But by 1977 there were growing signs of unrest and strikes increased again. The situation was exacerbated by the public spending cuts agreed as part of a deal with the International Monetary Fund to overcome a major sterling crisis: many in the labour movement felt the government had lost its way.

A third year, with pay rises limited to 10 per cent, was not agreed by the TUC, though few unions breached it. But a further attempt to impose a 5 per cent limit in 1978 collapsed amid considerable acrimony between the unions and Labour leaders.

The result was the 'Winter of Discontent' of 1978–9, with widespread strikes by low-paid public service workers and others: from August 1978 to May 1979, 13,500,000 working days were lost.

Labour's credibility as a government collapsed, and Mrs Thatcher's Tories swept into power in May 1979. During the election, the previous winter's strikes figured strongly. Typical of the Tory attacks was that from a senior party figure, Lord Hailsham:

We have seen the gravediggers refusing to bury the dead; we have seen refuse accumulating in the streets; we have seen schools shut in the faces of children because the caretaker has walked off with the key and now we see the teachers making them do without their lunches. We have seen cancer patients having to postpone their operations because hospital laundering is not done, floors not swept, meals not cooked.[64]

The political consensus originating in the war had already started to splinter. Now it collapsed, the unions finding their position under attack from all sides. There seemed a wide range of agreement that the unions had got out of hand, itself signifying the emergence of a new political consensus to the right of the post-war one. Repeating a familiar theme, the conservative *Sunday Telegraph* argued in an editorial: 'Who can doubt that the greatest single obstacle to a competitive British economy today lies in the obstructive power of the unions?' The Labour leader, James Callaghan, said: 'The workers' power in combination is greater today than ever before', adding later: 'Let those who possess industrial muscle or monopoly power resolve not to abuse their great strength.'[65]

In 1980 an illuminating interview was given by a leading Tory, Lord Carr. Although he had been the minister responsible for introducing the controversial 1971 Industrial Relations Act, Lord Carr was by then firmly on the moderate or 'wet' wing of the Tory Party, his basic ideology being hardly distinguishable from the Labour right or the soon-to-emerge Liberal/SDP Alliance. Lord Carr made it clear that he considered that union power had to be tamed by the end of the 1970s, primarily because it was becoming too 'political':

When I first got involved in politics the trade unions had considerable political power because of their industrial strength and because of their organic link with the Labour Party. But then they always reserved industrial action for industrial purposes . . . they now tend to use their industrial power for political purposes, which is both wrong and dangerous . . . Now we have some trade unionists who are politicians first and trade unionists second . . . as the 1950s and then the 1960s passed it became clear to many people in this country . . . that the old voluntary concordat was breaking down. More and more of us began to feel there was a need for a legal framework within which trade union power would not be diminished but controlled and channelled.[66]

Another 'wet' Tory, the new Employment Minister in Mrs Thatcher's government, added: 'Many people feel about the trade unions today the same way they felt about the industrial barons of the nineteenth century or the landed barons of the seventeenth and eighteenth centuries. The unions should not be seen as constituting an estate of the realm.'[67]

The evidence for unions having *of their own volition* become 'too political' is scant indeed. By and large, unions were only driven into political conflicts by *government-initiated* policies. Britain's historic economic problems – of under-investment, industrial backwardness, a declining manufacturing sector and share of world trade – had increasingly come home to roost. British capitalism's inability to continue to deliver rising living standards to the organized working class forced governments to attack union power through incomes policies or through changing the law – and in turn forced unions to resist these attacks.

Nevertheless, in the 1980s the Conservatives were able to draw on a deep reservoir of public feeling that something had to be done about the unions: the climate was ripe for the Thatcherite attack.

5
THE THATCHERITE ATTACK

The Conservatives came into office in May 1979 armed with a distinctive 'new right' philosophy described as 'Thatcherism'.[1] Determined to achieve a radical restructuring of the economy to boost the position of private capital and market forces, they made a decisive break with the post-war consensus and set about creating a new mood. The extent of the break was shown by acid criticisms of previous Tory administrations which had been part of that consensus. Heath's government in particular was ridiculed for its 'wetness', despite its early right-wing platform and its bitter confrontations with the unions.

The Thatcherites had a multi-pronged strategy, including a restructuring of the party system. Since it would not cooperate, the Labour Party needed to be broken as an electoral force and thus prevented from providing an alternative government which could undermine the new, rightist consensus. It might be risky to allow a regrouping of the centre which could challenge the Tories' claim to 'middle ground' opinion. But at least the option of a centrist alternative government – later offered by the SDP/Liberal Alliance – was preferable to a socialist one, particularly if it did not threaten the Thatcherite market economy.

The economic policies to be pursued included giving an absolute priority to controlling inflation (even if in practice this meant *de*flation); exposing the British economy to the full glare of international competition by abandoning subsidies, tariffs and exchange controls; and cutting public expenditure in order to provide room for the private sector. There was to be a much smaller state sector, selective rather than universal welfare provision and lower personal taxation. Accompanying this was a concerted drive to boost a form of privatized individualism at the expense of collectivist values.

In line with the 'new right' thinking of 'liberating' the private market, the whole corporatist edifice of the post-war consensus needed to be replaced.[2] The labour market needed to be freed from the distortions of official regulation, and industrial relations restructured in order to curb working-class power. This meant above all a concerted drive to weaken trade unions.

Workers' wages needed to be cut to boost profits. Indeed pay seemed at times to provide an explanation for the whole British economic crisis, as the Chancellor told the House of Commons: 'The main cause of high unemployment in Britain today . . . is the determination of monopolistic trade unions to insist on levels of pay that price men [sic] out of work. Some of them, not content with pricing men out of work, do their best to strike them out of work, too.'[3]

But the Thatcherites dismissed a formal wage restraint policy as just another 'corporatist device'. Instead they imposed an indirect one through rigid public-sector cash limits, a tight monetary policy, curbs on local authority spending power, privatization and a deliberate decision to allow unemployment to rise to record levels.

A rejection of corporatism was also evident in the approach to labour laws which, instead of relying on *government* intervention to be activated, forced *employers* to initiate court action. At the same time they boosted court and police powers, so encouraging a genuinely authoritarian, 'strong' state to control dissident forces and shield private capital from union power. All in all, the Thatcherite strategy amounted to one of 'coercive pacification' of organized labour.[4]

· UNION REFORM ·

Union leaders quickly found themselves out in the cold. Strong management was encouraged and attacks on union militants were publicly welcomed by ministers. Thatcher's approach to union reform was also deliberately populist. The Tories had constructed their election appeal around detaching a section of working-class voters from their traditional allegiance to Labour. And the 1979 result showed they had indeed managed to secure a significant extra slice of support from manual workers; they also achieved a 7 per cent swing among *trade unionists*, a third of whom voted Tory.

The government was particularly aware of the opportunities afforded by public disaffection with unions. For example, an ORC poll published in *The Times* on 21 January 1980 showed that 83 per cent believed the unions had too much power and that a similar proportion favoured restrictions on union rights and immunities. Even among trade union members questioned there was overwhelming support for reforms to limit the ability to strike and to picket.

However, Thatcherism's approach to trade union reform was both more tough and more subtle than the 1971 Act. Under the 1980 Employment Act picketing was restricted to the point where the only pickets not open to legal challenge were those attending in small numbers where they themselves worked, who kept out of everyone else's way and who, consequently, were virtually impotent. In particular, it was illegal for trade unionists to be involved in 'secondary picketing'. But this provision was to be enforced through civil proceedings rather than application of the criminal law. Thus the government avoided being embroiled as a direct protagonist in legal action against strikers, as it had been under the 1971 Act.

Similarly the 1982 Employment Act placed the onus on employers or interested private parties to sue unions for damages if its provisions were breached, so avoiding the Heath government's problem of creating martyrs by imprisoning strikers for refusing to pay fines if they had breached the law. The 1982 Act significantly reduced union immunities so that they applied only in the very limited circumstances of a trade dispute between worker and employer where the dispute related wholly or mainly to terms or conditions of employment. Sympathy strikes or any industrial activities with wider political connotations were outlawed.

The 1984 Trade Union Act carried the Thatcherite programme of reform a stage further. Besides requiring union leaderships to be elected by individual member ballots and forcing unions with political funds to win membership ballots to retain them, it also stipulated that there had to be membership ballots before strikes could legally be called. Though undoubtedly an attack on unions' bargaining strength and capacity to wage strikes, this could be presented as an extension of democracy – or 'giving unions back to their members', as the Tories argued.

·TORY THINKING·

Thatcher's strategy towards the unions had been carefully planned from the time she became Tory leader in 1975. One of her first steps was to set up a small group chaired by Lord Carrington to see what lessons could be drawn from the Heath government's problems with strikes. Evidence was taken in confidence from businessmen and from senior civil servants involved in the 1973–4 conflict. The subsequent report recognized that key groups of workers, such as in the electricity supply industry, had considerable power and it was not easy to confront them. It also rejected the use of troops to break strikes. Instead it called for higher priority to be given to emergency planning and to the careful use of publicity to rally the population against strikes by workers strategically placed in the economy.[5]

But the Conservative Party's policy group on the nationalized industries went one stage further. The group was chaired by the radical right-wing Tory MP, Nicholas Ridley, and its report was leaked to the *Economist* who published it on 28 May 1978. The Ridley recommendations were quite blunt. They included using government financial controls over nationalized industries in order to regulate wages with the specific objective of 'buying off' powerful groups. Although nationalized industries would have to achieve a set rate of return on capital employed in order to reduce costs, the report argued that the figures for return on capital could be rigged 'so that an above average wage claim can be paid to the vulnerable industries'. It added: 'Every precaution should be taken against a challenge in electricity or gas.'

Instead a Tory government should choose its field of battle carefully, only taking on groups in the public sector where decisive victories over strikers could be won – these included the railway and steel workers, civil servants and British Leyland car workers. Ridley also argued that although a battle with the miners was undesirable it was probably unavoidable, and the report suggested detailed tactics, which will be discussed later, to prepare for this.

State powers should be used quite deliberately to break strikes, Ridley argued. The group believed 'that the greatest deterrent to any strike would be to cut off the money supply to the strikers and make the union finance them'. (By this it meant restrictions on state benefits for strikers' families.) And: 'There should be a large, mobile squad of police, equipped and prepared to uphold the law against violent picketing. Good, non-union drivers should be recruited to cross picket lines with police protection.'

·EMERGENCY PLANNING·

This thinking was complementary to the contingency planning that had been evolving during the 1970s. Here again the significance of the victory by miners' pickets at Saltley in 1972 is apparent. A senior adviser to the Tory Chancellor of the Exchequer later wrote of Saltley:

At the time many of those in positions of influence looked into the abyss and saw only a few days away the possibility of the country being plunged into a state of chaos not so very far removed from that which might prevail after a minor nuclear attack. If that sounds melodramatic . . . it was the analogy that was being used at the time. This is the power that holds the country to ransom: it was fear of that abyss which had an important effect on subsequent policy.[6]

There was a determination not to have another Saltley, and a feeling that the old Industrial Emergencies Committee was not up to the job. An official review of civil emergency planning was conducted by Lord Jellicoe. It proposed a reconstituted emergencies organization, to be called the Civil Contingencies Unit (CCU), nicknamed 'Cuckoo'. Unlike previous emergency units which were coordinated by the Home Office, the CCU was made equivalent in rank to a Cabinet standing committee and was based in the Cabinet Office Briefing Room. Known as COBRA, this room contains high-technology systems to communicate directly with Chief Constables, military leaders and other government departments. It is also linked to eleven regional Emergency Committees comprising police chiefs, local authority representatives and central government civil servants.

The CCU's contingency plan for nation-wide strikes calls for about 15,000 troops – the total available without affecting commitments to NATO and in Northern Ireland – including 3,000 technicians and 2,200 drivers and vehicles.

Within a few years the CCU had been developed so that it was on permanent stand-by, not just for industrial crises but also for other civil emergencies such as natural disasters, terrorist threats and hijackings. The Secretary to the Cabinet, Sir Robert Armstrong, wrote: 'What was required was an organization which could be brought into effective action at an hour's notice, at any time of the day or night, and stay in action, day and night if necessary, for as many hours, days or weeks as circumstances demanded.'[7]

It constantly updates files on sixteen essential services and industries, monitoring industrial relations in these and the options open for deploying police or troops in the event of a strike. The list of sixteen is topped by electricity supply, and includes water supply, the docks, coal, oil, rail and road haulage.

The CCU has been activated on a number of occasions, including the 1972 dock strike, the 1973–4 miners' strike, the 1974 Ulster workers' strike, the 1977 firemen's strike, the 1978–9 'Winter of Discontent' and the 1983 water strike. Although it was also operational during the 1984–5 miners' strike, monitoring power supplies and so on, the main mobilization of state resources on that occasion was through the police National Reporting Centre.

·THE USE OF STATE POWER BY THE TORIES·

As it embarked upon its strategy of undermining the unions, the Tory government armed itself with a formidable battery of powers to confront strikes. An emergency organization was already in place. New anti-strike legislation was introduced. Additional resources were given to the police force which was expanded while expenditure on other public services was being cut; furthermore, the trend towards highly organized, strong policing was intensified after 1979.

In addition, the government used the welfare and taxation system to penalize strikers, the Secretary of State for Social Services, Patrick Jenkin, informing the House of Commons in April 1980 that the object was 'to fix responsibility for the support of strikers' families where it rightly belongs, namely, upon the unions'.[8] This marked a sharp break with tradition. As far back as 1900 the High Court ruled that Poor Law Guardians could relieve the dependants of strikers. And well before legislation following the Second World War gave strikers' families rights to benefit payments, they had been eligible for support under National Assistance.

But in 1980, under the Social Security (No. 2) Act, the entitlement of strikers' families to social benefits was reduced by the device of 'deeming' them to be in receipt of £12 weekly strike pay from their union (by 1984 this figure had been uprated to £16): this amount was deducted from supplementary benefit payments to their families. (Benefit is not payable to single strikers, but the change further restricted their ability to make hardship claims on grounds of urgent need, leaving some striking miners in 1984–5 with no income at all.)

Then in April 1982 new regulations were introduced to freeze all income tax rebates to strikers until they had gone back to work. The tax system assumes that the taxpayer is receiving full pay throughout the year, and if that pay ceases at any point, there is an immediate entitlement to a rebate. Prior to 1982, this was invariably paid to strikers a fortnight after they stopped work and, like supplementary benefit, was a major source of income for those on strike – and often the only one, since unions rarely give strike pay.[9] In addition, from July 1982 the supplementary benefit strikers could claim in respect of adult dependants was made taxable for the first time – meaning a further cut in their income.

The government also encouraged managers to 'take on' the unions, especially militant shop stewards. A public example was made at British Leyland in the winter of 1979–80 when the communist convenor of the shop stewards' committee, Derek Robinson, was sacked – and the unions were unable to mobilize support from their own members to take industrial action to resist this. When major groups of workers did strike, the Thatcher government kept a studious distance, in public at least, decrying the 'beer and sandwiches' interventions of Labour governments. In its first period in office it was successful in curbing strikers, mainly because of unemployment, which quickly doubled.

In 1981 and 1982 the number of days lost through strikes fell to a level close to the average for the century, the Tories adopting a particularly uncompromising stance in the public sector, resisting strikes by steel workers in 1980, by civil servants in 1981 and by health workers in 1982. Although the government denied it was operating an incomes policy, the Chancellor announced annual 'guidelines' for public-sector negotiations. The system of cash limits in the civil service, coupled with new spending restrictions on local government and health services, was used directly to limit pay rises. In the nationalized industries, strict financial targets – echoing the recommendations of the 1978 Ridley report – acted as a severe constraint on pay bargaining, with management negotiators in any case looking over their shoulders through Whitehall to 10 Downing Street where the Prime Minister used her powers of appointment ruthlessly, placing in key positions public servants in her own image.

As the Employment Acts of 1980 and 1982 began to bite, the role of the courts as agencies of the government's anti-strike policy became clearer. For example, in November 1983 the Appeal Court granted an injunction to Mercury Communications instructing the Post Office Engineering Union to drop its industrial action against the company; POEU members had been refusing to make the vital connection Mercury needed into the main British Telecom network.*

·NGA STRIKE·

Meanwhile what was to become a major dispute had been brewing in Warrington between the National Graphical Association (NGA) and the Stockport Messenger Group of newspapers. This was the first time the anti-strike provisions of the 1980 and 1982 Employment Acts were used fully. The dispute concerned maintaining a closed shop – agreements over which were almost universal in the print industry and were the key to the NGA's strength and high degree of discipline. An associated issue was the management's insistence on new technology which threatened the craft skills of the NGA membership.

The strike began in July 1983 after the Managing Director of the Stockport Messenger Group, Eddie Shah, set up non-union subsidiaries. When NGA members elsewhere in his company were instructed to handle work from these non-union firms, they refused, and the strike started. Attempts at arbitration failed, as Shah displayed an intransigence which recalled the behaviour in 1976–7 of George Ward, Grunwick's Managing Director. (Like Ward, he developed close connections with Tory right-wingers.) When journalists refused to hand copy to non-union print workers, Shah issued a writ in August against the National Union of Journalists. In September he went to court again and issued another writ against the NGA for its attempt to dissuade advertisers from taking space in the Group's papers.

It was evident that this would be a test case, both of the NGA's determination to maintain the closed shop and also for

* It later emerged that Sir John Donaldson, the Master of the Rolls, who had presided over the case, held £5,000 worth of shares in Cable & Wireless, which in turn owned 40 per cent of Mercury – though his wife told the *Guardian* newspaper that it was wrong to think that this financial interest could have in any way affected his judgment.

employers thinking of resorting to Tory legislation rather than negotiation. So the NGA organized picketing and demonstrations; it also appealed to other unions for solidarity. On 14 October Manchester High Court granted Shah two interim injunctions. One restrained the NGA from unlawful picketing, the other ordered the union to refrain from blacking the Group.

But the NGA decided to step up its action and the picketing continued more frequently and with larger numbers of pickets. By now the strike had escalated into a major political conflict: Shah's uncompromising rejection of arbitration was couched in terms which made it clear he wanted a clear-cut victory which would inflict a general blow against union power; government ministers made public statements in his support; and the right-wing Institute of Directors, it was later disclosed, gave him constant advice and help.

On 17 November, Manchester High Court heard another application by Shah. He wanted the sequestration of the NGA's funds for its defiance of the two injunctions previously issued. Mr Justice Eastham fined the union £50,000, awarded costs against it and warned that, if there were continued breaches of the two injunctions, then 'the time might come when this union must be taught to obey the law by having all its assets sequestered'.

The NGA was still defiant, however. Picketing continued and the numbers grew, until the night of 29–30 November when 4,000 pickets 'were dispersed by police using new riot control tactics implemented with unprecedented ferocity'.[10] The police, publicly urged on by the Prime Minister and the Home Secretary, were determined to break the strike by preventing the mass picketing. Even more completely than at Grunwick, the ghost of Saltley was being exorcized. Television and press covered the clashes from behind the police lines, presenting a one-dimensional picture which completely distorted responsibility for the violence and left the pickets to take the full blame.[11] The result was widespread public horror and antagonism towards the strikers.

In this climate the NGA suspended the picketing and opted for negotiations through ACAS. But Shah remained intractable and on 9 December he again applied to Manchester High Court for contempt orders because of the continued picketing. The court imposed record fines totalling £525,000 for two contempts of the injunctions previously granted against the NGA.

Now boxed in both by aggressive policing and hostile courts, the NGA appealed to the TUC for support in general and, most immediately, backing for a one-day national print strike. But although its Employment Policy and Organization Committee voted by nine to seven in favour of a 'sympathetic and supportive attitude' to the NGA's request, the TUC's General Secretary, Len Murray, angrily told waiting journalists outside Congress House that the committee had no authority to take such a decision which would put the TUC in breach of the law. He declared his intention to get it reversed by the full General Council, and this indeed occurred a few days later amid bitter recriminations, the left arguing that failure to back the NGA would signal the labour movement's unwillingness to resist the Thatcherite attack.

Later, the NGA decided it had no alternative but to purge its contempt. By the end, the union had paid fines and legal costs totalling nearly £1 million. The Institute of Directors hailed the result as an 'NGA climbdown', adding in a statement: 'It is important to note that there has been an important change in the balance of power between employers and employees due to the enactment of the employment legislation.' In an interview afterwards, one of the local NGA officials involved commented on the way in which they had been forced into a political confrontation with the new Tory laws:

I have never personally been a very political animal. And I would agree with you that the NGA has always tended to be a little bit right of centre. But when one looks at the events of the past months, when one sees how politics have been used against our union, then I think it *has* to affect people, it *has* to make you more politically aware.[12]

Within weeks, the government had announced on 25 January 1984 its intention to outlaw trade unions at GCHQ, the intelligence-gathering centre in Cheltenham. As the year drew on, the 1980, 1982 and then 1984 Acts were used with increasing frequency. On 27 November 1984, the *Financial Times* carried a major feature under the headline: 'The law begins to bite', listing a series of cases in which unions had been forced to back down from strike action because of injunctions taken out by employers.

The labour movement's weakness when faced with a major *political* challenge had been exposed in the defeat of the NGA strike. Shortly afterwards the stakes were raised even higher, with the government determined both to inflict another political defeat on strikers and to break the power of the National Union of Mineworkers.

·PREPARING FOR THE 1984–5 MINERS' STRIKE·

Ever since their humiliation by the miners in 1972 and again in 1973–4, the Tories had been anxious to take revenge. The Ridley report, leaked in 1978, had anticipated the strategy of the Thatcherites, many of its recommendations being directed at the coal industry. The report argued that the most likely battleground for a Tory government would be in the mines and a number of steps were suggested to strengthen the government's hand. First, maximum coal stocks should be built up, particularly around power stations. Second, contingency plans should be made for the import of coal. Third, recruitment of non-union lorry drivers by haulage companies should be encouraged to help move coal where necessary. The report also advocated the privatization of sections of the coal industry.

Much of this thinking was soon implemented. Coal stocks were allowed to build up, partly because of a productivity scheme implemented in 1977. In October 1979 a Cabinet paper noted that giving preferential treatment to nuclear power 'would have the advantage of removing a substantial portion of electricity from disruption by industrial action of coal miners and transport workers'.[13] Britain's energy policy was switched, with nuclear power under the Tories playing an increasingly strategic role and being much more heavily subsidized than the coal industry. In line with Thatcherism's determination to maximize profits and

restructure production by cutting subsidies to traditional industries, the 1980 Coal Industry Act required the National Coal
Board (NCB) to break even by 1983-4. This was tantamount to
an ultimatum for colliery closures, since the coal industry (like
those in other countries) had needed large subsidies for years.

In 1981, Mrs Thatcher made a tactical retreat – again echoing
the Ridley report. The NCB had announced a sudden pit closure
programme and, as details emerged, the South Wales miners came
out on strike and there were strikes at pits in other areas. Almost
immediately, the government backed down and conceded extra
funding for the NCB. Coal stocks then stood at 37 million tonnes;
three years later they had risen to 57 million. The popularity of
the government was also at its lowest. Afterwards a key Thatcherite minister, John Biffen, said in a frank television interview
that he hadn't 'come into politics to be a kamikaze pilot' and that
to take on the miners then would have been a suicide mission.[14]
The Secretary of State for Energy, David Howell, also admitted
that the government was not ready for a coal strike at that time
and that the retreat was 'entirely tactical'.[15]

Meanwhile the Treasury continued to turn a blind eye to wage
settlements for the miners which were better than most others in
the public sector, and coal stocks were deliberately increased. In
1982 the head of the Central Electricity Generating Board, Glyn
England, was replaced by Sir Walter Marshall. A pro-nuclear
energy Thatcherite who publicly criticized the 'monopoly power
of the miners', Marshall dramatically increased oil imports from
3.1 million to 12.5 million tonnes. (Glyn England had been
opposed to this switch, his opposition being seen as a reason for
his replacement.)[16] The CEGB's capacity to switch to oil-fired
power generation was also increased, giving added protection to
the country's electricity supply in the event of a coal shortage.

The day after the Tories had won their second term of office
with a landslide election victory in 1983, Peter Walker was appointed as the new Secretary of State for Energy, the Prime
Minister reportedly telling him: 'We're going to have a miners'
strike.'[17] Within four months of the election, in September 1983,
Mrs Thatcher personally appointed Mr Ian MacGregor as

Chairperson of the NCB. He had been Deputy Chairperson at British Leyland, supervising job cuts of over 34,000 during his five-year stay. Then the Thatcher government appointed him as Chairperson of British Steel in May 1980. So keen were they to obtain his services that the government even agreed to pay a 'transfer fee' to the merchant bankers, Lazard Frères, which he had joined in the meantime. The 'up front' fee paid to Lazard's was £675,000, with over £1 million payable in addition depending on his results at British Steel. In fact, BSC's workforce was halved during his tenure, with a loss of over 80,000 jobs.

Before holding these prominent positions in Britain, MacGregor had been President of the giant AMAX corporation which, as well as its extensive interests in minerals, became America's third-largest producer and ninth-largest owner of coal reserves; it also had large coal reserves in Australia. While with AMAX, MacGregor gained a reputation for hostility towards unions and for strike-breaking: for example, when miners went on strike in Wyoming over medical cover, safety measures and pensions, their two-year-long struggle was crushed; armed security guards were brought in and trade unionists were later victimized.[18]

Consequently, his appointment was seen by the miners as deliberately provocative – a view also shared by some media commentators and Conservative MPs. Soon his presence was being felt. He altered the traditional nationalized industry management style of the NCB – a style based largely on 'in-house' promotions to management positions which the Thatcherites regarded as leading to far too cosy a relationship with the unions. The degree of flexibility accorded to the miners over pay in previous years gave way to rigidity, as the NCB stuck to a 5.2 per cent offer that became the norm in the public sector for that wage round. In response the NUM instituted an overtime ban in November 1983. By then industrial relations in the industry were deteriorating, with localized disputes breaking out regularly and the miners increasingly feeling that a confrontation was inevitable.

The main issue was not pay, but jobs – the subject of a developing conflict for at least a decade. Concerned in 1972 about irresponsible pit closures in the 1960s, the NUM had adopted a policy rejecting all pit closures except when they were necessary because of exhaustion of reserves. This policy was embodied in the 1974 'Plan for Coal' agreed with the government and the NCB. It seemed to operate for some years, though the miners remained suspicious that pits were being closed when they were still workable. In 1980 the NUM's annual conference agreed to take whatever action was necessary to oppose closures on grounds other than exhaustion. Then came the crash programme of closures announced without warning early in 1981. Unofficial strikes broke out and escalated, a national strike becoming likely – but the Thatcher government backed down, the programme was withdrawn and new subsidies announced. During this time and afterwards, Arthur Scargill, NUM President from 1982, continued to allege that the NCB had a hit-list of pits to be closed, producing leaked documents to back up his argument. Meanwhile a number of NUM regions – the national union is essentially a federation, with regions having considerable autonomy – agreed after membership ballots that they would take industrial action to resist unilateral pit closures.

·THE STRIKE BEGINS·

One of these regions was Yorkshire, as management were fully aware. Nevertheless, the NCB decided to announce without notice on 1 March 1984 the closure of Cortonwood colliery in South Yorkshire – where the men had been assured there were another five years at least of life in their pit. The next day the closure of nearby Bullcliffe Wood pit was announced. Soon afterwards it became clear that the NCB intended to close five pits immediately, with more to follow in a closure programme in which at least 20,000 jobs would go, with compulsory redundancies likely.

In accordance with their membership mandates, Yorkshire, Scotland, South Wales and Kent areas called area disputes, receiving authority on 8 March from the NUM's National Executive to take official strike action from the next day. What was to become Britain's longest-ever national strike had begun.

The miners themselves recognized that they had been forced into a political confrontation and their union seemed more willing to accept the consequences than many others. Arthur Scargill as NUM President never pretended that the strike could be divorced from the wider political environment, saying in October 1984: 'We want to save our jobs. But more – we want to prepare the way for a transformation, rolling back the years of Thatcherism. We want to pave the way for an economic recovery, a general election and the return of a Labour government.'[19] His members showed no enthusiasm for taking on the government, their determination springing more from a belief that Tory policies had made the conflict *inevitable*. One activist expressed a typical view amongst rank-and-file miners:

Thatcher wanted us, she has been planning to repay us for 1974. We beat her to the punch in 1981 and because she was not ready she gave us a body swerve . . . I also think that 1981 proved that we at least were not trying to make this a political strike. If we were, we would have gone on strike in 1981 when we had her and the rest of them in a corner.[20]

·STATE OPPOSITION TO THE MINERS·

For its part, the government made little attempt to hide its ultimate political objective: defeat of the miners. As one Fleet Street labour editor wrote, six months into the strike: 'For the government and for Mrs Thatcher the strike has become a political battle she dare not lose as she looks over her shoulder to what happened to Mr Heath ten years ago.'[21]

It seemed to the striking miners as though the whole apparatus of state was ranged against them. A Cabinet sub-committee called MISC 101 was established immediately and met twice a week. Chaired by the Prime Minister, it was composed of seven senior ministers with two officials of the Civil Contingencies Unit present. The strike-breaking role of the courts and the police will be discussed in following chapters. But government ministers were not slow to demand that the law be applied stringently. A week into the strike Mrs Thatcher made it publicly known that she was angry with the failure of the police to prevent mass picketing in Nottinghamshire and criticized some Chief Constables at an internal Tory meeting with backbench MPs.[22]

At one stage the Home Secretary called for tougher sentencing of convicted miners, while the Attorney-General called for heavier fines to be imposed before the union's assets were sequestered. Later the Attorney-General came under fire in Parliament for taking the unprecedented step of funding the firm of accountants employed to sequestrate the assets of the NUM; the firm incurred expenses estimated at over £100,000 in trying to trace the union's funds, which had been sent abroad. Although it was technically a *civil* action to which the government was not a party, this did not deter the Attorney-General from authorizing unlimited public funding to carry through the sequestration.

The NCB was encouraged to undertake a costly secret operation to switch movement of coal supplies from rail to road to compensate for the lack of trains after the refusal of the rail unions to handle coal. More than 800,000 lorry journeys kept coal moving to power stations, factories and domestic consumers. Drivers were equipped with CB radios to warn each other of trouble-spots at pits and power stations, and the operation was so successful that 26.5 million tonnes of coal were delivered during the strike, only 8.5 million tonnes less than normal.[23] In another unusual step, the NCB commissioned extensive poll research into the attitudes of the striking miners and their families. Surveys were done at regular intervals and the results used to influence the NCB's negotiating strategy, its publicity campaign encouraging miners to return to work, and the way it framed its popular press advertisements.[24]

Electricity supply was maintained by sharply reducing dependence on coal, at massive extra cost. Normally, 80 per cent of electricity is generated in coal-fired stations, 14 per cent by nuclear power and the remainder – just 6 per cent – by oil-fired stations. During the strike, coal-generated electricity was reduced to 40 per cent, oil increased to 40 per cent and nuclear power to 20 per cent. During the winter weeks, the Electricity Board was spending over

£100 million *weekly* on imported oil, equivalent to one third of OPEC's total fuel oil production.[25]

At a time when public expenditure was being ruthlessly trimmed, the government seemed quite content to meet the escalating cost of the strike, the Chancellor of the Exchequer even telling the House of Commons on 31 July that, in 'narrow financial terms', the additional public expenditure on the dispute was 'a worthwhile investment for the good of the nation'. He said much the same thing in his 1985 Budget speech after the strike had ended, even though expenditure upon it had severely reduced his ability to cut taxes.

Official figures showed that the direct cost to the government was well over £3 billion, the policing costs alone being over £225 million. Massive losses were suffered by the NCB and the Electricity Board (the latter's loss resulting mainly from having to import coal and oil). When account was taken of the impact on the economy as a whole, the total cost of the strike jumped to well over £5 billion. The balance of payments was adversely affected by about £4 billion and economic growth was reduced by 1.25 per cent. The actual cost to the government of keeping more pits open would have been trivial by comparison (indeed when the full costs and benefits of closures on mining communities were calculated, it was actually *cheaper* to keep them open).[26] But the Thatcherites were less concerned about the *financial* cost of the strike to the public purse than the *political* cost of losing it. It was crucial to their overall political project to alter the balance of power and class forces in Britain.

· MANIPULATING THE WELFARE SYSTEM ·

Ministers also took administrative action to increase the pressure on the strikers, even though the government maintained (at least at the beginning) that they were not intervening directly in the dispute. This affected the miners in many different ways. For example, those who accepted early retirement at the end of 1983, but whose formal date of retirement fell after 1 March 1984, were told they could no longer claim redundancy pay, even though this had been an agreed part of the early-retirement scheme. Electricity Boards started threatening to cut off supplies to the homes of strikers unless weekly payments were made on such a scale as to use up virtually all their income from benefit. Officials from the Ministry of Agriculture employed various bureaucratic procedures to impound 137 tonnes of food which had been sent to families of Durham miners from the Soviet Union.

In addition, the whole welfare system was manipulated. Workers laid off by companies indirectly affected by the dispute found themselves treated as strikers and denied benefit. At the start, local social security offices delayed the payment of benefit, almost as if they were trying to deter the miners from staying on strike. Entitlements to supplementary benefit – or, if a miner's wife was working, Family Income Supplement – were denied. Pregnant wives of miners were denied grants for baby clothes and other essentials. Undernourished expectant mothers had difficulty in obtaining cash for diet supplements, and in Yorkshire one miner's wife was told by the DHSS that nappies were not a necessity for a six-week-old baby. There were many other cases of special hardship treated callously by local social security offices and by local councils too.

Seven months into the strike, documented evidence of abuse was so widespread that the Opposition spokesperson on social services, Michael Meacher, protested: 'The government are using every possible delaying tactic, loophole and manoeuvre to deny miners benefits they should be entitled to.'[27]

It was evident that senior officials in the Department of Health and Social Security were utilizing their powers of discretion at best to display insensitivity and at worst to discriminate against miners' families. This was confirmed by a pilot survey by the National Association of Citizens' Advice Bureaux. It also found wide variations in treatment between different parts of the country. For example, in some areas payments for sickness benefit were made to miners simply on production of a doctor's certificate, while in others claims had to go before a medical board and then were sometimes refused.

The Miners' Welfare Centre in Maltby, South Yorkshire, gave a fairly typical report which illustrates the manner in which the administrative apparatus of the state could be used to undermine the strength of the strike, in some ways more effectively than aggressive policing of pickets:

The miners' strike has seen a political manipulation of DHSS rulings and guidelines . . . Study the typical case of an NCB trainee coming into our Advice Centre. He, like all other trainees, had been receiving unemployment benefit due to a tribunal victory. This has now been suspended because of evidence supplied by the NCB showing that since the strike is about pay and trainees stand to benefit they are unable to continue claiming.

This man has been served a notice to quit because of rent arrears. The housing benefit office is so inundated with claims it is taking about three months to send out rent cheques rather than the obligatory fourteen days. In fact our man may not receive any help with his rent after deductions have been made for his two sons, both striking miners receiving no benefit, who are living in his house.

The lights may not be going out over Britain but they are certainly going out down his street. His neighbour has already been disconnected and he is unable to get help from the DHSS for electricity payments. As for Family Income Supplement this will not be paid, even when the wife is working over thirty hours per week, because the DHSS interpret 'normal income' as the miner's income way back from when the strike began.

In despair our client asks if he can claim single payments for his wife who is pregnant to buy maternity clothes and safety equipment. 'But,' says the DHSS manager, 'all grants will be repayable, phone up nearer the expected date of delivery.' The only trouble is that the phone has been disconnected. British Telecom will only allow the bill to be paid in instalments once the phone has been cut off.

Miners' claims are being dealt with slowly and inconsistently to make it as difficult as possible for them to receive financial assistance from the state.[28]

Then in November 1984, with the dispute eight months old, the government announced an increase in the amount which strikers were 'deemed' to be receiving in strike pay from £15 to £16. This effectively cut the income of miners' families by £1 weekly – a large amount relative to their total income from benefits. The timing of the announcement was heavily criticized, on the grounds that it had been left to the last possible moment. Under the Social Security (No. 2) Act 1980 an increase was required in line with inflation. But this was calculated on the basis of the Retail Prices Index declared in June and could have been announced then as had been the case in previous years. The suspicion was that the government had timed the announcement to accelerate the drift back to work which had started in November.

One way or another, therefore, the 1984–5 miners' dispute showed more vividly than ever before the extent to which the procedures of the modern welfare state could be used against strikers. Because the poor are now more dependent on state benefits than in pre-welfare days when they had to rely on community self-help, they are more vulnerable to attacks on these benefits. The miners found such attacks coming in various forms. These ranged from the openly political decisions and departmental instructions of government ministers, to the exercise of discretion by local officials. The latter was more ubiquitous and, although local officialdom disclaimed political motives for the way discretionary powers were used to penalize the miners and their families, the fact is that their decisions were taken within a climate made hostile to the miners by the government: where there was any doubt the regulations were interpreted against the welfare of the strikers.

·DIRECT GOVERNMENT INTERVENTION·

Direct government intervention was felt in other ways. Ministers mounted a concerted propaganda battle against the NUM, Mrs Thatcher's language being especially colourful. She denounced 'the emergence of an organized revolutionary minority who were prepared to exploit industrial disputes', but whose real aim was 'the breakdown of law and order and the destruction of democratic parliamentary government', and she also urged the British people to fight this 'enemy within'.[29] As one analysis showed at the time:

The great advantage which the government enjoys in the miners' strike is that it is fighting on ground which it has prepared more thoroughly than any other. Industrial Luddism and revolutionary extremism are portrayed as the enemies that the whole community, not merely the government, has to fight ... so long as the issue can be displaced from the industrial sphere into the political sphere, it can be treated as a problem of law and order – the defence of the right to work against mob picket violence – and all the powers of the authoritarian populist consensus can then be enlisted on the government's side. The public can be rallied much more easily in defence of social order than in defence of market order. The skill of Thatcherism is to present the two as the same.[30]

Two aides of the Prime Minister actively assisted 'Working Miners' Committees' set up mainly in the Nottinghamshire coalfields where the majority had decided not to strike. The National Working Miners' Committee also received support and advice from the National Coal Board and from wealthy businessmen with close Conservative Party connections.[31] It is doubtful whether the many legal actions against the union by working miners would have been brought without such support. Active promotion of a return-to-work movement, exploiting divisions within the National Union of Mineworkers, became an increasingly important part of the government's handling of the strike. Significantly, in its latter stages Mrs Thatcher repeatedly insisted in public that she would not agree to a settlement which undermined the 'working miners' whom she regarded as the real heroes of the dispute.

Indeed as it drew to a close the government abandoned any pretence at non-interventionism, with Mrs Thatcher demanding virtual surrender terms from the NUM as a precondition for negotiations. In January 1985, the Prime Minister's office blocked informal discussions between Coal Board officials and miners' leaders which looked likely to produce a settlement. At a critical point, Mrs Thatcher's press officer, Bernard Ingham, briefed journalists in the Parliamentary Lobby that these informal talks 'were a waste of time'.[32] A few days later, one of her special advisers, David Hart, a go-between with the working miners, wrote an article in *The Times* under the headline 'Nothing short of victory', insisting that there should be no 'compromise or fudge' with the union.[33] Subsequent press reports and statements by Mrs Thatcher confirmed that that was her general position too. Later, the NCB's former Director-General of Industrial Relations, Ned Smith, confirmed that there had been 'a dramatic change' in the government's role in the last two to three months of the dispute, with the government 'prescribing what management negotiators could or could not do, indeed what they would or would not do'.[34]

The strike ended with the miners going back to work in March 1985 without a settlement. Their dignified return could not hide the reality of a defeat for the NUM. Despite the extraordinary resilience of the strikers in staying out for a year in the most difficult of circumstances, and despite the determination of the union's leaders, the Tories had been successful in the most comprehensive political attack ever mounted on a strike in Britain.*

· THATCHERISM IN PERSPECTIVE ·

But the government did not emerge politically unscathed. The tax-cutting policy so crucial to its populist appeal was damaged (at least for the Budget year 1985–6) and, immediately after the strike finished, its standing in the opinion polls fell, the evidence suggesting that the public was dissatisfied with the hard line taken against the miners in the final stages.

This underlines the importance of making a careful assessment of the impact of Thatcherism on union power. There is no doubt that it encouraged strong management and significantly undermined the trade union movement's ability to advance and defend its conditions of work. In the private sector decentralized bargaining increased, with management often by-passing unions and approaching employees directly. 'No-strike' agreements started to

* The total cost of the strike to the NUM was estimated at £24 million, including legal fees and fines, the cost of transporting pickets and subsistence allowances for the strikers.

spread. Public-sector trade unionism was particularly sharply hit by a hard-line government stance and by privatization. Any strikes which had a serious political impact on the industrial climate or the government's policies were ruthlessly opposed. Overall, union confidence and militancy declined.

But while union strength at *local* level was also severely reduced, the evidence suggested that industrial relations within those private companies which survived the Tory recession had not been affected as much as may be supposed. Real earnings in manufacturing companies continued to rise much faster than productivity, union membership remained relatively stable, the frequency of strikes even edged upwards and management attempts to 'put unions in their places' were mostly ineffectual.[35] For all male manual workers, the average earnings of trade unionists rose sharply compared with *non*-trade unionists after 1979; this represented the steepest climb in the relative superiority of trade union members for a decade.

Although strikes did drop to a new plateau, it was one still well above the average of the 1950s of 3 million *days lost* annually due to industrial disputes. Days lost totalled 12 million in 1980, 4.3 million in 1981, 5.3 million in 1982, 3.8 million in 1983 and 4.8 million in 1984, excluding the special effects of the miners' strike. Days lost in 1984 were up by over a quarter on 1983, largely attributable to public-sector stoppages.*

Moreover, the *number of workers* involved in stoppages outside mining was 1.2 million in 1984 – double the 1983 total and comparable with the annual average of 1.5 million workers over the ten-year period from 1974 to 1983. Commenting on this in its annual report for 1984, the Advisory, Conciliation, and Arbitration Service (ACAS) detected 'indications that the trade unions and their members were becoming more willing to consider the possibility of industrial action', greater resistance to closures and redundancy proposals and 'more combative bargaining over pay' in companies and sectors where financial problems had eased.

---

* With the miners included, the 1984 figure leapt to 27.1 million – the biggest total since the 1926 General Strike, with the exception of 1979 when 29.5 million days were lost.

In 1985, however, it seemed as though the 1984 Trade Union Act's requirement to have a membership ballot before a strike was having some effect. Major strikes at Austin Rover in late 1984 and in the Post Office and London's underground in early 1985 were called off after court injunctions to enforce ballots. The national leadership of the railway workers narrowly lost a recommendation for strike action in a membership ballot over one-person-operated trains in August 1985.

By contrast, the industrial relations director of the Ford Motor Company complained in January 1986 that the Act had forced the company to concede a higher pay settlement: a ballot by workers had overwhelmingly backed strike action during the negotiations and strengthened the union's bargaining position.

But in February 1986, after a calculated manoeuvre designed to shift production to a new high-technology printing plant at Wapping in East London, Rupert Murdoch's News International Corporation sacked 5,500 Fleet Street print workers. Despite having been among the most militant sections of the trade union movement, the print unions were unable to prevent the Murdoch titles from being printed by an entirely new workforce and distributed with the assistance of unionized road-haulage firms. The fact that the unions had dutifully balloted under the 1984 Act and won massive votes to strike cut no ice with the union-busting tactics of the Murdoch management.

By the mid 1980s, Thatcherism had not crushed unions' *defensive* strength so much as severely reduced it and limited unions' capacity to alter the wider social and political environment within which they had to bargain. Perhaps because of this, 'radical' Thatcherites such as Sir John Hoskyns, Director-General of the Institute of Directors and head of the Prime Minister's Policy Unit in 1979–82, urged the government to go much further and introduce a new system of contract law binding employees to employers. In an article in *The Times* in February 1985 entitled 'No recovery until the tyrants are tamed', he insisted that 'perhaps *the* major cause of UK unemployment is the rigidity of the labour market', and asserted: 'Collective bargaining is an inherently destabilizing device.'[36]

MILITARY
INTERVENTION
IN STRIKES

Like other agencies of the state, the armed forces are widely believed to play an impartial, neutral role on behalf of the nation. Thus, for example, when soldiers put out fires in a fire brigades workers' strike or move rubbish during a dustmen's strike, they are seen to be helping the ordinary citizen, rather than to be strike-breaking. Perhaps because of this, remarkably little attention has been paid to the role of the military in industrial disputes. Yet it is a role which has become an increasingly important component of the government's strategy towards major strikes.

Until the emergence of a properly constituted police force in the mid nineteenth century, the authorities relied mainly on the armed forces to deal with turbulent strikes and associated political unrest. Although it was sometimes extremely controversial – as at Peterloo in 1819, when troops killed eleven people and injured many others after opening fire on a peaceful assembly – military intervention was excused as being necessary to control rioting. The principal function of troops in strikes was a *public-order* one. During the 1820s and early 1830s, strikes, especially in the coalfields, were tantamount to 'civil wars in miniature' [1] and were forcibly put down by marines and cavalry. Between 1839 and 1842, when radical Chartism was at its peak, troops were used regularly to suppress outbreaks of working-class agitation in which the boundaries between political and industrial action were extremely blurred.

But by 1848, when there were pitched battles and Chartist uprisings all over the country, the armed forces had started acting more in cooperation with local police forces. The subsequent decline in union militancy during the moderate 'New Model Union' era saw troops having to deal less frequently with riots. Instead, they increasingly acted in reserve, as back-ups for police. From time to time they were also used either as blacklegs or to protect blacklegs, notably in building or farm-worker strikes. This provoked protests from the London Trades Council, which managed to win a change in the Queen's Regulations forbidding the use of troops 'where strikes or disputes between farmers and their labourers exist'.[2]

Towards the end of the century, however, economic recession, combined with the more militant 'new unionism' of unskilled workers, led to renewed unrest and a spate of strikes. By the 1890s clashes with troops were more frequent again, such as in the 1893 dock strike, when soldiers were deployed to protect blacklegs and two gunboats were dispatched up the Humber river to intimidate the strikers. A few months later, during a miners' strike at Featherstone in Yorkshire, there were two deaths and many injuries when troops fired on crowds around the local colliery.

· REORGANIZATION ·

The worst such incident for a long time, Featherstone encouraged an official reassessment of the procedure for calling in the military. The outcome was that the powers held by local magistrates to summon the aid of the armed forces were curbed, and in future any requests had to be channelled through Chief Constables.[3] By this change it was hoped that military intervention would secure public legitimacy which had been undermined by the insensitivity of the magistrates, particularly at Featherstone.

Growing working-class organization and the resulting extension of democratic rights forced the government to introduce a more ordered and regulated basis for dealing with strikes, so that, by 1909,

Governments had realized for decades that troops should only be used in strikes or riots as a last resort as their presence often caused more trouble than it quelled. The growth of the police from the mid nineteenth century had enabled the military to withdraw from public order and strike duties to a large degree as the unarmed police proved a more publicly acceptable instrument of control, although troops were called out to aid the civil power on twenty-four occasions between 1869 and 1908.[4]

However, at this stage the government's stance towards major strikes was very 'reactive': police or troops would be deployed, or government departments involved, as and when circumstances required it. Control over public-order enforcement was gradually being taken away from local elites, but there was still no real capacity for forward planning.

Then came the turbulent period of 1910 to 1914, which stretched to breaking-point the government's ability to control strikes and working-class agitation. The police were unable to cope and the military intervened regularly, frequently with bayonets drawn and guns ready. Some strikers were killed and many were injured. Conventional channels for calling in troops were by-passed, with scant regard for constitutional procedure. The real sense of panic which gripped the government in the railway strike of 1911 was expressed by the rhetoric of Churchill, then Home Secretary, who declared: 'I do not know whether in the history of the world a similar catastrophe can be shown to have menaced an equally great community . . . The conditions which have undoubtedly occurred in the last week have been without any previous experience in this country.'[5] The government tried to break the strikes by using the military in a manner which it conceded was illegal but which it felt was justified by the extreme emergency conditions of the time. This provoked Keir Hardie to protest in the House of Commons: 'The law of England has been broken in the interests of the railway companies', and he asserted that strikers shot in South Wales were 'murdered by the government in the interests of the capitalist system'.[6]

In fact the degree of violence used against strikers by the troops was counter-productive and the authorities recognized that a different approach was necessary if they were to retain public support. There was also concern about the vulnerability of key services such as the railways and essential industries such as the mines. As Peak shows in his study, *Troops in Strikes*, 1911 'was the watershed between the old and the new approach to military strike-breaking'.[7]

· AN ALTERNATIVE LABOUR FORCE ·

The new approach was much more centralized. It included the use of the military in a more peaceful role as an alternative labour force to replace strikers and maintain emergency services. The government also started to develop the capacity to organize strike-breaking more effectively by planning ahead. In 1919 and 1920, troops were used again in fresh outbreaks of industrial militancy. Railway and mining strikes led to widespread breakdowns in public order, and considerable violence, with troops once more thrust into the front line of opposition to strikers. However, military leaders were by now displaying some reluctance to perform strike-breaking duties, which they saw as the responsibility of the civil power, partly because they felt this was undermining the armed forces' constitutional position and partly because there was growing resistance among rank-and-file soldiers to being turned into 'blacklegs'.

The culmination of these pressures was the introduction of the Emergency Powers Act in 1920, under which the statutory basis for military intervention was clarified. Although a residual back-up role to the police remained, it was clear that the armed forces' main purpose was now to run essential services as part of an overall plan for dealing with emergencies. This was emphasized by Churchill, when he carefully distinguished between ordinary strikes and those which disrupted services essential to the life of the country:

To use soldiers or sailors, kept up at the general expense of the tax-payer, to take sides with the employer in an ordinary trade dispute

... would be a monstrous invasion of the liberty of the subject, and ... would be a very unfair, if not an illegal, order to give the soldier. But the case is different where vital services affecting the health, life and safety of large cities or great concentrations of people are concerned.[8]

This meant a more limited role in 'ordinary trade disputes'. But it also legitimized military intervention against strikers whose strategic position in the economy created serious political problems for the government.

The first major test of the new emergencies organization came with the General Strike in 1926. Three days before the strike started, the government declared a state of emergency and immediately activated a well-prepared plan for dealing with essential supplies and emergencies. An official press statement was issued 'making it clear that the troops were intended for protection purposes only and not for taking sides'.[9]

The armed forces adopted a low profile, though they gave some assistance to the police to maintain public order, and they also did some strikers' work. Soldiers escorted food convoys through picketing dockers, protected key installations like power stations and cordoned off central government buildings. The army occupied special camps at all large cities, naval ships went to all major ports, and fighter planes patrolled railway lines. Submarines provided electricity for the London docks. Some troops were used to run London's docks and power stations. These military operations were successful, as was the overall emergency plan: the government's authority was maintained with relatively little difficulty.

The General Strike also marked a turning-point by being the last occasion on which the army intervened in an industrial dispute to keep the peace:

Before 1926, troops had primarily been called on in strikes to display or inflict force that the police either did not possess or could not be relied upon to deploy effectively. Since 1926, however, the police have been responsible for public order and troops have only intervened in strikes to replace the strikers or ameliorate the effects of their actions.[10]

·POST-WAR INTERVENTION·

Afterwards, there was no military intervention in strikes until the Second World War had ended. Under the 1945–51 Labour government, the armed forces were used at least fourteen times to do strikers' work, provoking newspaper criticism at the time that the Ministry of Labour seemed 'almost an appendage to the service departments'.[11] The military were deployed so frequently in this period because of the persistent problem of unofficial strikes, especially in the docks. In contrast, troops intervened only four times from 1951 to 1970 to do strikers' work: during the 1953 oil tankers dispute; the 1955 railway strike; and the 1960 and 1966 seamen's disputes.

However, the confrontational stance adopted by the Conservative government elected in 1970 marked a further turning-point, opening the way towards a new era of military intervention in strikes. Although the Tories publicly threatened to use troops in the dock strike of July 1970 to maintain essential services, this did not prove necessary. The first occasion on which they called in the military was in October 1970 during the refuse collectors' strike. That followed a request from the Labour-controlled council in the London Borough of Tower Hamlets where piles of rubbish had become a health hazard. But even such a limited use of troops was provocative: *all* the council's workers went on strike in protest until the dispute was settled.

In December 1970 troops were used to deliver army generators to a number of hospitals during industrial action by power workers. But the government said it would not be practical for troops to run power stations. Nor was any attempt made to use the military to break the 1972 miners' strike. Even the humiliation the government suffered by the closure of Saltley coke depot did not deflect the Secretary of State for Trade and Industry from the view that it would be 'highly unwise' to send in troops.[12] Reginald Maudling, Home Secretary at the time, later wrote:

Some of my colleagues asked me afterwards why I had not sent in troops to support the police, and I remember asking them one simple question: 'If they had been sent in, should they have gone in with their rifles loaded or unloaded?' Either course would have been disastrous.[13]

The government's diffidence about deploying troops was also apparent during the 1972 dock strike. A state of emergency was declared and there were two instances of limited assistance by the military: one at Dover's ferry terminal, the other to transport emergency supplies to Scottish islands. Such emergency measures, the Home Secretary, Robert Carr, insisted, were 'not directed against the dockers or their union. Their purpose is not to break the strike. It is to protect the life of the community.'[14]

But during the Glasgow fire brigades strike in 1973, an open strike-breaking role was adopted by the troops. Army leaders felt less constrained because the strike was unofficial, and it lacked the backing of either the Fire Brigades Union or the TUC.

Then came an episode which, though not constituting direct military involvement in a strike, underlined the drift towards a more important role for the armed forces in maintaining public order. In January 1974, during the 1973-4 miners' strike (and the longest state of emergency declared since 1926), armed troops were deployed at Heathrow Airport to assist the police. Soldiers with sub-machine guns patrolled the vicinity for several days in armoured cars. The first such case of military aid to the civil power, it was ostensibly undertaken because of a suspected terrorist attack. In fact the evidence suggested it was 'basically a public relations exercise to accustom the public to the reality of troops deploying through the high street'.[15] After Labour came to power there were similar exercises in June, July and September 1974.

A special Tory Party study group reported in 1977 that troops could not be used to break strikes for two main reasons: 'first, that Britain no longer had enough troops, and second, that it would permanently damage the fabric and practice of the country's politics'. But this conclusion seemed almost a reluctant one, provoking Labour's Denis Healey, then Chancellor of the Exchequer, to complain that the Conservatives wanted to use the armed forces 'to win a confrontation with the working people of Britain'.[16]

In the event, the 1974-9 Labour government deployed troops in strikes more often than the Tories had done: directly in six disputes, with a stand-by role in others.* The first occasion was in 1975 when 2,000 soldiers cleared 41,500 tons of rubbish in the Glasgow refuse collectors' strike. Here troops were clearly performing the role of an alternative labour force. But two years later they assumed a more overt strike-breaking role during a strike by Air Traffic Control assistants. In October 1977, pickets outside West Drayton Air Traffic Control Centre were suddenly cleared by police to allow the passage of twelve military oil tankers driven by members of the Royal Air Force. They contained diesel fuel for generators which supplied the computers controlling air traffic over London. Although the official reason given was to keep computers controlling military flights operational, the assistants' union argued that these could have been isolated from the civilian computer system, and that the intervention of the military was decisive in undermining the strike which ended a fortnight later.[17]

·FIRE BRIGADES STRIKE·

Soon afterwards the use of soldiers in the national fire brigades strike marked a new era, in which military intervention in strikes became both more frequent and more decisive than for decades. Over two months in the winter of 1977-8, some 20,000 military personnel replaced about 30,000 members of the Fire Brigades Union (on a national strike for the first time in their history). The dispute was for higher pay and reduced hours and it came during the third year of the Labour government's pay restraint policy. As *The Times* explained: 'At stake in the dispute, apart from the dangers to life and limb, is the future of the government's pay policy, and thereby its political credibility.'[18]

* Between 1945 and 1983, Labour governments called in the military twenty-one times and Tory governments fifteen times.

The operation had been carefully planned in the weeks before by the Civil Contingencies Unit (CCU), which supervised a country-wide command structure bringing together the military with civilian organizations from the Home Office down to local councils. County emergency committees of councillors and officials met in county control rooms (some of these being wartime county control centres), at which were also based military liaison cells.[19]

The troops used 800 'Green Goddesses' – fire engines built in the 1950s and kept, regularly serviced, in mothballs by the Home Office since that time. In all, they assisted at 39,000 fire incidents across the country, keeping an elementary fire service going and thereby helping to break the strike. After two months the union was forced to accept a 10 per cent increase, exactly in line with the government's pay norm, though the union also won a beneficial index-linked pay agreement for the future and a reduction in hours staged over several years.

Those responsible for contingency planning certainly benefited from the experience gained. The Chief of the Defence Staff later described it as an 'invaluable' operation and, as Peak adds,

the military showed they could take over an unaccustomed national role with only a few days' direct preparation and sustain it for a prolonged period. And perhaps almost as significantly, the public and the strikers reacted with markedly less hostility to the use of troops than in the past, thus immeasurably aiding the policy of 'normalizing' the use of troops in strikes that the contingency planners appear to have been following.[20]

Furthermore, *The Times* noted shortly afterwards how the government's resolve in handling civil emergencies had 'stiffened noticeably in the past few months, with ministers overcoming their fastidiousness about strike-breaking. Success in handling the firemen's dispute has strengthened their determination.'[21] The CCU prepared for troops to be introduced when petrol tanker drivers started an overtime ban a fortnight later and again during a prison officers' dispute in October 1978; but in the end neither dispute escalated to a point which could have made military intervention necessary. However, the Royal Navy did intervene to

replace civilian shipyard workers who blacked work on three Polaris
submarines at Scotland's Faslane base in the summer of 1978.

· 'WINTER OF DISCONTENT' ·

During the 'Winter of Discontent' between December 1978 and
March 1979, there were strikes in several key areas: by oil tanker
and lorry drivers, local government workers, water and sewage
workers, and ambulance crews. The Labour government's attempt
to impose pay restraint for the fourth successive year provoked
hostility throughout the trade union movement, and the strikes
quickly became a direct threat to the government's policy and its
standing in the country.

Early on, the *Daily Mail* reported: 'The army has been told to
stand by to enforce the government's pay policy', and, later,
leaders of the Transport and General Workers' Union were warned
by Cabinet ministers of plans to use troops to move petrol and
break the strike.[22] As it happened, the dispute ended soon afterwards. On 10 January the tanker drivers accepted a revised pay
offer of about 15 per cent – though markedly less than their 30–
40 per cent claim, it was well above the government's 5 per cent
norm.

But a contingency plan had been drawn up by the CCU. Called
'Operation Drumstick', it was ready for implementation late in
December when there were media reports of a likely state of
emergency. The plan was very detailed and the Home Secretary
later made it clear that the government had been ready at any
time to activate it and call in the armed services. The public
leaking of its broad outline was a good example of the government
using the option of military intervention to 'soften up' striking
trade unionists, with an eye not merely on the tanker drivers but
major strikes looming elsewhere. The other significant feature of
the episode was the absence of real political controversy about the
threat to use troops. Military intervention in strikes in essential
services was becoming almost normal: testimony to the state's
success in preparing the ground during the 1970s.

During the lorry drivers' strike which followed soon afterwards, the government also made clear its willingness to call on the military, though it was doubtful whether they could have moved more than a small proportion of strike-hit goods. In practice, the contingency plan activated by the CCU for dealing with the strike proved effective and there was no need for either a state of emergency or for troops to be deployed. Much the same pattern followed in the local authority manual workers' strikes and sporadic action by water workers which broke out that January: the CCU was once more in action and troops were standing by, but the unions eventually settled for increases well above the 5 per cent government target.

However, the armed services were called in during industrial action by ambulance crews between January and March 1979. There was also an unusual – and almost certainly illegal – use of troops at this time at London's Westminster Hospital. During the local authority manual workers' dispute, two vans were left in the entrance to the hospital with their tyres slashed, blocking the movement of essential supplies. Hospital officials called in soldiers from a nearby Royal Yeomanry Garrison to move and repair the vans. But no proper authorization had been given through the accepted legal procedures.

·THATCHERISM AND TROOPS·

The armed services were again called in to replace strikers during two separate civil service disputes in the summer of 1979. The first was by members of the Institution of Professional Civil Servants, and civilian strikers in naval dockyards were replaced by servicemen. Then, during selective strikes by industrial civil servants, service personnel were increasingly used to do the work of civilians at military airports, Royal Ordnance factories and dockyards.

In 1979–80, Tory government ministers let it be known during several strikes that plans were in hand to deploy troops should this prove necessary. One of the strikes was at London's Charing

Cross Hospital, and in November 1979 Mrs Thatcher herself indicated that the government was considering deploying soldiers to break a picket line. The following April, it emerged that the government had recently revised its contingency plan for the health services, enabling health authorities to make use of troops during strikes.[23] This additional opportunity for military intervention in strikes was determined by *administrative* action, with no prior parliamentary debate or agreement. Six months later, in November 1980, when it looked as though there might be another fire brigades dispute, the Transport Minister signed an order permitting military personnel to drive fire engines; it was slipped through without proper parliamentary consideration.

Such use of the armed forces showed a casual attitude towards due procedure and was probably illegal. Manipulation of the law was also evident in October 1980 when the Imprisonment (Temporary Provisions) Act was pushed through Parliament in thirteen hours and twenty minutes, to give the government the power to break industrial action by prison officers. The Act gave sweeping powers to the government, overriding the judiciary and the legal rights of prisoners. It also enabled troops to run prisons and, for the first time, to perform the duties and assume the powers of police constables while acting as prison warders. It was passed on 28 October. Four days earlier, the Emergency Powers Act 1964 had been invoked to authorize the general use of troops in the dispute, but extra powers were needed to permit them to run prisons. The dispute lasted over three months, during which 1,000 military personnel were used for a total of 17,000 'staff weeks', with an unspecified number of additional troops putting in the equivalent of another 60,000 weeks.[24] Military leaders again expressed satisfaction with their contribution and the extra experience gained.

In 1981 there were two further uses of the military in strikes. They replaced strikers at nuclear submarine bases in Scotland in April during selective strike action by civil service unions, and were called in to perform other duties before the strike petered out in July with the government having stood firm.

Meanwhile plans had been refined for the limited use of service personnel to do certain health service work. When health service disputes started breaking out early in 1981 and it looked as if the pay negotiations for ambulance crews might prove difficult, details leaked out of alternative plans either to replace ambulance crews with troops, or to use military ambulances. A national official of the Transport and General Workers' Union commented angrily: 'They are trying to put the scares on our people. Here is a government that publicly deplores military intervention against workers in Poland and yet is planning the same thing itself.'[25] The dispute dragged on into July, and troops were deployed in only a few isolated incidents.

In the long-running health workers' dispute of 1982, troops did ambulance work on only one occasion in London, though they were on stand-by throughout. Also in 1982, troops were used to prepare extra parking places in London parks during a two-day national rail strike in June. Then in January 1983, water workers went on their first-ever national strike. For some years a water and sewage strike had been regarded by planners in the CCU as a potential 'nightmare',[26] and it was clear that the government would only risk using troops if the system was on the point of collapse. The strike, by 29,000 manual workers, lasted a month before they won a pay increase that went significantly beyond the government's guidelines for the public sector. Its effect was less catastrophic than had been feared, partly because of action taken by the CCU under its plan called 'Operation Keelman', partly because managers in the industry continued to work, and partly because the government did not adopt as hard a line against a pay rise as it did with other, less powerfully placed, workers.

· A TOTAL STRATEGY ·

By the mid 1980s a distinctively modern pattern of military intervention in strikes had become apparent. The military's traditional role of public-order enforcement, first performed alone and later in support of the police, had, from 1926, been gradually overtaken. In modern times the armed forces have increasingly been used as a replacement force for strikers, especially in essential services. Since the fire brigades strike of 1977–8, troop deployment to perform strikers' work in strategic services has been refined to the point where it is now part of a total strategy by the state towards industrial action which threatens its interests.

Military intervention in strikes is no longer *ad hoc* – a pragmatic response to a crisis with which other state agencies cannot cope. It is now carefully planned well in advance. The CCU has available comprehensive proposals for strike-breaking in each sensitive area of the economy. These plans are given special code names and are regularly updated. Military intervention is simply one of a series of options available, according to the circumstances. Use of the armed forces is now a purely *tactical* question determined by the CCU and ministers, the basic principle of military intervention having been endorsed by successive governments.

The contingency plans are also tailor-made to account for both the logistics of the strike-hit work and the nature of the relevant trade unions. For example, troops have not been deployed in miners' strikes, because the contingency planners felt that they could not do miners' work and that any attempt to keep mines open would provoke a militant reaction from the miners' union. In the electricity supply industry, the government acknowledged on more than one occasion the limited scope for army personnel who lack the required skills and experience. Much the same is true for the water industry. When troops have intervened during the 1970s and 1980s this has increasingly been part of a wider plan involving both other contingency measures and political action by the government.

·POLITICAL ATTITUDES·

The growing use of the armed forces in politically sensitive strikes has made the attitudes of service personnel towards trade unions more important. In earlier periods, from time to time there were signs that rank-and-file soldiers might be unwilling to carry out strike-breaking duties. Immediately after both the First and Second World Wars, the use of soldiers against workers with whom they had recently fought side by side was a sensitive matter. During industrial unrest in 1919, for example, local army commanders reported that troops might not be reliable if they were called in to tackle strikes threatened by miners and railway workers.[27] And in 1950 the Cabinet was told that the army 'viewed with some disquiet the repeated demands which were being made upon them in connection with strikes'.[28]

There has been a long tradition of radicalism which has attained wider appeal within the armed forces from time to time – for example during the Second World War military leaders were most concerned at the spread of left-wing ideas.[29] But it has normally had only minority support and in recent years the evidence suggests a predominance of right-wing and anti-union views within the military.

The authors of a study of government strike-breaking interviewed members of the armed forces, and although they recorded a range of views, some 'very moderate', they found particular antipathy towards trade unions at private soldier level – for example:

'I'm pretty convinced that the services would enjoy breaking up a massed picket. It would be the same as rioting. Riot drill is something we know about. The mass riots in Northern Ireland were good fun. No other military in the world is better at breaking up riots than the British.'[30]

Senior soldiers were also anti-union, though less vehemently so, and they seemed more concerned to maintain the armed forces' position, as they saw it, of constitutional 'impartiality'. Nevertheless, in capitalist societies high-ranking officers 'have constituted a deeply conservative and even reactionary element in the state system and in society generally'.[31]

Few could deny the existence of a right-wing bias within both the leadership and the rank-and-file of the armed forces. But it is often argued that such opinions are 'personal and private', and would not be allowed to prejudice the professional duty of soldiers to the 'whole country'. This is coupled with an insistence that the military's function is 'impartial', as the *Manual of Military Law* claims:

The merits or demerits of such disputes or unrest are of no concern whatsoever to soldiers, who are solely concerned with the duty and obligation common to all citizens of assisting the civil authority in the maintenance of law and order, and in these situations their principal duty will be the protection of persons and property.[32]

But, as one legal analyst has shown, 'One of the inevitable consequences of military intervention as a weapon in the arsenal of government is . . . the strengthening of the bargaining power of management, at the expense of those taking part in industrial action.'[33] Nor can military intervention in the public sector be 'impartial': since the government is the employer, the military are automatically acting in support of the particular political policies of the government. Furthermore, although great play is made of the armed forces' solemn duty to 'protect essential supplies', in practice the 'distinction between strike-breaking and safeguarding essential supplies is a very fine one'.[34]

As an agency of the state, the armed forces are no more neutral or apolitical than the state itself. When they are brought into a strike by the government, the military are forced to take sides in a class conflict – a self-evidently political act. And to the extent that such intervention has been growing, their political role has been growing too.

· 'COMING OUT' POLITICALLY ·

During the 1971–5 period of crisis in Britain, with trade union militancy relatively widespread and the left advancing within the Labour Party, there was some discussion in senior military circles as to whether the armed forces should intervene in a more open political role, possibly by organizing a coup. Field Marshal Lord Carver, Chief of Defence Staff in 1974, later acknowledged that such discussion had occurred among 'fairly senior officers', but said he personally 'took action to make certain that nobody was so stupid as to go around saying those things'.[35] It seems that Harold Wilson, then Prime Minister, was not consulted about the three joint army–police exercises that took place at Heathrow Airport when Labour was in office in 1974. At the time he privately expressed concern that the troops manoeuvring there 'could be turned around against the government, totally'; later, he also complained that there was a right-wing faction within the security services which was seeking to undermine his administration.[36] It later emerged that military leaders and MI5 in particular secretly backed the Protestant Ulster workers' strike in 1974 'as part of a strategy to unhinge the newly elected Wilson government'.[37] The success of the strike in paralysing Northern Ireland provoked a collapse in the government's policy of 'power sharing' between Protestants and Catholics.

In 1974–5 there were reports of private 'citizens' armies' being prepared by prominent eccentrics and retired military figures. They included General Sir Walter Walker (until 1972 Commander-in-Chief of NATO's Northern Command in Europe) and Colonel David Stirling (known for his wartime exploits in the Special Air Service). The purpose, as Stirling expressed it, was to 'provide on a volunteer basis the minimum manpower necessary to cope with the immediate crisis following a general strike or a near general strike in the knowledge that the government of the day must welcome our initiative'.[38]

The 'government of the day' happened to be a Labour one, at that stage still pursuing a relatively left-wing programme, and, although these private armies were ridiculed by some commentators, it may be that 'the real purpose of these organizations was to push the *government* into making more preparations'.[39] David Stirling explained later that he thought a general strike was likely and that he was forming a group of trained cadres because Labour was unwilling to make the necessary preparations for an appropriate military response.[40]

It is also significant that around that time the ideas in Brigadier Frank Kitson's book, *Low Intensity Operations*, were being widely canvassed. Published in 1971, it argued that the army might have to intervene in conditions of rapidly falling living standards caused by high inflation and industrial unrest. His general approach seemed to be reflected in a series of events and preparations undertaken between 1971 and 1975, including joint police–military exercises, joint seminars and conferences on urban political, social and industrial unrest.[41]

The experience gained by the armed forces in Northern Ireland has accustomed them both to the task of controlling civilian populations and to a more overtly political role. As was argued in 1976,

the British army's record in the Northern Ireland campaign shows clearly that it is fully capable of playing an influential role in the political arena. The Irish campaign has forced a greater political awareness on the officer corps. Through the coordinated civil–military–police operations ... the army has gained experience for the first time of running a province of an advanced capitalist country at grass roots level. As one major put it, 'now we have very much closer insight into the working of the political mind'; and generals too have become involved in intimate political relationships and are learning how to wheel and deal.[42]

Because a tour of duty in Northern Ireland is limited and members of the armed forces resume their role on the mainland afterwards, their experience can be passed on and so becomes directly relevant should they be required to intervene in any other conflict, such as a major strike.

·AN EXTRA-DEMOCRATIC FORCE?·

Growing military intervention in strikes raises important issues of democratic accountability. There has been a distinct lack of clarity surrounding the constitutional basis for deploying troops. They have sometimes been used to meet the circumstances of the moment with little regard for legal niceties:

Whether the government has the power which it claims to use troops to intervene ... remains unresolved. But a strong case can be made that governments acted illegally when they sent in troops on some if not the majority of occasions since the Second World War. On many of these occasions the orders given to the troops may not have been lawful.[43]

The government's order to use troops is transmitted through a division of the Ministry of Defence called Defence Secretariat Six (DS6) to the headquarters of United Kingdom Land Forces near Salisbury. The main legislation on the use of troops in strikes – the 1920 Emergency Powers Act – was introduced after secret legal advice during the industrial conflict of 1919 showed that the growing practice of deploying armed forces personnel to do the work of civilian strikers was actually illegal. The Act allows for the declaration of a 'state of emergency' when the government considers that 'the essential services of the country are threatened'. Although the declaration has to be reported to Parliament, it is the Cabinet advised by the contingency planners which determines whether the circumstances justify an emergency. The 1920 Act was buttressed by the 1964 Emergency Powers Act which directly legitimized strike-breaking and, crucially, allowed troops to be used without a state of emergency being declared and without requiring parliamentary approval.

In practice, very little democratic control is maintained over the use of the military in strikes. The law has been continuously updated by governments through new interpretations of its scope to meet new situations, thereby short-circuiting parliamentary accountability to an even greater extent. Furthermore, as the contingency and military planning apparatus has been extended and refined, power has shifted away from the Cabinet, so that now:

The official strike-breaking machine is run by civil and military contingency planners who operate largely independently of the ministers who theoretically control their work. These planners decide which strikes are potential threats and how they can be brought to an end. Military strike-breaking has developed as a covert activity, often unseen.[44]

The implications of this go beyond the important question of accountability in general, to the specific position of a *Labour* government. The record suggests that the state agencies involved in strike-breaking have sought to push Labour towards using troops. For example, Labour MP Brian Sedgemore, Parliamentary Private Secretary to Tony Benn, Labour's Secretary of State for Energy in 1975–9, wrote: 'The [Civil Contingencies] Unit was constantly meeting when Labour was in power and preparing behind the scenes for troops to break strikes.'[45] He also described how the government was almost manipulated into using troops to break an unofficial strike at the Windscale nuclear reprocessing plant in March 1977. The CCU advised that troops be called in on the basis of an assessment of the situation which was so false as to imply it was deliberately misleading Tony Benn, perhaps with a view to discrediting his status as a leader of the left. In the event he went to some trouble to prevent military intervention and instructed the authorities to reopen negotiations, after which the strike was settled.

By the mid 1980s military leaders, together with other members of the state elite, had been able to carve out for themselves a certain autonomy of action, allowing them to pursue their own interests with little real democratic check. The implications for major strikes in the future are far-reaching.

7
POLICING THE WORKERS

The picture of police forming up against strikers is now a familiar one. But, more than is generally acknowledged, the way policing has evolved in Britain is intimately bound up with the way strikes have evolved. To a considerable extent the character of policing has been altered to meet the political threat strikers have posed to the state in particular periods. In turn, the nature of police intervention in industrial disputes has considerably affected their outcome.

The police have been called upon to maintain order during the industrial unrest which has invariably occurred at crisis-points in British political history. Although they have traditionally been anxious to protest their independence from partisan or political influences, as one history of the police explains:

... when a situation of internal 'crisis' develops, the police become preoccupied with their order-maintenance function and become involved in vital encounters with the public over highly emotive, sensitive issues, such as industrial relations ... It is in such areas that they are presented as the first line of defence of authority against challenge; it is in such areas, when public order is challenged, that they become most visible as the symbolic and actual representatives of the state.[1]

Perhaps more than anything else, police intervention in strikes has challenged the conventional wisdom that they act 'impartially': as agents of the state their role has gone beyond simply holding the ring between employer and striker, and has instead reflected the objectives of dominant interests in society.

·ORIGINS·

The origins of the modern police force lie in the state's reaction to the growth of the working class from the beginnings of industrial capitalism in the late eighteenth century. Prior to this, law and order had for some six hundred years been maintained by a diffuse system of local policing. Its agents were parish 'constables' and 'watchmen'. Answerable ultimately to the Crown, they came increasingly under the direct control of local elites, in which the key figures were magistrates.

The functions of these magistrates had been formalized under the Justices of the Peace Act 1361. They were effectively responsible not simply for maintaining the peace, but also for administering the law, running such local authority provision as then existed and even regulating wages and hours of work. The vesting of these political and legal responsibilities in the same individuals –who tended also to be drawn from among local landowners – underlined the difficulty of separating the political and law enforcement functions of parish constables.

This system began to collapse with the onset of the industrial revolution, the movement from rural into urban areas and the rise of a new urban-based working class. Rapid population growth, social dislocation, poverty, rising crime – the consequences of an emerging industrial capitalism – provoked deep anxiety in the higher classes at the danger to public order and therefore to their interests. This anxiety turned to panic in the aftermath of the French Revolution of 1789. As Frances Lady Shelley noted in her diary of 1787–1817, 'the awakening of the labouring classes, after the first shocks of the French Revolution, made the upper classes tremble. Every man felt the necessity for putting his house in order . . .'[2]

However, there was also a strong tradition of resistance to the centralization inherent in a properly organized system of policing, with widespread fears expressed that it could lead to 'a system of tyranny', or an 'engine . . . invented by despotism', as E. P. Thompson explains:

Tories feared the overruling of parochial and chartered rights and of the powers of local J Ps; Whigs feared an increase in the powers of Crown or of government; Radicals ... preferred the notion of voluntary associations or rotas of householders; the radical populace until Chartist times saw in any police an engine of oppression.[3]

· THE 'NEW' POLICE ·

In the early decades of the nineteenth century the dominant classes at least began to shed such inhibitions. They felt *individually* threatened by rising working-class crime and *collectively* threatened by rising working-class industrial and political militancy. These tended to be linked together in the eyes of the authorities, particularly since this was a time when workers' organizations had been driven underground, when there were Luddite attacks on factories and when trade union struggles were spreading.

In London the problem seemed acute. Dock workers had been paid partly in kind, but this had developed to the point where port authorities felt that dockers, sailors and port labourers had 'a general licence to plunder for their remuneration', as Patrick Colquhoun, the Chief Magistrate for the City of London, described it.[4] On his recommendation, the system of 'watchmen' who guarded the docklands was replaced in 1800 with a properly constituted river police. Under the 1800 River Police Act the magistrates presiding over this 'new' police force were also made accountable to the Home Secretary. Thus a model was established for later police organization.

The formation of the river police 'was, however, significant for another reason. It led to the establishment of the money wage in the docks. The theft of goods from the docks represented not just a criminal act, it was a substantial threat to the profits of the merchants.'[5] Hence from its origins the police force of Britain was inextricably bound up with the defence of dominant interests.

Meanwhile the government was becoming more conscious of the provocative role of the armed forces when they were used to maintain public order, such as at Peterloo in 1819. In 1829 the Home Secretary, Sir Robert Peel, introduced a Police Act to set up the Metropolitan Police Force. By 1835 similar police forces were being officially set up in towns outside London, and by 1839 in the counties too. Their immediate tasks were protecting middle-class areas from crime and maintaining public order.

From the 1840s onwards the police began increasingly to intervene in industrial disputes, often using violent tactics against strikers: 'Where labour disputes were concerned the police everywhere protected the interest of the industrialist against the workers.'[6] Their lack of impartiality derived most immediately from the fact that those responsible for directing local police forces were also local landowners and businessmen. For example, a revealing study of unrest in Black Country areas between 1835 and 1860 recorded how the police acted against the working classes, because

power lay with the Lord Lieutenant and the JPs who, collectively in Quarter Sessions, were the local legislative, administrative and judicial authorities for the whole country; in Petty Sessions they dispensed local and summary justice for their districts; they had influence over the county police force through the Chief Constable, whom they appointed. They could command bodies of police, troops and special constables in times of emergency; and in the Black Country, a large number of the JPs were themselves large coal and iron masters, the largest employers and the most powerful economic forces in the region; they could exercise this power to protect their own interests and property through the normal forces of law and order.[7]

·INDUSTRIAL CONFRONTATIONS·

There were other instances of police confronting strikers in the Scottish coalfields of Lanarkshire and Ayrshire in the early 1880s, prompting Keir Hardie to complain that the police were lackeys of capital, happy to ride down 'inoffensive children nearly to death and felling quiet old men with a blow from a baton'.[8] Elsewhere, troops were also called out periodically to aid the police to put down strikers and pickets. There were brutal clashes after police had attacked strikers at Tonypandy in 1910 and in other colliery areas in the South Wales valleys.

The country-wide unrest and union militancy between 1910 and 1914 saw thousands of police being marshalled to break strikes, not just in Wales, but also in Liverpool, Hull and Salford. During this time, 'Frightened police going beserk in baton charges was almost a commonplace during a large strike.'[9] Another study records: 'The police were, quite simply, used as a battering ram in such situations. All their methods and training were aimed at strike-breaking rather than the impartial preservation of the public peace. Thus while blacklegs received sufficient police protection to prevent pickets and strikers getting at them, when workers resorted to *mass* pickets the police simply charged, with the intention of scattering strikers to the wind.'[10]

However, this overtly political policing in strikes was complemented by a far less controversial role in the ordinary life of the community, where a tradition was gradually built up of the amiable British 'Bobby'. An unarmed body of men was created which was intended to win, and to a great extent did win, the confidence of the public right across class boundaries. Unlike the continental police tradition, where the public are not expected to come into regular contact with the police, except as law-breakers, the British police developed a tradition in which a great deal of time was spent patrolling alone. It was never envisaged that they should enforce the law as a small elite capable of implementing the wishes of the government by superior force of arms, and doing so, if necessary, against the wishes of large numbers of people. Instead, the police are supposed to act in accordance with the wishes of the majority, against a minority of law-breakers. 'The British political genius was to make this police force, clearly taking side in a class struggle, appear to be an independent, non-partisan agency simply enforcing the law. It is a political illusion that has been increasingly difficult to sustain during more recent class confrontations in Britain.'[11]

Despite the fact that the police have always sought to present themselves as standing between conflicting social forces, this has never been the case. In his semi-official history of the police, Critchley gives away the falsity of the carefully fostered 'man in the middle' image when, referring to the nineteenth century, he writes: 'They stood (as they sometimes do today) at the storm centre of the conflict between two naturally antagonistic and mutually uncomprehending systems of virtue – radicalism and authority.'[12] But 'authority' in the nineteenth century, before the advent of democracy, was little more than the power of businessmen and landowners. The police could not play the role of referee between 'authority' and 'radicalism' and somehow remain neatly in the democratic middle, because they were part of that authority then, just as they are today.

· POLICE ORGANIZATION ·

The way the police developed from the time of Robert Peel's pioneering legislation – the main features being better organization and greater centralization – largely reflected the political function the force was asked to perform. Peel had declared that he intended, as the police became publicly accepted, to extend the operation of the Metropolitan Police beyond the districts of London to which the 1829 Act applied. In other words, he wanted to win public acceptance of the need for a national police force. But it was not until 150 years later that this started to occur.

Peel's hopes were initially stifled by the strengthening of local government and the desire to retain local control of policing. The rising middle class in the towns used the new local government structures established after 1835 to set up Watch Committees, which took control of law and order from the multiplicity of watchmen and parish constables. Although the counties were not to elect local councils until the 1880s, in 1839 legislation provided for the magistracy to set up county police forces under their control. But the picture across the country remained patchy, with local elites and emerging local government structures each being anxious to retain their local autonomy.

Further pressure for the rationalization of policing came from the challenges posed to dominant interests by Chartism and trade unionism. In 1856 the government introduced legislation making the creation of proper police forces compulsory and set up an Inspectorate of Constabulary in the Home Office to supervise the standards and operation of police forces.

Consequently, the modern policing system developed explicitly as a response to working-class movements struggling for greater democracy. The division of responsibility for policing between local elites (represented on Watch Committees) and central government (represented through the Home Office and the Metropolitan Police) amounted to the maximum degree of centralization which local elites would tolerate. There is no doubt that the alternative of a single national police force would have been preferred by the Home Office if it had been politically acceptable.

However, the limited amount of central control instituted in 1856 gradually began to take effect. There were 259 separate police forces in 1859, dropping to around 200 by the end of the century. Central government's share of police financing rose from a quarter to a half after 1874. Meanwhile both Head Constables commanding police forces in the towns and Chief Constables those in the counties began to take greater control, the role of Watch Committees in practice diminishing as policing became more organized.

By the end of the century there began to emerge an increasingly professional group of senior police officers who, under the guidance of the Home Office, began to shape the direction of policing. They began to refine policing policy, though its overall priority remained to combat the 'twin threat' of working-class crime and militancy – rather than, say, enforcing early laws on public health and industrial safety. Thus the history of the police came to be the story of a slow eclipse of the power of local political elites and the establishment of a unified, national force – albeit divided into regional components – strongly influenced by the national government and commanded by a group of men with professional and political concerns of their own.

Before and after the First World War the police were heavily involved in strike-breaking, and there were bitter clashes with trade unionists. In the General Strike they confronted thousands of workers in picket-line clashes: although they played a 'tactful' role, and there were instances of strikers playing football with local officers or organizing other joint sporting ventures, there were also violent attacks by police on workers.[13]

Later, unemployed workers found themselves particular targets for police attention, representing as they did, after the trade union movement had been defeated in 1926, the most visible source of resistance to the state. During the 1920s the police constantly harassed the National Unemployed Workers' Movement, and between December 1931 and January 1932 they were involved in violent clashes with workers in major cities across Britain. Conflict with the unemployed lasted through to September 1932 when there were three days of open combat between police and workers in Birkenhead culminating in what has been described as a 'reign of terror', when working-class areas were raided by police who forced their way into homes and attacked individuals.[14] During the Second World War, the police assumed a quasi-military role: 'they acted throughout the war as a kind of intelligence service, reporting ... on the state of public order and civilian morale ... the effect of enemy propaganda, and signs of industrial unrest'.[15]

· CENTRALIZATION ·

Between the two World Wars, rationalization of police organization and resources gradually went ahead. All the time, centralization of policing was proceeding. Organizational efficiency was one reason for this. Politics was another, for the Labour Party was coming into office with increasing frequency, not only nationally but also in local government. Police chiefs were determined to retain and indeed increase their control – and keen to ensure that effective policing of the working class was not undermined by Labour-controlled police authorities. This tension was to surface far more openly in the 1970s and 1980s.

By the time the system of policing was subject to a major review in 1962, the number of forces had dwindled to 117. Though rejecting a single national force, the Royal Commission set up that year recommended that the number should be further reduced, and this was done in 1966 when the Home Secretary used new powers provided under the 1964 Police Act to compel amalgamations. The effect was drastically to increase the separation of the police from effective public control locally, and to consolidate the power of Chief Constables.

This combination of organizational centralization and increased political independence of police forces went a stage further after the 1970s reorganization of local government, when there was a further reduction in England and Wales to forty-one provincial forces (on top of the separate Metropolitan and City of London forces). Even then, pressure remained to centralize still further, with a growing consensus among police chiefs that their political role in a time of industrial strife, political protest or street disorder would be enhanced by a police service more unified and therefore more able to act with a degree of political cohesion. In 1979, after the 'Winter of Discontent', a joint conference of police and local government chiefs discussed the idea of a 'fully national police force' along the lines of most other EEC countries. By 1984 this was already beginning to occur, as a National Reporting Centre, based in Scotland Yard, coordinated policing of the miners' strike on a nation-wide basis.

· POLICING WORKERS IN THE 1970s ·

With the trend towards the centralization of policing has come a much greater readiness by the police to intervene in strikes in a manner which goes far beyond holding the ring between employers and workers. Whether by design or by default, the police in the 1970s and 1980s have become a strike-breaking force again – much as they had been historically at previous crisis-points.

Coming on top of the spate of militant political demonstrations that stretched police resources for several years after 1968 –

notably in the universities, against the Vietnam War and on South African sports tours – was the period of intense industrial militancy in the early 1970s.

But the watershed for policing was the 1972 miners' strike, in particular the success of mass pickets in forcing closure of the Saltley coke depot in Birmingham. This amounted to a serious defeat for the police, and the government's reaction illustrated very clearly how police practice could be altered specifically to curb union militancy, but in a way that had a much wider impact on the whole society.

In March 1973 a National Security Committee (NSC) was established, with representatives of the police, the armed forces, intelligence agencies, the Home Office and the Department of Trade and Industry. Another miners' strike was anticipated and the NSC began preparations to cope with it. Additionally, the Home Secretary announced that 'flying pickets' would be intercepted while travelling to power stations, it being reported that an 'intelligence bureau has been set up at Scotland Yard to give police forces throughout the country early warning of when industrial unrest may turn to violence'.[16] This amounted to an embryonic police National Reporting Centre, though its existence was not officially acknowledged until March 1984 when it began to play a key role in the miners' strike. These three steps – the setting-up of the NSC; the unprecedented interception of strikers moving about Britain; and the new coordination of national intelligence – were all taken without prior public debate or parliamentary sanction.

· 'THIRD FORCE' POLICING ·

So was another step: the establishment of what was effectively a 'third force' role for the police, between civilian policing and the army. The problem after Saltley was not simply one of maintaining essential services and keeping the economy going in the event of widespread strikes, but defeating mass pickets without politically risky intervention by the army. Shortly afterwards, the dilemma was revealed by Brigadier Brian Watkins of the Army General Staff:

The whole period of the miners' strike has made us realize that the present size of the police force is too small. It is based on the fundamental philosophy that we are a law-abiding country. But things have now got to the state where there are not enough resources to deal with the increasing numbers who are not prepared to respect the law.[17]

But the dilemma went beyond the question of police numbers to ones of basic organization, training and equipment. At that time the only group capable of defeating such a determined, organized and potentially militant group as the Saltley pickets was the army. There was no equivalent of a paramilitary force like the 15,000-strong French CRS, notorious for its ruthless response to political or industrial unrest. Back in 1961, a Home Office working party had considered the need for a 'third separate policing force', but had rejected the concept on the basis that the public would not support it.[18] Although much the same conclusion was reached by the NSC, it recommended far-reaching changes in policing practice. Drawing on experience of the conflict in Northern Ireland, a number of changes were introduced, including more comprehensive police training in riot control and firearms, joint police–military exercises, and a permanent stand-by role for plain-clothes units of the crack Special Air Service in any conflict the police might not be able to control.

The Special Patrol Group was also reconstituted. Originally formed seven years earlier with the task of combating rising crime in inner London, and having been used in a public-order role at the Vietnam demonstrations in London in 1968, the SPG was now turned into a paramilitary group, part of the main police organizationally and operationally, but nevertheless acting as a highly mobile, elite force. The Metropolitan Police Commissioner, Robert Mark, later recalled how at the time he saw the police 'as very much on their own in attempting to preserve order in an increasingly turbulent society'.[19]

During the rest of the 1970s, the SPG was on duty or was held in reserve at every major industrial dispute, gaining a national reputation among trade unionists for its aggressive strike-breaking tactics. By the time of the Grunwick strike in 1977, Robert Mark had been succeeded as Commissioner by David McNee, formerly Chief Constable of the Strathclyde police. He had refined the role of its SPG equivalent, the Strathclyde Support Unit, and had also overseen joint police–army operations to break strikes by Glasgow firemen and dustmen.

Under McNee's direction, the SPG was sent to Grunwick where violent incidents provoked by its activities were widely criticized by strikers, MPs and journalists. The police quite clearly sided with management, drinking tea in the company's canteen and keeping on first-name terms with its managers while rigidly restricting numbers of pickets and making arrests for obstruction on the flimsiest of pretexts.[20] In 1978, the TUC's annual conference called for a public inquiry into the SPG. However, this call was ignored, for by then the SPG and its companion Police Support Units (PSUs), numbering 416 up and down the country, had become crucial instruments in the maintenance of public order, especially in industrial disputes.

They also took on a wider significance that was to emerge dramatically in the 1984 miners' strike. PSUs play a key role in 'mutual aid' operations, where officers are sent into the areas of other police forces as reinforcements. 'Mutual aid' as a doctrine was formally instituted in 1925 in the lead-up to the General Strike, and the ability of police officers to serve outside the area of their own force was extended by the 1964 Police Act.

Until 1980, mutual aid was obtained by local initiatives and local arrangements between forces. But in April 1980 operational weaknesses in the system were revealed during an urban riot in Bristol. The experience of the extensive mutual aid and finance needed to police pickets in the 1980 steel strike also led the Chief Constable of South Yorkshire (where most picketing had occurred) to ask his fellow police chiefs at their annual conference that summer whether there was a need for 'a stand-by force when national emergencies or problems arise, formed from officers seconded from police forces on a temporary basis and with the units being on permanent stand-by, and totally financed and equipped from national resources'.[21] His proposal for a mobile national reserve force was not accepted. But in August 1980 the Home Secretary did implement a reorganization of police command structures and operational plans for dealing with public disorder, encouraging Chief Officers to invoke mutual aid immediately the need for it arose.

During the early 1980s police tactics towards strikers were further refined. In 1981, 390 engineering workers at an East London firm, Staffa Products Ltd, occupied their factory in protest at management's decision to close it down, move the plant and create some 300 redundancies. In the early hours of a Saturday morning in November, police moved in, evicted the strikers and stood guard while equipment needed by the owners was moved out. A few days later, workers occupying the Laurence Scott engineering works in Manchester experienced an even more dramatic police operation. With full police cooperation, two helicopters moved in and masked men lifted out goods and equipment from the factory. The action of the police undermined both strikes. It also proved decisive in breaking picketing of the Stockport Messenger newspaper group in 1983.

·POLITICAL POLICE·

The familiar police denial that they play a political role in industrial disputes is even harder to sustain when their surveillance and intelligence activities are examined. From their earliest days, trade unions were infiltrated by spies and police and their communications were intercepted.[22] Later, the Special Branch undertook the main responsibility for this. Originally set up in 1883 as a small section of the Metropolitan Police after a series of bombings by Irish nationalists, it evolved to monitor working-class organizations.

In 1916 the Branch was asked to investigate industrial unrest in the arms production industry. From this relatively limited task its wartime role was extended in the classic fashion of British policing – step by step on a pragmatic basis – first to monitor radical political groups, then to take on a still wider remit: 'surveillance was not limited to revolutionary groups; it extended to many of liberal inclinations, including members of the Labour Party who became involved in anti-war activity or industrial action. In short everyone who was ideologically to the left of the Tory Party became a potential subversive.'[23] In May 1917 there were a number of strikes in which key activists were arrested on the recommendation of the Branch.

In the turbulent years of widespread industrial action after the war the Special Branch was given specific responsibility for gathering intelligence on the trade union movement. When the police went on strike in August 1918 it infiltrated the strike organizers and reported directly to the Cabinet on their activities. In this way, a wartime precedent established a practice which further politicized policing.

In the 1930s, the Special Branch infiltrated the National Unemployed Workers' Movement and encouraged wider police harassment of its activities. In 1966 it briefed the Prime Minister, Harold Wilson, on the seamen's strike, encouraging him to allege publicly that it was instigated and manipulated by communists – an allegation unsupported by the facts. Evidence later emerged that the National Union of Seamen had been closely monitored. There was regular contact between the Branch and some officials of the union, and in 1970 a Branch officer tried to persuade one official that his proposals for a merger with the Transport and General Workers' Union 'would not be good for the country'.[24]

In the 1970s, the Branch stepped up its activity to keep pace with rising industrial militancy. When a strike broke out, Branch officers developed a practice of briefing police on known 'ring-leaders' who were often the ones then arrested on picket lines. It also took a close interest in the factory occupations, of which there were over a hundred, between 1971 and 1974.[25] In January 1985 the former Chief Constable of Devon and Cornwall, John Alderson, confirmed to a House of Commons select committee that Branch officers compiled detailed daily reports on all Britain's industrial disputes and forwarded them to the Home Office.

But the activities of the Special Branch go well beyond intervention in strikes. As a matter of routine its officers often make

contact with senior members of companies and then establish a
working relationship with personnel officers:

It is their indirect intrusion into industrial affairs which is the more
pernicious. Collusion between management and the Branch can lead
to dismissal, blacklisting, or the continual failure to get promotion.
Once sacked militant workers can find themselves blacklisted throughout the industry in which they are skilled. For many years such a 'black-
list' has existed in car-making, building, engineering and aircraft-manu-
facturing. At other times it may be the firm which approaches the
Branch for information on a prospective employee, which is usually
readily given. This practice is quite normal for foreign firms based in
this country.[26]

Increasing suspicion that the Special Branch was also organizing
widespread telephone-tapping of strike organizers was confirmed
during the Grunwick strike in 1977, when the offices of the strike
committee were tapped.[27] Leading members of the Fire Brigades
Union had their phones monitored during their 1977–8 strike, and
a key shop steward at the Ford Motor Company had his phone
tapped at a crucial stage in pay negotiations in 1978 (Merlyn Rees,
Home Secretary at the time, took the unprecedented step of
publicly denying he had authorized these taps, suggesting they
were undertaken without proper legal authority).[28]

In the 1984–5 miners' strike, there was evidence of 'a blanket
tapping operation involving strike centres and personal phones of
many union activists'.[29] The massive increase in the scope of
Special Branch and police intelligence-gathering illustrates the
way in which the police have been able to extend their powers on
purely operational grounds and according to priorities which *they*
determine.

New techniques of surveillance and new technology have been
introduced by the police without prior debate or parliamentary
approval, with the police and the security services operating
'almost entirely outside the law. This is not to say they *break* the
law: quite simply, there are hardly any laws for them to break.
The methods of surveillance are effectively uncontrolled by the
law. The terms within which the political police operate are a

matter of executive, not parliamentary or judicial, decision-making.'[30]

MI5 has also been deeply involved in surveillance of trade unionists. In July 1984 one of its former senior officers, Peter Wright, claimed that in recent years, instead of concentrating on foreign subversion, MI5 had 'taken the somewhat sinister decision to divert resources away to working against domestic groups – trade unions and so on'.[31]

In February 1985 a former MI5 intelligence officer, Cathy Massiter, revealed that the security services had tapped the phones of miners' leaders Arthur Scargill and Mick McGahey. She described how other trade unionists had been placed under surveillance, despite the fact that they had done nothing illegal, and how the home of Ken Gill, General Secretary of TASS, had been broken into and bugged in order to monitor discussions of a merger with the engineering union.[32]

· DISCRETION ·

Time and again during strikes, the immense operational discretion accorded to police officers plays an important role. It can be applied to cool tempers and permit orderly dispute procedures to occur. Alternatively, it can create circumstances in which quite ordinary strikes escalate into outright political confrontations between police and pickets.

The courts have consistently supported the police in such circumstances. As one legal authority confirmed, 'the court will always uphold the instructions issued by a policeman, however slight the evidence is, that a breach of the peace might occur', while another stated: 'a court will not be over anxious to discuss the assessment of a policeman on the spot'.[33]

As a leading law lord, Lord Scarman, acknowledged in 1981,

the exercise of discretion lies at the heart of the policing function. It is undeniable that there is only one law for all and it is right that this should be so. But it is equally well recognized that successful policing depends on the exercise of discretion in how the law is enforced. The good reputation of the police as a force depends upon the skill and judgment which policemen display in the particular circumstances of the cases and incidents which they are required to handle. Discretion is the art of suiting action to particular circumstances. It is the policeman's daily task.[34]

But Lord Scarman failed to point out that such discretion can be applied in a politically biased way and that it is not amenable to legal or parliamentary challenge. This was evident in the role of the police in the industrial emergency created by the 1978-9 'Winter of Discontent'. When ambulancemen went on strike in early 1979 the police maintained emergency services in areas where no cover was being provided. But although this was the first occasion police had actually performed strikers' work rather than simply maintained order, it was done entirely at the discretion of the relevant Chief Officer of Police.

Section 15 of the Police Act 1964 enables chief officers to provide what are termed 'special police services' at their own discretion. However, as one legal expert pointed out, 'It is unclear whether these "services" are limited to activities of a kind within the range of police duties.'[35] As she also argued, in performing the work of strikers police cannot possibly be neutral. On the contrary, in the 1979 dispute their role was politically significant. Yet it was undertaken on a purely administrative and expedient basis, giving the police considerable political autonomy in a highly sensitive matter.

Although police forces are nominally answerable to police authorities outside London and to the Home Secretary in the capital, the 1964 Police Act makes it clear that the 'direction and control' of a force is the sole responsibility of its chief officer. Thus, chief officers have *statutorily based* powers of discretion which are very wide indeed. Furthermore, the responsibility of chief officers for law enforcement has been repeatedly defined by the courts as one of accountability only to the law – as *they* interpret it – and not to their police authority or the Home Secretary. In the face of this there are considerable limitations on the extent to which police authorities are able to influence local policing policy. This was vividly shown in the 1984-5 miners' strike, where a number of authorities found themselves in fundamental disagreement with police handling of picketing and restrictions on the movement of individuals across their areas.

Indeed, police chiefs have more discretion than possibly any other individuals in the system of law enforcement and administration. Even though judges and magistrates, for example, have considerable discretionary powers, they at least are constrained by formal rules and procedures. The police are much less so, since their work is in practice heavily dependent on the way they choose to respond to particular circumstances, which in turn reflects their own personal feelings and social and political attitudes.

·POLICE ATTITUDES·

The most comprehensive survey yet done of police attitudes, Robert Reiner's *The Blue-Coated Worker*, showed that the rank-and-file police officer was 'inclined to adopt a hostile stance towards trade unionism outside the force, and was prepared enthusiastically to support government attempts to curb union power with their help'.[36] This hostility is not merely greater than that of the population at large, but is also expressed more vehemently. Reiner quotes a number of individual policemen who express views on trade unionism which, he says, are typical: [37]

'When they were instigated they did a fine job, Tolpuddle Martyrs and all that jazz, to secure better conditions for people who had no say. But now the wheel's turned full circle. One of the fundamental reasons of the country going to pot is that workers don't work hard enough. All they're interested in is arguing about things which don't concern them, like making policy. As far as I'm concerned you can take all the unionists away, line them up against a wall and shoot the lot.'

'A lot of the trouble with strikes is primarily to do with the leaders, and obviously to my mind backed morally, physically and financially by communism.'

'People get their knickers in such a twist about where peaceful picketing ends and rioting begins. If I was an officer in charge down there I'd knock the lot off as soon as a person is physically prevented from going about his lawful business.'

Reiner's survey was conducted in the year after the 1972 miners' strike, and often such views were accompanied by comments about strikes becoming 'too political' and being overly influenced by 'rent-a-pickets' and 'industrial agitators'. He also found that right-wing attitudes predominate among police officers.

When this is viewed against the tendency since the 1970s of police leaders to become identified with the Conservative Party, then it is possible to see why the police have increasingly acted towards strikers in a politically hostile fashion. Rank-and-file officers are represented by the Police Federation, whose leaders have been willing to speak on Tory platforms and express public admiration for Tory leaders; in the 1979 general election the Federation gave thinly disguised support to the Conservatives.[38] After the October 1984 Labour Party Conference had given full support to the miners' strike and had censured police handling of it, a leading officer of the Federation even announced that the police might not be able to work under a future Labour government.

· POLICE CHIEFS ·

During the last two decades the Association of Chief Police Officers has adopted a steadily higher political profile, on occasion resorting to public campaigning techniques more associated with non-governmental pressure groups. For example, the pro-union reforms of the 1974–9 Labour government enraged the ACPO. When proposals were before Parliament to regularize picketing by giving pickets the legal right to stop vehicles in order to communicate with their occupants, the ACPO chose a dramatic and publicity-worthy method to 'consult' its membership, sending telex messages to each Chief Constable. Their predictable response – outright opposition – attracted the desired publicity. The proposals vanished and the determination of the police to exercise maximum freedom of action was rewarded.

Since then the ACPO has taken every opportunity – such as the submission of evidence to official inquiries, the meeting of its annual conference, the sitting of parliamentary committees – to publicize its views. Invariably these have been antagonistic to policies supported by the trade unions and the Labour Party (in office or not).

Although the ACPO has no direct control over government policy, it has become increasingly influential. This is particularly significant because, unlike the Police Federation and the Superintendents' Association, it is not a statutory body and in recent years has become something of 'a law unto itself'.[39]

In July 1985 it emerged that, after the inner-city riots in 1980 and 1981, the ACPO had drawn up a confidential manual entitled 'Public Order Tactical Operations'. It advised how pickets could be broken up by charging at crowds with truncheons, 'striking in a controlled manner' and 'incapacitating' ringleaders. Mounted officers should also use 'fear created by the impetus of horses'. And there should be a 'tactical use of noise' such as 'chanting and rhythmic sounds' and 'battle cries'. The manual was used in the 1984–5 miners' strike to promote the kind of paramilitary police tactics evident, for example, at a major picket at Orgreave in South Yorkshire.

Until its existence was revealed during a trial of miners prosecuted for riot at Orgreave, it was considered so secret that no officer below the rank of Assistant Chief Constable was allowed to see it. No police authority was consulted upon it and Parliament was not informed of its existence. Perhaps this was because the manual took discretion so far as to contain instructions which were actually illegal: as one barrister who acted for the Orgreave defendants told the *Observer*: 'They are quite clearly an incitement to police officers to commit criminal offences.'

Chief Constables themselves have also been much more willing to 'go public' and campaign for their own views in a way that can only be described as 'political' and, on the whole, right of centre.[40] Sir Robert Mark, Metropolitan Police Commissioner from 1972 to 1977, was perhaps the first police chief to do this, developing a taste for expressing his views publicly.

After he had retired, his pronouncements became even more pungent. In the middle of the 1979 election, for example, Mark received front-page treatment for his criticism of the then Labour government's treatment of the unions: 'Not only do the unions enjoy a high degree of immunity from the law; in any critical situation in which the law does not support them the government of the day – their partner or their puppet according to your view – declares its intention to change the law in their favour. This is not unlike the way in which the National Socialist German Workers Party achieved unrestricted control of the German state between 1930 and 1938.'[41]

At about the same time, Mark wrote: 'The police are . . . very much on their own in attempting to preserve order in an increasingly turbulent society in which Socialist philosophy has changed from raising the standards of the poor and deprived to reducing the standards of the wealthy, the skilled and the deserving to the lowest common denominator.'[42] Quite apart from being a serious distortion of the purpose and practice of modern British socialism and trade unionism, these statements are notable for the fact that they also represented the views of most of his former police chief colleagues.

·NATIONAL REPORTING CENTRE AND THE MINERS' STRIKE·

Although the behaviour of the police in the 1984–5 miners' strike shocked many people – not least those living in mining communities – it was actually more an extension of a long-term trend in policing than something basically unique or unprecedented.

As part of the Thatcher government's preparation for a miners' strike, serious consideration had been given to the role of the police, and on 9 February 1984 – a month before the strike started – the Home Secretary met with all Chief Constables and the Attorney-General at the Home Office. They considered the effectiveness of the police operation during picketing in the Stockport Messenger dispute which had just finished; but it seems that they also discussed law enforcement in a possible miners' strike.[43]

Right at the start of the strike – indeed, within three and a quarter hours of miners organizing mass pickets of their working colleagues in the Nottinghamshire coalfields – the police claimed to have mobilized 1,000 officers from different forces. Within the next couple of days more than 8,000 officers from all but two of the forty-three forces in England and Wales had been deployed to control the strike.[44]

Certainly, the police National Reporting Centre (NRC) was very quick off the mark with its response to miners' pickets. By 14 March, the President of the Association of Chief Police Officers, Humberside's Chief Constable David Hall, had travelled to London and set up shop on the thirteenth floor of Scotland Yard 'to mastermind the police operation against the pickets', as the *Sunday Times* put it. Staffed twenty-four hours a day throughout the dispute, the NRC operated a computer-based communications link to all forty-three police forces and was able to call on 120,000 officers, including a pool of 13,500 specially trained members of Police Support Units around the country.

The NRC was originally set up in 1972 'to help in the national coordination of aid between chief officers of police in England and Wales under section 14 of the Police Act 1964'. In 1980–81 it was used in a purely informational role during four months of industrial action by the Prison Officers' Association. It was then used to coordinate police activity on just two occasions: for six weeks in 1981 during the summer riots in British cities, and for five days during the Pope's visit in 1982.

But the third time it was used to coordinate policing – in the miners' strike – it took on the new role of a command centre. The political importance of this was revealed as the strike progressed and it became increasingly evident that the NRC had no clear lines of accountability to any democratically constituted authority. It was not answerable to any of the police authorities whose forces it commanded, nor was it controlled by the Home Secretary. The latter sought, publicly at least, to distance himself from influence over its operational role, while David Hall continually insisted that no directions were given to him by the government: 'I want to be very very forceful on the fact that there is no discussion between the police service and the civil servants acting on behalf of the politicians, or the politicians themselves, as to the way we should react,' he maintained at the time.[45]

A less sanguine view was taken by the Chairwoman of the Merseyside Police Authority, Lady Margaret Simey. She explained how the NRC overrode local police responsibilities during the miners' dispute and complained that the Association of Chief Police Officers had 'become an executive arm of the state, without any authorization and without any public control'.[46]

Claims about the NRC's 'independence' from central government sat uneasily with the report of the Home Secretary's Chief Inspector of Constabulary, who noted that it was 'operated by a team under the direction of the President of the ACPO, my representative and one of your officials'.[47] In reality the Home Secretary was much more involved in the day-to-day management of the miners' strike than was ever publicly admitted.[48] As the *Economist* reported early on in the strike:

Officially the police have been keeping the peace on their own initiative. Not in reality. But all government preparations for dealing with the miners' strike have been by word of mouth and informal. The Cabinet Office has taken care to ensure that there are no traceable links with the Coal Board or the police. Even the Prime Minister has been persuaded to restrain her normal eloquence.[49]

· CRIMINALIZING THE MINERS ·

As an independent state agency, the NRC may not have been at the beck and call of the Home Secretary. But it nevertheless acted entirely in line with the government's strategy to break the strike. Indeed, the role of the police became the anchor-point of this strategy, for the government chose not to rely on the 1980 and 1982 Employment Acts. These made virtually all *effective* picketing illegal and also made unlawful other activities which characterized the miners' dispute, such as sympathy action. During the

Stockport Messenger Group dispute at the end of 1983, an injunction taken out by the Group's Managing Director, Eddie Shah,
led to the union involved, the NGA, being fined and having its
assets sequestered for organizing 'secondary picketing'. But
although civil action under the new legislation, backed up by aggressive policing of pickets outside the company's premises, was successful in the NGA dispute, a different approach was felt necessary to
respond to a strike that was not concentrated at a single location.

There was also a recognition that to invoke provisions of the
1980 and 1982 Acts against the National Union of Mineworkers
might immediately escalate matters and push the struggle on to
territory less favourable to the government. Activation of the new
laws would probably have resulted in the imprisonment of miners'
leaders or immediate sequestration of union assets. This could
have drawn the rest of the trade union movement into a fight
around anti-union laws – a fight which would probably have
commanded much broader support for the miners from the rest
of the labour movement than in fact materialized. Confident of
ultimate victory, the last thing the government wanted was a re-
run of the 1972 'Pentonville Five' fiasco. An early legal action
initiated by the National Coal Board was allowed to lie on the
table and instead the government's major weapon became the
power of the police.

Effectively, this amounted to a strategy of breaking the strike
by 'criminalizing' the miners, as one study demonstrated: '. . . the
strategy had three objectives: firstly to criminalize the strikers
both within their own organizations and in the eyes of broader
society; secondly to physically thin out the numbers of men available for picketing; and thirdly to gather masses of intelligence on
activists for use in a post-strike situation'.[50]

The key role of police *discretion* was never more evident than at
the outset of the strike. Charged with what amounted to a straight-
forward political task of defeating the miners' union, the police
acted as a political agency, using their discretionary powers almost
as they saw fit. This role led the former Devon and Cornwall
Chief Constable, John Alderson, to complain that the police had
been 'pulled into backing a political choice by the government'.[51]

The crucial early period of the strike set the pattern. If the early miners' pickets of their colleagues in Nottinghamshire had been successful, then the strike could have achieved a national solidity, the absence of which was later to undermine its legitimacy and weaken its strength. The police interpreted their duty as being to protect the ability of working miners to cross picket lines. They explained this in terms of 'upholding the law' and 'defending individual rights'. But in reality they had made a political choice from the beginning: to defend the *working* rather than the *striking* miners – a choice which happened to coincide with government's wishes. It was later to mean utilizing massive police resources to enable even a single miner to go through the ranks of thousands of his colleagues, rather than to allow the collective will of the majority to prevail. Throughout the dispute the police worked closely with the National Coal Board and with ministers, varying their tactics accordingly.[52]

Normal court procedures – being more cumbersome and more constrained by due legal process – were not sufficiently flexible tools to stem the strike's early momentum: such flexibility was provided by the police. A study in Yorkshire and Kent showed how the police acted punitively *prior to trial* by magistrates:

1. Men who were stopped on the way to picket were told to present their driving documents to their local police station within five days. For men from Kent who were out of their area for periods of up to three weeks this presented problems.

2. Car drivers simply had their keys taken from them, effectively impounding the car.

3. Conditions of bail were demanded by magistrates on the instructions of the police. These were such that men were unable to travel to counties outside their own while awaiting trial.

4. In one case in South Yorkshire and one in Kent, both involving large numbers of defendants, the prosecution withdrew its case knowing that the men had been wrongly charged, in exchange for the defence agreeing that the men be bound over (in Kent for a sum of £100 a year). This tactic obviates the need for a trial and though the men had not infringed the law they were being contained and punished.

5. The most serious strategy . . . is that of 'remand in custody' . . . [some] men had not been found guilty of any offence, but simply broken conditions of bail.

. . . police . . . acted out their powers without recourse to the courts, statute or precedent, simply stopping people, searching their cars, breaking windscreens, and turning drivers back to where they had come from.[53]

A revealing experience was that of Ernie Way, a South Wales miners' lodge official:

On the first day of the strike Ernie Way received instructions to send fifty pickets to the Midlands. When he hired a bus, the company called back within a few minutes and said the police had restricted it. He arranged cars. The police called almost immediately and said they would be confiscated on the M4 [motorway]. So he rang British Rail and booked fifty seats. Within half an hour the police were screening the passengers at Newport station. Only a call to Neil Kinnock's agent cleared the police from the station – on the grounds that they were restricting public transport. 'Within ten days of the strike,' he said, 'we quickly realized that the agents of the government had abandoned their impartiality.'[54]

·PICKETING·

When the mass picketing got under way, the role of police discretion was also made more important than usual by the failure of the 1980 Employment Act to provide any clear legal foundation for police regulation of pickets. Instead, like the 1982 Act, it depended on *civil* action through the courts to enforce its provisions. There are picketing guidelines in the Code associated with the 1980 Act but no criminal law as such. This encouraged a blurring of the distinction between 'legal' and 'illegal' activity, so that the law became effectively what police on the spot declared it should be.

This was evident in June 1984 at the Orgreave coking plant outside Sheffield, where some of the worst violence of the strike took place. A policeman stopped a miner and a local union official as they were leaving the mass picket, and when the miner demanded to know what law gave the officer the right to stop him going home, the officer pointed at his blue uniform and said: 'This law'; while not being so specific, his boss, South Yorkshire's Chief Constable Peter Wright, admitted that some police tactics were 'a matter of practice, not law'.[55]

As one study reported:

On the picket lines the police define space as legal or illegal; sometimes pickets are allowed to stand in groups on one side of the road and at other times they are tightly herded together on the opposite side; sometimes shouting 'scab' is an arrestable offence, sometimes it is not. The general picture is of total unpredictability as to what will be allowed and what not.[56]

The extent to which such discretion was blessed, not just by the government but by the whole law enforcement system, is indicated in the refusal of the Director of Public Prosecutions to charge an officer who had gone berserk and repeatedly truncheoned a miner on the ground at Orgreave in front of television cameras. Documented evidence of police action against pickets suggests that it was an integral part of the government's strategy to defeat the strike. As Sheffield Policewatch reported:

We have observed that in the majority of cases where violence breaks out, this is due to police tactics and when there is what we describe as 'over-policing'. We have repeatedly noted that when the police arrive at a peaceful picket, even a large one, in overwhelming numbers and with dogs, horses, riot equipment and ambulances visibly in reserve, then the atmosphere changes. It is as though the police are preparing for and are expecting a violent confrontation. Time and again, we have seen this equipment violently deployed with little or no justification for its use. In our view it is inevitable that some pickets will retaliate when arrested arbitrarily and for no reason attacked by truncheons, chased by horses and intimidated by police dogs.[57]

There was violence by pickets too, and those who came to picket lines with various implements were clearly planning to attack the police. But they were in a tiny minority, and other independent studies, including one by the National Council for Civil Liberties, confirmed the view that most of the picket-line violence was provoked by police tactics.[58]

In an important case arising from the bitter clashes at Orgreave eight striking miners were acquitted at Sheffield Crown Court of unlawful assembly, after their defence had claimed that the men were arrested 'as a result of a police order to take prisoners' rather than because of any unlawful behaviour on their part.[59]

Then during a series of dramatic trials in July 1985, evidence emerged of what defence lawyers termed a 'frame-up' of miners picketing outside Orgreave. In all, 96 miners were charged with riot and unlawful assembly – extremely serious offences requiring full Crown Court jury trials – but all were acquitted. In one case, 13 pickets were cleared after an eight-week trial costing at least £250,000. In another, involving 14 pickets, the prosecution actually dropped their case after forty-eight days; this case cost over £500,000. Then the police decided to drop the charges against a further 79 miners. Defence solicitors maintained that this decision was taken to prevent further exposure in court of the illegal police tactics outlined in the secret ACPO manual 'Public Order Tactical Operations'. One solicitor, Gareth Peirce, analysed the transcripts of the court proceedings and found:

Orgreave on 18 June 1984 revealed that in this country we now have a standing army available to be deployed against gatherings of civilians whose congregation is disliked by senior police officers ... it is trained in tactics ... which include the deliberate maiming and injuring of persons to disperse them, in complete violation of the law.

If the pickets had succeeded in closing Orgreave, then the dispute might have taken a different course, with the strike strengthened. From the evidence given in court it was apparent that police chiefs were determined to avoid this. They had a carefully prepared plan to 'ambush' the pickets by charging into groups of miners, apprehending individuals and later prosecuting them with riot on the basis of evidence which, when tested in court, was found to be either contradictory or fabricated.

The results of police discretion were also evident when a miner's wife was arrested and charged with a breach of the peace for throwing an egg at a lorry being driven through a picket line in Port Talbot, South Wales, whereas no action was taken against a farmer's wife who had thrown an egg at Mrs Thatcher during her visit a month before to nearby Porthcawl.[60]

However, it is important to acknowledge that the policing of pickets varied considerably. For example, the West Yorkshire police force gained a reputation for relatively liberal behaviour and maintained some sort of working relationship with pickets; in neighbouring South Yorkshire the situation was radically different, with harsh police methods creating an atmosphere of virtual warfare between officers and strikers; while the Metropolitan Police were generally regarded as the most hostile. Such inconsistency underlined the wide scope of police discretion. It also confirmed that political judgments could determine how that discretion should be exercised.

· THE TOTAL OPERATION ·

Discretionary policing was not just directed at pickets but at whole communities of striking miners. The total operation virtually criminalized the daily life of strikers and their families in a manner which invited parallels with army and police tactics adopted in republican communities in Northern Ireland. Movement of individuals about counties with pits was heavily restricted, including interception of pedestrians even while going shopping.

There were regular roadblocks on an unprecedented scale. In Nottinghamshire alone, 164,508 pickets were stopped when entering the county in the first twenty-seven weeks of the strike. It was estimated that this prevented over half the pickets from reaching their destination.[61] These roadblocks represented a major erosion of civil liberties, the police extending their powers in an arbitrary fashion, including: forcing miners or their sympathizers to turn back; seriously delaying them; taking their keys; attacking them (including breaking car windows); and arresting them for such 'offences' as obstruction.[62] Protestations about infringements of individual freedoms were treated with derision as the police simply enforced their will, legal niceties being given short shrift.

In one incident, a group of miners parked their cars on a grass verge next to a slip road at the Tuxford junction on the main A1 trunk road in Nottinghamshire. As they left their cars to walk to Bevercotes colliery about a mile away, they came immediately upon a group of policemen who insisted that they should go no further. The miners tried to argue that the police had no right to stop them in that way, but the officers drew their truncheons and attacked. 'Some of them went berserk. They arrested and beat people up indiscriminately,' reported observers who complained of a 'police riot'.[63]

The total police operation extended well beyond its nominal target: the picket line. At the outset it had been decided that controlling pickets was the main job of the police. But as the strike progressed, the police interpreted this task in a much broader fashion, so that controlling pickets was not something limited to pit entrances. Since mining communities are often sited close by pits, it was inevitable that police criminalization of strike activists would spread to their home areas. Just as the police excused their tactics at roadblocks on the grounds that they were preventing potential 'breaches of the peace' on picket lines, so they excused harassing mining neighbourhoods in terms of pre-emptive curbs on potential pickets. Expediency assisted by un-constrained discretion led the police to behave in a way which perhaps only certain inner-city black communities had experienced in mainland Britain since the war. As one study showed, many of the arrests that followed resembled 'kidnap more than the due process of law'.[64]

One striker said on BBC TV: 'I think the police are under orders to harass us back to work. I think it is political.'[65] On the same programme an apprentice miner who was not on strike (having been given special dispensation to complete his studies) explained how he was on his way to buy some shoes at his local shops when he was stopped by police, questioned and then detained for nine hours before being released without charge. As a result he missed an important examination he should have taken the same day.

· MINERS' COMMUNITIES UNDER SIEGE ·

Many similar incidents of arbitrary arrests of individuals occurred throughout the coalfields. Even more serious, on numerous occasions whole communities came under siege from the police. In the South Yorkshire village of Armthorpe, local people's confidence in the police was shattered in August 1984. Tension had built up during a night of picketing – with miners complaining of Manchester police taunting them by waving £10 notes – and the police decided 'to "retake" not just the pit entrance but the entire village'.[66] Pickets were chased away, with officers in riot gear charging through streets and breaking into homes in search of fleeing miners, often beating them up if they were caught.

Even at times when there was no picketing, being subjected to regular police intimidation became almost a way of life for many pickets. For instance, in May 1984 there was the 'siege of Blidworth' (as it became known to villagers). Some eighty Yorkshire miners were staying at the homes of striking miners in this Nottinghamshire village. It was a particularly tense time for the government, with printers on the *Sun* newspaper refusing to print a picture depicting the miners' leader Arthur Scargill as a Nazi and with the strike poised to escalate into a wider political confrontation. During the night, police started searching tents and caravans where the miners were sleeping, attacking them and interrogating residents who had put them up. The whole operation lasted seventeen hours, with terrified residents being prevented from leaving their homes.[67]

Around the same time in the nearby village of Rainforth, a group of Yorkshire miners had just left a pub after closing time when they were set upon by police who had previously been spotted keeping watch on them. The police simply beat them up, chasing them as they tried to run away. There was no picket imminent and accounts of the incident state that the miners had been behaving in a perfectly orderly manner.[68]

After two days of particularly violent police behaviour in October in the Yorkshire village of Grimethorpe, South Yorkshire's Deputy Chief Constable made a public apology when he met angry residents. But such official apologies were rare. A *Daily Mirror* reporter who investigated incidents like this – an equally rare event for a Fleet Street journalist – concluded: 'This is an industrial war started by a government which is using the police as weapons.'[69]

Through such invasions of mining villages, the police not only aimed at potential or actual pickets; they also harassed strikers' families, threatening them and expressing extreme hostility to the strike. The fact that they were able to do this almost with impunity underlined the political role they were playing in the strike.

So did the manner in which support work for the strike was officially harassed and disrupted. All over the country police tried to prevent street collections for the miners' hardship funds, moving on collectors with threats to arrest for obstruction and in fact making arrests in many cases. At one stage people collecting food for miners' families were arrested under the 1824 Vagrancy Act. When it was discovered it was not an offence under this Act to collect food, arrests were made under the 1916 Police, Factories and Miscellaneous Provisions Act – until the dubious legal basis for *that* manoeuvre was shown when Clerkenwell magistrates' court dismissed a case in November 1984 against James Wood, a barrister charged with collecting under the Act. Six months later, however, the High Court overturned this decision and directed the magistrates to convict Mr Wood; the judges relied on a different interpretation of another law, the Street Collection (Metropolitan Police District) Regulations 1979. Meanwhile, strike supporters visiting mining areas were also harassed, as when a print worker trying to deliver food parcels to striking Nottinghamshire miners was stopped in his car by police, beaten up and told not to continue his journey.[70] It seems reasonable to ask whether such harsh police behaviour was in response to the success of the support groups whose work was so crucial to sustaining the strike – one estimate suggested that £60 million was collected.[71]

·USE OF THE COURTS·

Police powers were extended in other ways. One study listed a number of practices, most of which were clearly illegal. Miners were handcuffed indiscriminately; proper procedures for charging were abandoned; Judges' Rules covering access rights of suspects to relatives and solicitors were ignored; special court sittings were sometimes heard in private, with public access denied; rules governing identification of suspects were contravened; and *agents provocateurs* were used during picketing.[72] The photographing of strikers, whether or not they were charged, became widespread – and South Yorkshire's Chief Constable actually admitted that he could not think of any law permitting this.[73] Manipulation of prosecution procedures occurred frequently, with police threatening miners with additional charges unless they admitted guilt; or offering to drop all charges if they would agree to be 'bound over to keep the peace'; or introducing extra charges without notice at the start of trial proceedings.[74]

Bail procedures were also manipulated at the instigation of the police to undermine the strength of the strike. The National Association of Probation Officers complained at one stage that police had 'acted not to uphold the law but to render trade union activity ineffective'.[75] Magistrates agreed to police demands for bail conditions which were so stringent in their restrictions on pickets as to prevent those in houses owned by the Coal Board from continuing to live there with their families; some even missed Christmas at home because of this. One man was banished from West Yorkshire to live with relatives in Southport, 110 miles away. Others were subject to curfew-type restrictions preventing them from leaving their homes between the hours of 8 p.m. and 8 a.m. Many could not visit the pits where they worked. A proportion had to report to police stations three times a day. These unprecedented bail conditions, it should be remembered, were imposed on individuals who had not been convicted of an offence. They were simply police devices to remove more and more miners from participation in strike activity.

·POLITICS AND ACCOUNTABILITY·

It became increasingly apparent as the strike continued that such practices were being given a nod and a wink by the government. Even if each specific act by the police was not openly approved – certain behaviour was undoubtedly embarrassing to the authorities – the general thrust of policing was endorsed under the rubric of 'full support for the police'. Effectively this official blessing gave officers on the ground *carte blanche* to do as they pleased.

Indeed there was evidence that the government deliberately encouraged greater police autonomy and discretion than usual precisely to short-circuit normal processes of local accountability to police authorities, some of which were very critical of the behaviour of the forces over which they had supposed control. Seven months into the strike, the Home Secretary announced a definite limit on the amount of money any local police authority would have to find from local rates: 'Beyond that, any extra cost incurred in policing this dispute, for however long, will be met by the exchequer in full. Central government has never provided help on this scale before. But it is right we should do so now.'[76] The Home Secretary also stated that he was altering the law both to limit the control police authorities had over operational expenditure and to check their ability to suspend Chief Constables.

This was yet another twist in the spiral of centralized policing, because it reinforced the independence of Chief Constables from local accountability: it left less scope for police authorities to influence policing policy through their power to control the budget of the local force. The President of the Police Superintendents' Association said as much when, criticizing Labour-controlled local police authorities for their attitude to policing the miners' dispute, he said: 'A national police force strangely seems a little closer, brought about by the basic lack of support by certain police authorities who attempt to deny us the necessary resources to carry out our true function of maintaining the peace.'[77]

The strike made explicit a reality explained by the Chairwoman of the Merseyside Police Authority, Lady Margaret Simey: 'everything a policeman does has a political dimension and every financial decision we make has an operational one'.[78] As she also argued: 'The miners' dispute has highlighted the fact that Chief Constables can do what they like . . . They are out of democratic control. It is frightening.'[79]

The total number arrested in England, Scotland and Wales during the strike (excluding arrests of supporters on street collections) was 11,312, and 14 million hours were worked by police reinforcements outside Scotland.[80] The absolute priority the government gave to defeating the strike was also indicated by the cost of the police operation – put at over £225 million. And the movement of up to 7,000 officers from their local beats each week to the coalfields may have been at least partly responsible for an estimated 8 per cent increase in reported serious crime during 1984 against a decrease of 1 per cent in 1983.[81]

More than any other feature, it was the way in which the strike was policed that shaped the way it unfolded: the picket-line confrontations moulded public opinion by obscuring the real issues motivating the miners; and police power kept open working pits and crippled attempts at solidarity action. By the end of the strike, an embryonic national police force containing a paramilitary capability was in place for future industrial or political crises.

THE LAW AND UNIONS

'As individual members of the Bar who have become increasingly appalled at the various ways in which legal processes have been manipulated in favour of the National Coal Board and the government ... We declare this to be a misuse of the law for political ends.' So said four leading barristers when they took the unusual step of issuing a public statement during the 1984-5 miners' strike, criticizing the role of judges and magistrates in particular.[1] In another unusual incident, a Labour MP, Martin Flannery, was suspended from the Commons in July 1984 for refusing to withdraw a protest about 'tame Tory judges'.*

But the fact that the coal dispute produced a flood of such criticisms does not mean that there are no precedents for political bias in the application of the law towards strikers. The miners merely highlighted sharply a long tradition of such bias.

This is partly because the very foundations of British law favour the rights of the *individual*, rather than the rights of the *collective*. As one legal analysis explains:

In crude terms, the idea of individual freedom is a middle-class concept which is often in conflict with the fact of working-class advancement through solidarity. The middle class advance as individuals through educational advantage, promotion prospects and so on; the main instrument of working-class advancement is through collective action.[3]

* When a Labour MP referred to a senior law lord, Lord Diplock, as a 'Tory judge' in December 1980, the Speaker of the House of Commons ruled that 'it is offensive to refer to a judge of the High Court by anything other than as a judge of the High Court'. He added, 'it is wrong for any of us to attribute to any judge a bias'.[2]

Under the law, the *individual right* to cross a picket line overrides the *collective right* to take industrial action. The courts tend to view someone exercising such an individual right as an innocent citizen deserving of the law's protection, rather than as a strike-breaker undermining the collective right to solidarity of his or her fellow workers. Connected with this, the law assumes that 'the owners of capital should be entitled to more rights than the owners of labour. Property rights are regarded as sacrosanct except when the property concerned is someone's livelihood.'[4]

The history of trade unionism supports this view that the law has favoured the dominant class. 'Trade unions', stated a consultative document produced by the Conservative government in 1981, 'came into existence in the nineteenth century despite the law and not under its protection.'[5] This is an understatement: not only did working people and their unions lack the protection of the law, the courts positively obstructed the development of unions and their ability to strike.

From its beginnings, 'many judges regarded trade unionism as a criminal objective',[6] and they were able to pursue this belief by acting within a judicial tradition that has consistently encouraged them to use their common-law powers effectively to make law. Britain has a unique legal system under which judges are not merely charged with applying statute law passed by Parliament, but are required to find principles of common law where they cannot obviously apply existing statutes. Such judge-made law, in the form of rulings, and especially decisions of the Court of Appeal and the House of Lords, is as binding as legislation passed by Parliament and can lead judges to play an overtly political role.[7] This is clearly shown in the history of strikes in Britain.

Back in 1351 the Statute of Labourers had begun a tradition under which workers could not legally combine together to advance their interests and, thereafter, the judiciary frequently acted as the major instrument for state suppression or control of emerging trade unionism. Even when workers indulged in stoppages so parochial as to be otherwise incapable of being interpreted as politically motivated, judges were quick to invent new curbs that turned almost any strike into an act of political defiance or subversion.

·CONSPIRACY·

One of their prime instruments was the common-law-based offence of conspiracy. Because it makes into a criminal act committing the *agreement* to commit the offence rather than committing the *offence itself*, conspiracy is ideally suited to trapping workers who have agreed to undertake *collective* action. By its very nature a strike follows a collective agreement to take collective action and therefore automatically comes under the umbrella of a potential conspiracy.

When industrial capitalism first began to emerge in the seventeenth century, conspiracy was used to prevent workers organizing against employers. By the eighteenth century, the law on conspiracy

enabled judges to punish by criminal process such conduct as seemed to them socially undesirable, even though the actual deeds committed constituted of themselves no crime ... where the actual deeds were of doubtful criminality, it saved judges from the often embarrassing necessity of having to spell out the crime.[8]

For instance, judges in the 1721 case of the Cambridge Tailors ruled that something they called a 'conspiracy to raise wages' was a criminal offence. Even after the 1824 repeal of the Combination Acts (which had made unions illegal), conspiracy was interpreted by judges in scores of cases to make virtually any strike or picket a criminal offence.[9]

In 1851, nine tinplate workers were prosecuted after they had called a strike in protest against the dismissal of one of their colleagues – a senior member of their national union. All were convicted of conspiracy to molest and obstruct their employer, it being judged that they had interfered with his 'lawful freedom of action'. In the *Druitt* case of 1867 a group of tailors was convicted of conspiracy for picketing their masters' shops. Even though the judge acknowledged that their action was peaceful, he declared it amounted to conspiracy to molest because it included 'abusive language or gestures' and was 'calculated to have a deterring effect on the minds of ordinary persons, by exposing them to have their motions watched and to encounter black looks'. In 1871 a group of women was even convicted of conspiracy for saying 'Bah' to blacklegs.

A year later, a group of London gas workers was convicted of conspiracy to *threaten* to strike in protest against the sacking of a colleague for his union activity. They were sentenced to twelve months' hard labour because of a judgment arguing that they had been guilty of 'unjustifiable annoyance and interference with the masters in the conduct of their business . . . such annoyance and interference as would be likely to have a deterring effect upon masters of ordinary nerve'.

These cases illustrate the way in which judges were able virtually to make up the law on conspiracy as they went along in order to suppress strikes which they saw as a political threat to dominant interests. Eventually pressure for reform forced Disraeli's government to introduce the 1875 Conspiracy and Protection of Property Act. It gave strikers immunity from the simple crime of conspiracy if they were engaged in a trade dispute. Nevertheless judicial ingenuity still found ways of circumventing this.

The scope for deeming strikes to be *criminal* conspiracies was narrowed by the 1875 Act, but judges supported a series of *civil* cases for conspiracy brought by employers and other interested parties. In a series of cases, peaceful pickets – who had been granted the rights of 'peaceful persuasion' under the Act – found themselves caught by new, judge-made, conspiracy offences. They were deemed guilty of conspiracy to create a 'public nuisance', 'watch and besett premises', or 'intimidate'.[10]

In one case in 1896, involving the Amalgamated Trade Society of Fancy Leather Workers, an injunction was granted against *peaceful* pickets, the judges declaring that the right of 'peaceful persuasion' given to pickets under the 1875 Act really specified only the 'communication of information': a fine distinction but one sufficient to achieve the desired objective of restricting such industrial action. Furthermore, strikers still remained targets for ill-defined crimes like conspiracy to molest or to induce others to break a contract, if they strayed beyond the strict confines of a strike against their employer; even within these confines there was the possibility of conspiracy still being applied to certain offences.[11]

Thus, whatever extra protection they might have won from Parliament, strikers still faced curbs as the courts found new interpretations of the law to apply to them. The essentially political nature of judicial behaviour in relation to trade unionists is illustrated by contrasting it with the *Mogul* case of 1889. This involved a powerful group of tea traders who used dubious methods in a conspiracy to stamp out competition. But the judgment in the case declared it was not an illegal conspiracy because they had acted 'with the lawful objective of protecting and extending their trade and increasing their profits'.[12] Under capitalism, some conspiracies are clearly more acceptable than others, and, as one legal writer put it, 'the history of the law of conspiracy is the history of the class struggle and the regulation of wages'.[13]

The use of conspiracy laws to catch strikes which judges regarded as challenging the interests of private capital reveals them to have acted in a political manner which, while broadly compatible with the wishes of the dominant class, nevertheless displayed a certain *independence*.

· PICKETING ·

Judicial bias is also illustrated by the more recent experience of responses to picketing. Having been a major focus for political conflict over strikes in the last century, picketing became highly controversial again as the storm clouds of economic crisis began to gather over the post-Second World War boom. Once again the judiciary began to reinterpret and to narrow the law without prior parliamentary agreement.

In the 1960 case of *Piddington v. Bates*, local police decided that no more than two pickets were allowed to cover one entrance to a printing firm. Their decision was unilateral and without legal precedent. When a third picket attempted to join his colleagues he was arrested and charged with obstruction, even though all parties agreed that the episode was entirely peaceful. Later, in a court judgment upholding the decison of the police, Lord Parker said: 'I think that a police officer, charged with the duty of preserving the Queen's peace, must be left to take such steps as, on the evidence before him, he thinks proper.' Besides being a significant affirmation of the discretionary powers of the police to apply the law as they saw fit, this judgment effectively overturned picketing practice which strikers had for years considered to be theirs by legal right. The result of such judicial interpretations meant that, as one legal expert argued, the right to picket had 'no more substance than the grin of a Cheshire cat'.[14]

This was emphasized in 1973 when Lord Reid gave a judgment which further restricted strikers' rights by seeing picketing as equivalent merely to hitch-hiking: 'One is familiar with persons at the side of the road signalling to a driver requesting him to stop. It is then for the driver to decide whether he will stop or not. That, in my opinion, a picket is entitled to do.' In the same case, known as *Hunt v. Broome*, Viscount Dilhorne argued: 'To give pickets the right to stop persons and vehicles would involve a restriction of other people's rights.' The case was also important because it came just two years after Parliament had expressly legislated in the 1971 Industrial Relations Act to permit peaceful picketing; and there was no dispute that John Broome, a local trade union official, *had* been acting peacefully when he picketed a building site in Stockport in September 1972.

In the 1970s there was increasing public criticism of picketing in the media and by politicians of all parties. They saw it as the most threatening manifestation of the power of workers to further strikes. Being so visible, picketing made ideal television and began to attain a disproportionate significance in the public mind. After mass pickets had forced the police to close Saltley coke depot in February 1972, picketing was seen as a major *political* threat to the state. Mr Justice McKinnon warned one picket who came up before him: 'It is no use setting about a police officer because behind him stands the police force, behind them the Army, Navy and Air Force and behind them the whole state.'[15]

In this climate, judges were able to exploit the vague nature of the law. In 1974 a judge agreed that to shout 'Scab' on a picket line would give the police grounds to break it up. The police had argued that pickets gathering outside St Thomas's Hospital in 1973 shouting 'scabs and such names' could constitute 'insulting words' under the 1936 Public Order Act and lead to a breach of the peace. In his judgment on the case, the Lord Chief Justice, Lord Widgery, made it clear that there was no right to picket as such: the law only conferred immunities in certain restricted circumstances which were invariably open to judicial interpretation.

·JUDGES, STRIKES AND PARTY POLITICS·

During the late 1970s the judiciary went beyond the use of their historic common-law powers to curb strikes and adopted a more partisan political role, openly showing their displeasure with the Labour government's pro-union laws.

At one point, the Advisory, Conciliation, and Arbitration Service (ACAS) complained to the government that judicial decisions were denying it the discretion to carry out its statutory duties, making it increasingly difficult to do its job and specifically undermining its responsibilities under the 1974–6 legislation.[16]

The head of the Appeal Court, Lord Denning, made it clear that he resented the protection given in the 1974–6 Trade Union and Labour Relations Acts to strikers involved in a 'trade dispute'. In a public lecture he argued that the definition of 'trade dispute' was far too wide.[17] In a series of cases in 1977–8, the courts effectively redefined the law, so that the legal protection provided for strikers was much more restricted than Labour's legislation had envisaged.[18] Giving judgment which prevented the Association of Broadcasting Staff from blacking transmission of the BBC's live coverage of the 1977 football Cup Final to South Africa, Lord Denning complained: 'Parliament has conferred more freedom from restraint on trade unions than has ever been known to the law before. All legal restraints have been lifted so that they can now do as they will.'[19]

The behaviour of Lord Denning's Appeal Court during the late 1970s highlighted the tendency of senior judges to see themselves almost as bulwarks against advances won by the labour movement through Parliament. This was shown dramatically in an extraordinary confrontation between Lord Denning and Labour's Attorney-General in 1977 over the latter's decision not to proceed against Post Office workers who had decided to black communications to South Africa for a week (a case discussed in Chapter 2).

But very often it was less dramatic, with judges simply frustrating the spirit of legislation, as happened over the 1976–7 Grunwick strike, for instance. In a typically forthright speech in October 1977, Lord Denning reviewed such controversial cases as Grunwick and the Post Office workers' disputes, remarking at one point: 'By and large I hope we are keeping the [Labour] government in order.' And on his role and that of his judicial colleagues, he added: 'We have ways and means of getting round the law.'[20]

In 1979 a senior judge, Lord Salmon, criticized workers picketing a hospital, saying that if they were acting within the law, then 'surely the time has come for it to be altered'.[21] (In the 1978–9 'Winter of Discontent', police chiefs added their voice to that of judges by lobbying the Labour government for additional restrictions on pickets. Their views were given wide media coverage which increased public pressure for the kind of restrictions introduced by the Conservative government in 1980.)

However, when the Tories came to power in 1979 the higher judiciary began to play a different political role. Statements made at the time the Tories were introducing what was to become the 1980 Employment Act suggested that they were keen to 'push the Conservative government in what they saw as the right direction'.[22]

In one judgment, delivered in a case where transport workers had blacked a ship to try to secure decent wages, Lord Diplock spoke of the danger of wage demands bringing down 'the fabric of the present economic system'.[23] In a case before the House of Lords during the 1980 steel workers' strike, Lord Diplock again complained that the immunity given to trade unions was 'intrinsically repugnant', even though this immunity had expressly been granted by Parliament back in 1906. In the same case, Lord Edmund-Davies described the law as 'unpalatable to many', and Lord Keith saw trade unionists as 'privileged persons' able to 'bring about disastrous consequences with legal impunity'.[24]

· JUDICIAL DISCRETION ·

If these senior judges were attempting to increase the pressure for further limitations on unions' ability to strike, then they must have been gratified by the way the 1982 Employment Act did precisely that, historic union immunities being one of its main targets.

The 1980 and 1982 Conservative laws virtually invited the courts to become political agencies, being framed in such a way as to give wide discretionary power to judges to exercise their own political prejudices in curbing industrial action. Associated with the 1980 Act, for example, is a 'Code of Practice' on picketing which gives enormous discretion to police officers on the spot and is phrased in such a way that, as one labour lawyer put it, 'it is unclear where the law stops and opinion begins ... opinion masquerades as law'.[25] Even the British Institute of Management stated that the Code was 'seriously open to criticism on grounds of being over-political in parts',[26] while an all-party House of Commons Select Committee called it 'constitutionally undesirable'.[27] Not surprisingly, strikers caught by the 1980 and 1982 Acts feel they are victims of a politically partisan legal system.

Today, as in the past, the judiciary has used the discretion built into the British legal structure in order to defend dominant class interests. Judges have been called upon to play an overtly political role at particular historical junctures in class struggles. The labour lawyer, Lord Wedderburn, explains:

... the eras of judicial 'creativity', of new doctrines hostile to trade union interests, have been largely, though not entirely, coterminous with periods of British social history in which the trade unions have been perceived by middle-class opinion as a threat to the established social order. That was certainly true of the judge-made law of the periods 1961 to 1969, and 1976 to 1979. The lack of such 'creativity' by the courts in the 1930s can similarly be related to the extreme weakness of trade unions in that decade.[28]

Another such era began in 1984 when the courts played a demonstrably political role during the miners' strike. They gave a virtual blank cheque to authoritarian policing methods. And in a series of rulings the courts made a clear class choice, as a leading barrister, Helenna Kennedy, argued

the right to strike is not held as dearly by the judiciary as the right to work. They are making a choice about which of those rights is more important. So even if it is only the right of a very small number of people to go in to work in the face of enormous numbers of strikers, the judges are happily endorsing the government and the Home Office's view that enormous numbers of police and considerable expenditure is justified to protect the 'right to work' against the 'right to strike'. This is done on the pretext of 'protecting public order'. Yet the sure fire way to do this would be to say to the scabs that they should not fly in the face of the majority of their workmates on strike.[29]

· MAGISTRATES AND MINERS ·

Because most strikers appeared before magistrates' courts, the latter's role proved to be the most hotly criticized. Magistrates had used their powers to oppose strikes before: for example, in early periods of trade unionism they 'developed the habit of threatening strikers with imprisonment for breach of contract' under the Master and Servant law.[30] Until 1973, when the Queen's Regulations for the army were changed, magistrates had the power to mobilize troops in aid of the civil power.[31] The way they exercised this power was sometimes highly controversial – as at Featherstone colliery in 1893 when local magistrates were widely held to be responsible for the unnecessary deaths and violence that followed their decision to deploy troops.[32]

In 1977 during mass picketing in the Grunwick strike there were over 500 arrests and conviction rates were extremely high: about 75 to 80 per cent at Barnet magistrates' court and higher at Willesden, surprising even the police who had expected the rate to be no more than 55 per cent (the national average is about 50 per cent). There was evidence that local JPs were influenced by political hostility towards pickets they saw as disrupting the life of their area.[33]

This should not provoke surprise, perhaps, because the magistracy is overwhelmingly right of centre, middle-class, and dominated by supporters of the Conservative Party.[34] But, political opinions aside, independent studies have shown that magistrates tend to back the police and support their version of events. As one practising solicitor with some seventeen years' experience reported in 1980:

I have actually known cases where the police have reduced the charge from actual bodily harm to assault on police in order to keep it in the magistrates' court because they know full well that if a jury heard such a case justice might actually be done – the defendant acquitted and the police officer disciplined or expelled from the force. 'Justice' in the magistrates' court has become a joke . . . they used to be called and still are 'police courts'.[35]

Nevertheless, miners appearing before local benches in 1984–5 experienced a scale and intensity of hostility unprecedented in modern times.[36] One magistrate reported that the conversation in the 'retiring rooms' of local courts was 'strongly in favour of the miners who refuse to strike'.[37] A detailed account[38] by Suzie Gregson-Murray, a Nottingham-based solicitor who defended many pickets, described a general pattern confirmed by other evidence at the time:

Once charged, the men are then placed before special 'picket courts'. These are usually presided over by a sole lay magistrate . . . The majority are men without previous convictions and they confidently face the courts anticipating a fair hearing. They are horrified to find that this is not the case. It becomes clear that, before even hearing the defendant or his solicitor, the magistrates have pre-judged the case ... a fellow solicitor was recently informed by the chairman of the bench, before she had a chance to address the court, that whatever she said would make no difference at all for the magistrate had already made up his mind.

She also showed how the magistrates invariably accepted the police view, citing one case where

a magistrate (sitting alone) announced that he would grant unconditional bail to all the men. There was some mumbling among the police. The court clerk asked the magistrate to repeat his verdict, which he did. Unable to believe her ears, the court clerk asked the magistrate about the police request for conditions whereupon the magistrate hastily altered his decision to one of bail with the 'usual' conditions.

Another solicitor, appearing for miners at Chesterfield magistrates' court, confirmed that JPs were more reluctant than normal to be sceptical of the police:

It is very difficult for them. They have seen a succession of violent scenes on television news. I think this puts them under much more pressure to support the police. Secondly, the unlimited resources available to the police through the criminal justice system – in terms of witnesses, statements, availability of the courts – only reinforces the impression of the miners that there is a determined effort to smash them.[39]

Suggestions of party political membership influencing the choice of magistrates during the miners' strike emerged in St Helens, Lancashire, where it was reported that the nine JPs who were Labour Party members (out of a total of 100) were being excluded from hearing cases in which miners were accused of picket-line offences.[40] (In 1980 there were complaints of similar discrimination in the steel workers' strike.)[41] And the political temperature surrounding magistrates' justice was further increased six months into the strike when the government drafted in a special team of stipendiaries (full-time, professional magistrates) to hear cases in the Yorkshire and Derbyshire coalfields. These so-called 'flying justices' tackled a mounting backlog of cases, their appointment being described in the press as 'a signal of the government's determination to crack down' on pickets.[42]

But the role of magistrates should not be considered in isolation: it reflected a climate in which the criminal law was applied to striking miners 'with a ferocity which is unprecedented', reported the bulletin of the Legal Action Group. 'It is clear that in the mining dispute prosecutors are following a coordinated policy which accords with the government and police view that mass picketing is not a lawful activity.'[43] One prosecuting solicitor said in full hearing of a number of miners waiting in court: 'As far as I am concerned all striking miners should be locked up. I would prosecute them all, personally.'[44] Defence lawyers maintained that many charges (especially for 'riot') were brought to 'paralyse' strike activists even before their cases began; one explained: 'The prosecution really don't give a damn if the cases are thrown out. The point is that the prosecuting process itself has a self-justifying action. All they have to do is make the arrest . . . and the whole unwieldy procedure grinds on in the most slow-moving and oppressive way designed to crush the defendant before the case even begins.'[45]

The legal profession seemed to side with the government when a number of radical barristers who had defended strikers faced disciplinary hearings before the Professional Misconduct Committee of the Bar. The misconduct charges included appearing for miners for free, 'touting' (i.e. offering their services to miners rather than being introduced through solicitors), and attending meetings with miners' union officials to discuss problems of defending strikers in the conditions prevailing. One left-wing barrister protested that 'the rules of the Bar have been subverted to suit the political views of top judges and anti-trade unionists'.[46] It was difficult to escape the conclusion that the legal Establishment resented highly competent barristers travelling to mining areas and offering their services in support of the strikers.

·MINERS' BAIL CONDITIONS·

One of the most heated of the many controversies which surrounded the miners' strike concerned the unusual bail conditions imposed on pickets. This of course was not the first time attention had been drawn to variations in the granting of bail, with police, magistrates and judges exercising their wide powers of discretion to stipulate conditions which often reflected the social position or political opinions of defendants, rather than the gravity of the offence with which they were charged.

Black people, for example, have for a long time been subject to such discrimination. In one case, a magistrate hearing a formal application for bail asked the defending lawyer: 'Is your client black?' On being told he was, he replied: 'Then no bail.'[47] But the experience in 1981–2 of twelve blacks, known as the 'Bradford Twelve', most directly presaged the miners' treatment three years later.

That case arose out of the 1981 summer riots in British cities. Charged with conspiracy 'to manufacture explosives with intent to endanger life and damage property', the Bradford Twelve were eventually acquitted. But they had been subjected to what were then unique bail restrictions. Initially they were jailed for three months, the prosecution opposing bail on the grounds that political demonstrations were taking place in their support. (The Bail Act makes no mention of such a reason for denying bail.) When they were finally granted bail it was only on a basis amounting to house arrest. The Twelve were required to stay in their homes after 7 p.m. and could not leave Bradford. Nor could they attend any political meetings or take part in the activities of a defence committee which had been set up on their behalf.[48] But the full extent to which bail could be manipulated for political reasons did not become apparent until the miners' strike.

The 1976 Bail Act clearly sets out the principles governing the granting of bail, namely that an accused person has a *fundamental right* to bail and may be refused it or have conditions imposed only in certain statutorily defined circumstances. Under the Act the imposition of conditions is appropriate *only* where a person would otherwise have to be denied bail because it is believed that he or she would fail to surrender to custody, commit another offence, or interfere with witnesses or otherwise obstruct justice.

But in cases before Nottinghamshire magistrates, for example, conditions were imposed *en bloc* without considering the individual circumstances of pickets. Each defendant was required 'not to visit any premises or place for the purpose of picketing or demonstrating in connection with the current trade dispute between the NUM and the NCB other than peacefully to picket or demonstrate at his usual place of employment'. This was ready printed and stapled to each one's bail sheet. (Normally, any bail conditions would be handwritten on to the sheet by the Clerk of the Court at the end of the hearing.) In at least one case the Clerk completed these standard bail sheets for nine defendants *before* the prosecution even began their application for conditional bail.[49]

Clearly this practice was intended to limit the effectiveness of the mass picketing necessary to advance the strike. Magistrates' courts were effectively acting as the agents of the government in the dispute, there being no statutory authority for such behaviour. As a group of lawyers who had represented pickets said at the time: 'It is a policy imposed by the police and by the courts which is designed not to prevent further crime being committed but to prevent striking miners from taking part in lawful trade union activities.'[50]

Most of the charges they faced were 'summary' ones in which it would be normal to expect *unconditional* bail to be granted. Yet in the first six months of the strike, of the 1,745 miners charged, 94.5 per cent had conditions imposed on their bail.[51]

Nevertheless, the bail policy of the Nottinghamshire magistrates was upheld by the High Court when it rejected a challenge by a group of nine miners. Although they claimed in affidavits that they did not condone violence, the Lord Chief Justice, Lord Lane, said of the group: 'It must have been obvious to all those participating in the picketing that their presence in large numbers was part of the intimidation and threats. It must have been clear to them that their presence would, at least, encourage others to threats and/or violence, even if they themselves said nothing.'[52] In other words, even if these miners on bail behaved perfectly peacefully and lawfully, their mere *presence* was construed as tantamount to inciting *others* to illegality.

The High Court judges, like the magistrates before them, were virtually inventing a new legal control for activity they found distasteful. The crucial importance of this judicial stance arose out of the fact that the Nottinghamshire miners remained working during the strike, the coal they produced being vital to the government and the Coal Board in its efforts to defeat the vast majority of their colleagues who were on strike. By endorsing such draconian bail restrictions, the judges were limiting the effectiveness of picketing in the Nottinghamshire coalfields and thereby performing a valuable political service to the Coal Board and the government.

· SENTENCING AND LEGAL AID ·

There were other ways in which judicial discretion was used to penalize the miners. Independent studies had previously revealed wide discrepancies in sentencing by magistrates, some of which could be explained by the local social or political environment.[53] But in the miners' strike sentences often seemed wholly disproportionate to the offences.[54]

When imposing sentences courts have a duty not only to see that the punishment fits the crime but that, if it is financial, it takes account of the defendant's ability to pay. While some benches, such as a number of those in South Wales, suspended fine payments or allowed them to be paid over a long period in small instalments, Nottinghamshire magistrates tended to take a much harsher line, provoking complaints from lawyers. They required some defendants to pay their first instalment on the spot.

In one case where a striking miner was fined £20 for criminal damage, he was also ordered to pay £20 compensation and £33 towards prosecution costs – a total of £73, payable in fortnightly instalments of £2. He was married with two children, the family's weekly income was £45 in benefit, and he had weekly hire-purchase commitments of £12. This was just one of many sentences out of all proportion to the defendant's ability to pay and which could only be interpreted as a means of undermining the strike. There was also a practice of imposing terms of imprisonment on miners who had no previous convictions for offences, in circumstances where magistrates would normally at least adjourn the case for a social inquiry before considering a jail sentence.

Another way in which magistrates and police stopped miners from picketing was by 'binding them over' to keep the peace. The power to do this derives from the Justices of the Peace Act 1361. In many cases where the police were not confident that their evidence would stand up against pickets they had often plucked at random from a crowd, they dropped the charges at the trial and applied instead for a 'bind-over'.[55] This threatens a fine only if the defendant commits a breach of the peace within a specified time (often a year) in the future. Thus strikers could be prevented from picketing without being convicted.

Granting of legal aid was also an issue which provoked criticism of magistrates during the strike. In 1982, a four-year survey had shown wide discrepancies in the granting of legal aid by magistrates' courts.[56] But the miners found themselves refused legal aid 'in all but the most serious cases',[57] and so had to rely on their union to finance their defence – a convenient method of draining its finances and thereby undermining its ability to organize the strike.

·COURTS AGAINST MINERS·

But the most serious way in which the funds of the National Union of Mineworkers were attacked was in the High Court. In an 'interlocutory' (i.e. emergency) hearing some seven months into the strike Mr Justice Nicholls ordered the entire funds of the union to be sequestered as a result of an action brought by two working miners. They had asked the court to grant a 'declaration' that the strike was unofficial and that the miners' National Executive had acted in contravention of the union's rule book by not having a national ballot.* But it would have taken some considerable time for the court to have resolved whether such a declaration was in order, and so in the meantime the plaintiffs sought an injunction refusing the miners' leaders the right to call the strike official.

Usually an injunction is only used as an emergency procedure (for example, to prevent a road being built when it would be too late to have awaited the court's deliberations). It would not normally have been applicable in this case, where the strike had already been going on for seven months. But the judge made new law by using his power of discretion to grant the injunction. And when the NUM executive ignored it and continued to call the strike official, the sequestration order was issued.

The injunction was granted and the union was initially fined £200,000 within days of the Attorney-General calling for heavy fines to be imposed.[58] As is frequently the case, it was not obvious whether he was acting in his role as one of the highest law officers of the land or as a senior Conservative government minister. No doubt the judge, if asked, would have stuck to the fiction that the High Court is impartial and independent of politics. But even if he did not take the Attorney-General's public call as a direct instruction, the judge would have been acutely aware of the political environment in which he was making his decision and of its effect at that critical time in the dispute. When the NUM refused to pay the fine, the court ordered that its entire national assets (put at £4.7 million) should be sequestered. The court also appointed a Receiver, the first time this had been done at the same time as making a sequestration order during an interlocutory hearing.

* Quite a different attitude was taken by the High Court in November 1977 when it refused to grant an injunction to Kent, Yorkshire and South Wales areas of the NUM banning some local productivity schemes from being introduced in defiance of a national membership ballot which had rejected them. Then it suited the dominant class to ignore a national ballot decision. By 1984 political expediency allowed the court to stand on its head.

Litigation occurred throughout the dispute as both old and newly invented law was used against the strikers on a scale quite without precedent. The courts played a dutiful role within a multi-pronged strategy by the government and the Coal Board to break the strike.[59]

An additional example of one-sided judicial creativity came early in 1985. During another interlocutory hearing, this time for an injunction to be granted against miners picketing a pit in South Wales, the judge conceded that the action of the pickets did not come within any known crime, or 'tort' (i.e. civil wrong). However, he overcame this obstacle by inventing a new one – namely 'unreasonable harassment'; it was probably the first tort to have been created during interlocutory proceedings.

Previously the judiciary had effectively made new law to curb the strike when the High Court refused an application from Kent miners in March 1984 to declare illegal police roadblocks preventing them travelling through the Blackwall Tunnel to join picket lines further to the north. This police action was repeated elsewhere and upheld by Mansfield magistrates' court in Nottinghamshire, turning parts of the country into 'no go areas' for striking miners.

When the NUM tried to challenge the legality of the Nottinghamshire magistrates' decision, they had to wait eight months for a High Court hearing. Eventually in November 1984 the High Court gave the police the go-ahead to continue stopping people travelling towards coalfields if they 'honestly and reasonably' thought there was a risk of a breach of the peace. In fact police officers consistently used roadblocks to harass supporters of the strike, even those who were not pickets, and this action played an important role in preventing the picketing from being effective.[60]

The contrast between the undue haste with which the courts moved to grant the declaration against the union and the slowness of their response when the union sought their help is another example of judicial bias in the miners' strike. However, other unions too have faced this problem. For example, in July 1984 the National Union of Public Employees (NUPE) complained to the

Master of the Rolls, Sir John Donaldson, of repeated delays in getting an Appeal Court hearing about the sacking of nineteen Kent school-meals staff. An industrial tribunal had found in October 1982 that the workers had been unfairly dismissed for refusing to take a 30 per cent cut in wages and conditions. This was upheld by an employment appeals tribunal in April 1983. When Kent County Council tried again to overturn this by lodging an appeal with the Appeal Court, the hearing was successively delayed until the following year, with the school-meals staff still not reinstated.

In a statement, NUPE contrasted this long delay with the Master of the Rolls' speed in fixing an appeal hearing, at the government's request, to overturn a High Court judgment against its 1984 ban on unions at GCHQ. The school-meals staff had to wait to see whether they might get their jobs back for over two years; the Appeal Court obliged the government in two weeks. As a NUPE official put it, the clout of low-paid women workers counted for nothing compared with the vested interests of the Prime Minister: 'Justice delayed is justice denied. This sorry episode calls into renewed question the way in which the law operates in favour of the rich and powerful and against the poor and defenceless.'[61]

· THE JUDICIARY, GOVERNMENT AND STRIKES ·

Perhaps it should come as no surprise that judges should have been hostile to unions and strikers when account is taken of their class background and political leanings. They are overwhelmingly middle- or upper-class, white, male and elderly, with political attitudes that range between the centre and the far right.[62] As has been shown, 'judges in advanced capitalist societies have generally taken a rather poor view of radical dissent, and the more radical the dissent, the greater has been judicial hostility to it'.[63] In a variety of judgments on controversial social, economic or political matters, the courts have invariably favoured private capital and property at the expense of the poor and the powerless; the dominant class at the expense of the subordinate class.[64]

Nevertheless, there is no direct, mechanical link between the policies of the government and the operation of the courts. In relation to strikes it is possible to discern a distinct role played by judges and magistrates who sometimes act autonomously to pursue their own specific political objectives. As one labour lawyer explained:

The historical development of labour law is explicable in terms of industrial and political conflict. Whether or not one approves or disapproves of trade unions or regards them as too powerful or not powerful enough, it would be difficult to deny that labour law's development has reflected attacks on trade unions and counter-attacks by unions ... One of the recurrent themes in this development has been the tension between two of the organs of the state, Parliament and the courts. Parliament has proved susceptible to trade union as well as employer pressure group activities, whereas the courts often appeared to be hostile to trade unions.[65]

Sometimes the judiciary may undermine strikers' rights against the explicit wishes of the government of the day, as during Labour's period in office in the middle to late 1970s. At other times it may sidestep laws passed by Parliament to place new restrictions on unions, as is clear from the history of strikes.

But much of the time the courts' hostility to strikes has reflected the wishes of governments, especially Conservative ones. Ministers have seen advantages, for example, in allowing judges to adjust the common law to changing circumstances. One reason is that judge-made law is more flexible than statute law. This was apparent from the government's willingness to let the High Court's ruling stand in the Nottinghamshire case. The ruling upheld police in turning back miners travelling by car. In a White Paper on public order issued in May 1985, the Home Secretary had the opportunity to introduce a statutory power to stop and turn back pickets, but he chose not to do so.[66]

Furthermore, the courts can become convenient vehicles for the government to fight industrial battles in a 'respectable' manner. Because the legal system is widely held to be impartial and fair, because implementation of the law is popularly viewed as a technical business, quite neutral as between the interests of conflicting groups, it has much greater legitimacy when used against strikes than would be gained through an overt political intervention by employers or politicians.

Legal intervention can transform a strike into a direct political conflict if the strikers are forced to resist the application of the law. They can be presented in a subversive light as 'defying the law of the land', even if that defiance simply developed naturally as they pursued their industrial objectives. Their 'real' objective can be presented as being to 'threaten society' because the aims of the strike become submerged under controversy about the illegality of their activities. Instead of a dispute about jobs and conditions of work, it can be presented as one about law and order, with unions effectively criminalized and thereby discredited.

LESSONS FROM
THE MINERS

The defeat of the miners will be seen as a landmark
in the decline of the industrial working class and the advocates of
political strike action.
(*Guardian*, 5 March 1985)

This conclusion appeared immediately after the 1984–5 miners' strike in an analysis by no means hostile to the National Union of Mineworkers' cause. Such views have been expressed after other major strikes (in 1926, for example), and history has proved them wrong. But whether or not this one proves correct could well depend on the extent to which a number of lessons of the strike are absorbed by the labour movement.

The year-long dispute was the longest-ever national strike in British history. It was also a 'classic' political strike. First, the government provoked the miners into striking at a time and in circumstances least favourable to the union. Second, the government was determined throughout to defeat the miners for political reasons, almost regardless of the financial cost to the nation or the disruptive effect on industrial relations in the coal industry. Additionally, the objectives of the miners' leaders – to save pits and their surrounding communities – required substantial policy changes from the government and the union's demands were often couched in terms alien to the pragmatism of traditional union bargaining.

Since this political dimension was both more visible and more important than is usually the case with trade union activity, the strike could not be confined to an *industrial* battleground: the *political* battleground was even more important. Any assessment of the strike must therefore include an assessment of the political tactics and approach adopted, not just by the NUM and other trade union leaders, but by their political supporters in the Labour Party and elsewhere on the left.[1]

· A NECESSARY STRIKE ·

Trade unionists were deeply divided about the strike, and many argued that it was 'unnecessary' and 'counter-productive'. Critics from within the unions and the Labour Party suggested that picket-line violence and the spin-off of lost output into neigh-bouring industries like steel and rail was damaging to the wider trade union movement. They argued that the 'brute force' image of trade unionism presented on the nation's television screens would undermine public sympathy for unions; and that it would encourage support for even more stringent legislative restrictions on strikers than had already been imposed by the Thatcher government. They also maintained that it would seriously impede the election of a Labour government. Although many union *activists* rejected it, this general view was held by a majority of leaders and rank-and-file members within the trade union movement which refused to face up to the central fact that it was an *inevitable* strike.

British labour history shows that unions can seldom pick the time and place that suit them best for a confrontation. Invariably they are forced to react to decisions made by employers or governments: if they do not react effectively, then their position is undermined. Furthermore, labour movement critics of the miners in 1984–5 seemed at times to be calling in aid a British union tradition which was mythical. It was as if public-order illegality, picket-line clashes and political strikes were alien to Britain, as if unions had only ever won strikes by be-having with polite circumspection and dutiful obedience to hostile laws. The argument seemed to verge on saying that the miners could have won by offending nobody – as if that were really a serious option in a strike provoked by a bitterly hostile government.

The government had for some time been determined to take on the NUM and defeat the political power which it had seemed to possess in the successful miners' strikes of 1972 and 1974. A confrontation was thus inevitable in that it was so clearly part of the Thatcherite strategy. Only its timing was in doubt – and that too was controlled by the government and the National Coal Board. As described in Chapter 5, the Thatcherites had in the late 1970s formulated detailed tactics (contained in the 'Ridley document') to build up coal stocks; develop nuclear energy resources; cut back on benefits to strikers' families; refine strike-breaking police tactics; and encourage 'scab' labour. This was all part of a calculated plan to defeat the miners as the 'leading arm' of the labour movement.

Mrs Thatcher had climbed down in the 1981 confrontation over jobs and investment, when strikes started spreading in the coalfields, because the plan had not yet reached fruition. But the Tory election victory in 1983 was a turning-point. Soon afterwards the experienced Peter Walker was made Secretary of State for Energy and personally told by Mrs Thatcher to prepare for a miners' strike. Within weeks came the deliberately provocative appointment of Ian MacGregor as Chairperson of the National Coal Board, with his reputation for militant anti-unionism.

The way in which the NUM leadership was defeated in three successive membership ballots over pay, and then pit closures in 1981–3, virtually gave a green light to government ministers who fervently believed union leaders were out of touch with their members. This view seemed to be confirmed by the unwillingness of members to strike against pit closures in South Wales and Scotland in the winter of 1983–4. The sudden, rather clumsy, announcement of a national pit closure programme in early March 1984 may not have been planned in all its detail, but something like it was bound to happen at some time. As the *Sunday Times*, a supporter of Mrs Thatcher's policies, reported: 'There are good reasons for thinking that the timing of the dispute, and the choice of battleground on which it was fought, was deliberately engineered by the government.'[2] The NUM had to stand and fight or lose any credibility as a force of resistance as pit after pit was closed.

Although the media personalized the issue by maintaining it was 'Scargill's strike', the pressure to strike actually came from local NUM *activists*, not from the leadership; similarly, picketing of the Nottinghamshire coalfields was initiated by activists, with area and national leaders being initially unenthusiastic.[3]

· PRECONDITIONS FOR A MINERS' VICTORY ·

However, 'standing and fighting' could be seen in two ways: *either* as setting down a marker that the union would not tolerate being trampled all over – that it was prepared and able to resist unilateral management decisions; *or* as overturning the pit closure programme of the Coal Board and the government. In practice it aspired to the latter and ended up being the former.

The closure programme was part of an ambitious Thatcherite project to restructure manufacturing industry, substantially reduce the public sector and eliminate public subsidies. To have had any chance of overturning this would have required, as an absolute minimum, several conditions to be met. First, the miners would need to be as united as any big group of strikers could realistically have been. Second, major solidarity action would be needed among key workers in power stations and transport. Third, the government's political offensive through the media would need to be effectively countered on a political basis by mobilizing the broadest possible political constituency of support. The reason why the strike was defeated is that none of these conditions was met.

But this was not simply because of leadership shortcomings in the NUM, the TUC or the Labour Party, as many ultra-left critics maintained in their predictable search for scapegoats during and after the strike. Serious leadership failures unquestionably occurred in all three groups, and they undoubtedly weakened the strike. But the problem went much deeper.

·INTERNAL DEMOCRACY·

The NUM's own failure to maintain internal unity was critical. Unlike 1972 and 1974, a hard core of the union, constituting about a third of its members, mostly in Nottinghamshire, never agreed to strike and worked throughout the dispute. The Nottinghamshire members argued that the absence of the union's traditional *national* ballot over strike action meant they were not bound by the decision to strike because they had not been properly consulted on it.

The NUM leaders had faced a major dilemma. They knew they had to stand and fight or the closure programme would be forced through. Yet they also knew that they had failed to convince their members to take industrial action in three previous ballots over pay and jobs. They did not trust 'moderate' areas like Nottinghamshire to obey the result of a national vote, particularly after the experience in 1977–8 when a national membership ballot had voted to reject a productivity scheme, only to find Nottinghamshire, followed by other areas, agreeing to its introduction on a local basis.

There was also a real problem posed by the fact that the dispute was over jobs. In 1972 and 1974, when Nottinghamshire miners voted to strike, the issue was pay and, because of national pay rates, all miners and all NUM areas were affected in *exactly the same way*. But in 1984 jobs were more under threat in areas like South Wales, Scotland and Yorkshire than in Midland areas like Nottinghamshire, with its new-technology pits: the workers in the former areas had a greater reason to fight. Moreover, Midlands miners had higher earnings and the evidence suggests that their life-style had made them more susceptible to Thatcherism's appeal to skilled workers.[4] Several traditional mining constituencies there swung to the Tories in the 1979 and 1983 elections. Coming on top of the right-wing tradition among Nottinghamshire miners in the inter-war years, this meant they were less sympathetic to an appeal based on traditional class solidarity.

Against this background, NUM leaders made disparaging comments about the dangers of 'ballotitis' and expressed a determination 'not to be constitutionalized out of a defence of our jobs'.[5] And the left on the union's National Executive adopted as a calculated policy what was termed a 'domino' approach: an area-based strike escalating on a national basis.[6] In terms of the NUM's rule book this was strictly constitutional, because areas had the ability to decide on strike action and then seek ratification from the National Executive or a special union conference. The Yorkshire region had already achieved a membership ballot in favour of strike action against closures and it was in Yorkshire that the confrontation started with the closure of Cortonwood colliery. The 'domino' approach also proved successful in getting men out in some areas – Lancashire, for example.

Understandable though the leadership's response was in the circumstances, the absence of a ballot proved a major handicap. It intensified divisions in the union's membership. It resulted in attempts to 'picket out' Nottinghamshire miners in the early weeks of the strike, embittering an already adverse situation. And it meant that the very *legitimacy* of the strike – crucial in such a highly politicized environment – was undermined by constant accusations that the NUM was 'frightened' to consult its own members.

Whether a membership ballot would have produced a majority for strike action is open to question: certainly, union leaders did not think so. In an interview some weeks after it had ended, Arthur Scargill said he believed the union 'may well have lost' a ballot, but was faced with a 'stark choice' between accepting or resisting pit closures and job losses.[7] At the very start a MORI poll on 9 March found that 62 per cent of miners favoured a strike; on 10 July a Harris poll found the figure was 61 per cent. But it was subsequently revealed that the Coal Board had commissioned its own private polls from ORAC and Gallup, and, using more intensive interviewing techniques, these found that there would not have been a majority for strike action in a ballot.[8]

Internally, the absence of a ballot gave the working miners a plausible excuse to defy the strike on the grounds that it was undemocratic. Externally, it enabled fellow trade unionists to turn down pleas for solidarity action on the grounds that the NUM could not even get all its *own* members out. Overall, it allowed the strike's opponents to exploit the issue of democracy in their attacks on the NUM's leaders. The union was presented not merely as 'subversive' for waging a 'political strike', but as 'undemocratic' for refusing to allow its own members a vote: this was extremely damaging, not least because it encouraged the public debate around the strike to be conducted on territory favourable to the government, rather than on an alternative agenda of energy policy and jobs where government ministers were vulnerable.

Of course, there is a sense in which right-wing critics of the strike merely seized upon the ballot issue out of expediency. They would have found something else to exploit if they had needed to, as the experience of the pit supervisors' union, NACODS, illustrated. Despite winning an overwhelming membership ballot for strike action, the normally conservative NACODS was still criticized by government ministers and by the media for threatening industrial action in the autumn of 1984. The NUM could also be forgiven for a jaundiced view of those critics in the media and Parliament who had happily endorsed the implementation of local productivity schemes in 1977–8, despite a 55.75 per cent vote *against* doing so in an NUM national membership ballot.

Nevertheless, the lack of a ballot became a major millstone round the NUM's neck. It could not be confined as an 'internal NUM issue', as most sympathizers in the labour movement found themselves forced to argue in public. The lesson was that in such a political conflict *every* aspect of a union's conduct is potentially a matter of public interest.

Even from the NUM's internal standpoint to argue, as union activists did, that no one should have a vote on another's job was to sidestep the fact that this was precisely what the NUM leadership had previously asked its members to do, in a balloting procedure which went back generations. It failed to recognize that people have to feel they are part of a decision if they are being asked to make such a major sacrifice. If they are not, the basic principle of solidarity is seriously damaged.

However, sympathizers who held back from full support because there was no ballot have to concede that it may well not have produced a majority for the strike, in which case they need to suggest what the NUM should then have done, faced with the gauntlet of closures thrown down by the government. Such a transparent act of class confrontation had surely to be met by determined resistance. On the other hand, the NUM leaders and activists who shunned the ballot need to acknowledge the principle that democracy is not an expendable luxury to be discarded when the going gets difficult – and that any attempt to do so is ultimately self-defeating, as it proved to be in this case.

·VIOLENCE AND ILLEGALITY·

Perhaps the most serious issue of public debate around the strike was violence. The unprecedented level of police aggression and harassment of strikers created conditions in which violence both on and away from the picket line was inevitable, almost regardless of the stance of the union. But the blame for this was never perceived by the public to lie with the police and the government, partly because the strike organizers dealt inadequately with it. Instead of publicly urging their members not to be provoked by the police, they remained silent, only condemning attacks on working miners and their homes late in the strike. In the face of the horrifying police operation it is understandable that the NUM leaders were reluctant to make such public criticisms: they felt that to do so would betray their members, who were at the receiving end of brutal police behaviour which the public rarely saw because of biased media coverage. But the leadership's stance appeared to legitimize violence on and off the picket line which was not provoked by the police, and which started to gain a life of its own as frustration and bitterness spread.

The role of the media proved very significant. A daily torrent of abuse was hurled at the NUM in the tabloid papers. They painted the strikers in the most unfavourable light imaginable, constantly focusing public debate on the issues of violence and the ballot, and invariably giving prominent and sympathetic coverage to the public statements of government ministers and working miners; the only major criticism of the Coal Board was over Ian MacGregor's awkward and inept public behaviour. There were regular instances of political censorship, as when an article on government contingency measures for rationing of power supplies was removed from later editions of the *Sunday Telegraph* on 25 March 1984 after the direct intervention of the Secretary of State for Energy.[9] News coverage of picket-line clashes usually relied on the police version of events, and television cameras were based behind police lines, which emphasized aggression by pickets rather than by police officers.

There were several television programmes which gave a fairer picture. Balance was added by daily coverage given in Channel 4 News, the *Morning Star*, and to some extent the *Guardian* and the *Financial Times*. (But between them these covered only a small minority of readers and viewers.) In general the media effectively acted as another agency of the state in the dispute, joining the government, the police and the courts against the strikers. By outright suppression of news or biased coverage, the media set an agenda for public debate which was politically hostile to the NUM.

It would be naive to imagine that the miners could have obtained objective coverage from newspapers and television programmes so deeply biased and politically compromised. But public hostility could have been neutralized through a more astute presentation of the union's case by its leaders. As it was, the NUM was effectively 'criminalized' through the media by the government and the Coal Board. This ultimately damaged the political legitimacy of the strike, including its credibility among fellow trade unionists. It also meant that the full implications of the police operation were never brought home to the public in a way that might have been possible had the miners been correctly portrayed as the victims of it.

On the other hand, to imagine that the dispute could have been conducted entirely peacefully is to underestimate the authorities' determination to defeat the miners. From the Prime Minister down to local magistrates and police constables, there was an absolute commitment to do what was necessary to crush the

NUM, almost regardless of the human or financial cost, creating an environment in which police violence, manipulation of the law and authoritarianism became rampant.

This was the stark reality ignored by those who argued that any violence by strikers is enough to disqualify them from obtaining wider support. On that argument, almost no significant strike in the past would have received support either. Nevertheless, the daily conduct of the strike was altogether a different question, because the response of miners' leaders to media questions about violence was seen to be evasive, thereby conceding yet more territory to their opponents.

Some socialist feminists sympathetic to the strikers also questioned 'the tendency of the male left to equate "muscular militancy" and violence with political strength'.[10] The weakness of this criticism is that it did not suggest a positive or serious alternative in a traditional class conflict with the police being so determined to prevent effective picketing. It also ignored the fact that the vast majority of picketing was entirely peaceful, to the point of being tedious. Moreover, miners' wives and other women active in the strike did evolve their own methods of picketing. They appeared with their children during afternoon shifts and shouted at 'scabs'. They also went to the homes of 'scabs' and banged pots and pans. On the other hand, the labour movement has yet to face up to the barriers against wider involvement, especially of women, erected by *confrontational picketing* which is sometimes necessary to win a strike.

· PICKETING ·

Criticisms of the strike from those basically sympathetic to the miners' cause often displayed a fastidiousness which took no account of the seriousness of the class battle being waged and the issues at stake in picketing.

In a capitalist society workers can influence their pay, conditions and future employment only by acting in concert. Their numbers are their main source of strength, and they are understandably hostile towards their fellows who threaten that strength. They are therefore justified in so organizing picket lines that they can only be crossed by very determined individuals, because otherwise the solidarity upon which trade union strength is built would be too easily undermined. Furthermore, if it is to have any effect upon those at whom it is directed, a picket must serve as a reminder of the workforce that it represents, and a mass picket is the authentic reflection of a large workforce.

The experience of miners' pickets contained additional lessons. Just as mass demonstrations can now be contained by 'total policing', so even the miners, with their long experience of 'flying pickets' and a record of militancy unequalled in the trade union movement, found mass pickets were no longer the all-powerful vehicles of struggle they had appeared in 1972 or 1974.

One difference was the much lower level of support on picket lines given by fellow trade unionists. The closure of the Saltley coke depot in February 1972 was secured only because of support from unions nearby in the Birmingham area. The day the police finally closed the depot's gates, the Transport and General Workers' Union and the Amalgamated Union of Engineering Workers called sympathy strikes, and tens of thousands of trade unionists took the day off work, 10,000 of them marching on Saltley. 'The picket line didn't close Saltley, what happened was that the working class closed Saltley,' Arthur Scargill explained later.[11]

However, by May 1984 when the biggest confrontation of the strike occurred outside the British Steel coking plant at Orgreave, near Sheffield, there was nothing like the same support from trade unionists, even in that part of Yorkshire which had a strong labour movement tradition. The miners were virtually on their own, were not as well organized as in 1972, and in the end were simply overwhelmed by the police in some of the ugliest picket-line scenes ever shown on British television.

Where Saltley exposed the inadequacy of police strength, Orgreave revealed the sheer scale and organization of modern policing methods, and the unshakeable determination of the government to deploy police power to the full. The police now have the technology, the equipment and the political willingness to take on pickets in a war of attrition which they are likely to win by superior force, as they did in this miners' strike. In an editorial on 20 July urging the government to use even greater state powers, *The Times* argued: 'There is a war on.' The Thatcherites were never in any doubt about that and about the necessity of defeating the potential strength of mass pickets. It was therefore an error to argue that bigger and better mass pickets were more important than anything else to winning the strike, as some left-wing groups did at the time and afterwards.[12] Mass picketing was essential and it will remain an essential part of strikers' armoury in the future, but it is a *tactic* and should not have been elevated in importance to a point where it became a substitute for a successful *strategy*.

·SOLIDARITY·

Much more important was the need for solidarity from fellow trade unionists. While left-wing activists in the unions did give support, neither they nor their national leaders could deliver the kind of rank-and-file industrial action which could have caused power cuts and an economic crisis that might have forced the government to make concessions. Some union leaders, notably in the electricians' and engineering unions, did not even try to persuade their members to take solidarity action. Others, for instance those in the transport, seamen's and rail unions, did try; but they frequently found their members unwilling to respond. A National Opinion Poll published on the eve of the TUC conference in September found that 69 per cent of workers would not strike in solidarity with the miners.

The labour movement as a whole had suffered a series of defeats over a number of years. It was demoralized and the militancy and confidence of the early 1970s had evaporated. It was not willing or able to assist the miners to *generalize* their strike into one seen to be fighting on behalf of all workers. The government was consequently able to portray it as a defence of *sectional* interest: 'a sectional strike in defence of subsidies', as the *Economist* described it.[13]

For its part, the NUM leadership insistently demanded solidarity action in a way that seemed sectarian, irritating even left-wing allies in other unions. Haunted by the memory of 1926 and understandably wary of allowing the 'new realists' at the TUC to take over their strike, the NUM sought to maintain the General Council at arm's length while simultaneously blaming it for lack of support. This helped to marginalize sympathy for the miners in other trade unions.

In such circumstances, calls for a general strike made by some on the left – though not by the NUM – were at best token and desperate ones, and at worst cynical attempts to 'expose' union and Labour Party leaders who, as everyone knew, simply could not deliver a general strike even if they had wanted to. At least two left-wing Labour MPs who made this demand represented constituencies with pits where the majority of miners were actually working.

·SUPPORT·

However, the strike did receive much greater practical assistance in the form of fund-raising and local community support work than any other British strike ever has done. There was a country-wide network of miners' support groups and appeals.[14] One estimate put the total raised at £60 million.[15]

Activity in support of the strike involved hundreds of thousands of people – probably around a million. Local Labour Parties raised money and organized meetings and benefits in a way they had never done for any strike before, breaking through the traditional demarcation line in the labour movement between political and industrial action. It became the most serious movement of resistance that the Thatcherites had encountered. As the Research Officer of the South Wales NUM wrote:

With no prompting from *Marxism Today*, the *New Left Review* or *Labour Weekly*, the people of the coalfields created the basis for a new politics which grew out of experience and necessity. Old politicos – especially many of the crocodile-skinned varieties from Westminster – found themselves straggling badly behind, lost in a mist of worries about parliamentary whips and TUC guidelines. Others became near-sighted, so hard did they search the small print of their constitutions and manifestos for guidance on how to relate Trotsky and Tawney to food-parcel distribution in Cwm Llantwit.[16]

The activity did draw in new layers of people, not simply those previously active in the labour movement. This was especially true of women, and a network of women's support groups sprang up, mainly under the umbrella of the organization called 'Women Against Pit Closures'.[17] The involvement of women was perhaps the most extraordinary feature of the strike. The miners had long been renowned as a bastion of working-class male chauvinism, a tradition exposed in a feminist critique written only just before the strike began.[18] Yet miners' wives quickly developed their own autonomous forms of action: organizing food kitchens; going on picket lines when their men had been barred from doing so by restrictive bail conditions; travelling up and down the country to speak at meetings; and playing the kind of prominent public role they would never have contemplated before.

Many of these women found their involvement exhilarating and liberating. They experienced real hardship, but their self-organization gave them new confidence, drawing them out from what had often been a lonely, 'privatized' domestic role. The communal activity and spirit of collectivism gave them new strength and, indeed, a new sense of purpose and self-worth. Their activity also broke down barriers between daily life and politics in a way that rarely happens: for example, the food kitchens they organized did not simply provide a much-needed service to maintain the strike, they also became centres for the women to organize politically.

This positive side of support for the strikers was, however, only part of the picture. Support undoubtedly went *deeper* than the miners' strikes of 1972 and 1974. But it was also *narrower*. Opinion polls in 1984 showed a majority of the population consistently antagonistic to the miners' cause, whereas they had won wide public backing in the earlier strikes, creating a public climate then in which the government was seen to be acting 'unreasonably'. In 1972 this was as crucial to the miners' ultimate victory as the mass picketing, the government being forced to treat them as a special case.

In February 1974, Gallup Opinion Polls asked the question: 'Are your sympathies mainly with the employers or mainly with the miners in the dispute which has arisen in the coal industry?' Despite the fact that the Conservatives had called a 'Who governs?' election, the responses were: with employers, 24 per cent; with miners, 52 per cent. In December 1984, responses to exactly the same question by Gallup were: with employers, 51 per cent; with miners, 26 per cent; roughly the reverse of the previous position.[19]

The national strike leaders in 1984–5 made little attempt to appeal to a broader cross-section of opinion. Indeed, in the language used and the tactics adopted, the miners' leaders seemed to be directing their appeal at the labour movement alone. This was very effective in motivating *activists* and in achieving a depth of commitment from them far greater than in most strikes. But it proved inadequate in appealing to the wider *public*, as was conceded afterwards in a remarkably frank discussion among several local and regional NUM strike leaders.[20]

In contrast, a deliberate effort was made in South Wales to build the broadest possible community support. Alliances were created which went well beyond the organizations of the labour movement to include the churches, Welsh Nationalists, the peace movement, women's groups, folk singers and others from the world of culture.[21] A conscious attempt was made to isolate the government rather than the strikers from public opinion, and if this had been replicated elsewhere in the country, the strike might well have been more successful. Moreover, the breadth of opinion directly involved in support work helped to make the striking miners more solid in this area than in any other in the country. The South Wales experience underlined how even internal union support can be dependent on the climate outside: unions no more exist in a vacuum than does any other group.

The possibility of winning wider support was indicated by the surge in public opinion towards the miners in the latter weeks of the strike. At this stage mass picketing and violence was limited, and the hardship suffered by the miners and the issues underlying the strike began to emerge. The government's hard line in refusing to make concessions in the final negotiations also became unpopular. As one analysis showed, there was 'a vast middle ground among the public whose sympathies must have swayed back and forth through the daily developments of an intense strike'.[22]

Despite Arthur Scargill's personal eloquence, the NUM 'did little to create the agenda or rebut the daily propaganda from the Coal Board', reported the *Guardian*'s labour correspondent. Perhaps it was impossible to do so, because the NUM had only one press officer who was inevitably inaccessible in the pressure of events and who had to contend with probably over a hundred journalists covering the strike each day. The Coal Board, on the other hand, had over forty press officers. Every morning they issued return-to-work figures and, with the aid of the police, detailed accounts of picket-line violence, thus setting the daily news agenda and giving their version of events which (in the absence of detailed evidence to the contrary) became 'facts'.[23] To have countered this the NUM would have required a national information and monitoring network beyond the resources of any union. However, the NUM leadership rarely used its press conferences to set their own agenda. Their leaders were invariably on the defensive, parrying reporters' questions rather than deciding what *fresh angle* the union wanted to put and which aspect would give the journalists something new to write about.

· SETTING AN AGENDA ·

The miners' cause was not assisted by the way in which their basic case was argued. They fought a political strike with industrial arguments laced with syndicalist rhetoric. Their whole case rested on the preservation of jobs and communities, but this was invariably presented in a defensive, sectionalist fashion. With a more imaginative approach it might have been possible to get the miners' case heard above the din of the argument about picketing and ballots: the case for an expanding coal industry as part of a radically different energy policy from the government's. Further, union leaders never managed to provide effective answers to allegations about 'uneconomic' pits, despite the fact that when the full social costs and benefits of closures were accounted for it was shown to be more economic to the taxpayer to keep them open.[24]

Partly, this was because the NUM had by tradition never challenged the Coal Board's 'right to manage'. The union was therefore in a weak position when it tried to argue for an alternative policy to that of the Coal Board and the government. Historically, there had been support in the NUM for workers' control, such as in a famous pamphlet produced in 1912, 'The Miners' Next Step'.[25] But when the mines were nationalized in 1947 the NUM refused the opportunity offered by the Attlee government for a role in the policy-making machinery of the new Coal Board, on the grounds that the union's role was to defend and advance its members' pay and working conditions, not to help run the industry.

In the 1970s the same position was expressed in the NUM's opposition to workers' participation. From the right, the miners' President, Joe Gormley, argued in response to the Labour Party's 'social contract' and to the industrial democracy proposals in the Bullock report: 'Our role in society is to look after our members, not run the country.' From the left, Arthur Scargill opposed the ideas of the Institute for Workers' Control, insisting that industrial democracy under capitalism was little more than collaboration and that workers' interests could only be protected by independent, free collective bargaining.[26] In 1977 the Coal Board was encouraged by Tony Benn, then Secretary of State for Energy, to introduce industrial democracy measures, but the NUM decided not to cooperate, their decision being based on a rejection in principal of workers' involvement in planning in a capitalist society. During the 1984–5 strike, the left-wing President of the Yorkshire miners, Jack Taylor, commented:

The NUM recognizes that it is the duty of the NCB to manage the industry efficiently and to secure sound developments in accordance with their responsibilities ... It's always been the statutory duty of the NCB to manage. Equally, it has always been the duty of the union to defend its members. We don't want to take away either right from either party.[27]

Although Taylor's statement was made in response to government insistence that the union was unreasonably defying 'management's right to manage', it reiterated the NUM's belief in an *oppositional* form of trade unionism which is basic to the tradition of the whole British trade union movement.

The limits of that oppositionalist stance were revealed by the strike. The NUM was not able to present its own programme on how the coal industry could be run, because it did not have one. While it had a generalized case for the expansion of the industry, this often seemed merely a self-interested pretext for the preservation of its own members' jobs at a time when other workers were losing theirs. If the union had been able to present its own detailed plans for the industry (broken down on a pit-by-pit basis if possible), then it might have been able to secure a more sympathetic public hearing.

However, the failure to set an alternative agenda was not simply that of the miners' leaders, but of Labour Party leaders too. The fact that the Thatcher government had been preparing for a confrontation with the miners, and that when it came the stakes being played for were so high, never seemed to be fully grasped by the Labour leadership. From the outset they acted as if the strike was an embarrassing diversion from 'real' politics in Parliament and the electoral arena. They then appeared to wait impatiently for it to end so that 'business as usual' could be resumed.

Although the parliamentary Labour leaders gave general support, they acted as if supporting the miners' *case* could in some way be separated from supporting the miners' *struggle*. This distancing from the daily action of the strike, combined with the failures of the NUM leaders discussed above, enabled the

Conservatives to set the agenda and put Labour on the defensive. The Labour leaders spent more time saying what they did *not* support (such as picket-line violence and the absence of a ballot) than in setting an alternative agenda on the political issues raised by the strike: economic priorities, energy policy, public order and social change. The government won on these crucial issues because Labour, time and again, ducked them.

The fact that Labour leaders saw the strike as an issue of crisis management, rather than a struggle to engage in with the aim of building opposition to Thatcherism, meant that the party was also unable to appeal to middle-ground opinion, which might have responded had it been given a sustained argument for doing so.

No serious socialist expected Neil Kinnock, the party leader, to become a 'flying picket'. But if he had given more *visible* backing by being seen regularly in mining communities, at strike kitchens, benefits and so on – those areas of support activity around which public opinion could more easily be rallied and which demonstrated an identification with communities under threat – it is likely that more public support could have been won to the miners' cause.

That was a minimum requirement of the Labour leader. More generally, the strike demonstrated the problem of trying, as he did, to divorce extra-parliamentary from parliamentary struggle. Both can be enhanced by being linked: both can be weakened if this does not happen. Although immediately afterwards Labour experienced a sharp recovery in its opinion poll rating which had declined during the strike – and this was used as evidence in support of the leadership's aloofness – it is quite possible that the party would have benefited to a greater extent had its leadership become part of the resistance movement around it.

For its part, the NUM certainly suffered by conducting a political strike without being able to rely on its traditional political arm: the Parliamentary Labour Party. A key lesson was the difficulty the miners faced by being involved in a political conflict without having an adequate political strategy of their own to fight it. But this handicap was not simply due to lack of support from the Labour leadership. The political inadequacies exposed in the conduct of the strike reached far beyond that to the roots of the trade union movement's traditional weakness: its reluctance to put politics in command.

Early on in the strike, the Communist Party's industrial organizer, Pete Carter, said: 'It would be dangerous and sectarian to think that a major industrial dispute of this character can be won by industrial muscle alone, even in the face of hostile public opinion . . . Any projection of the strike as a political strike aimed at bringing the government down will be of no help to the miners – quite the reverse.'[28] Other major public-sector strikes that have been portrayed over the years as 'against the government' faced similar problems.[29]

But that is not a reason for trade unions to back off from confrontations with governments. If the government's stance means that an escalation into a major political conflict is unavoidable, unions are faced with three options: to climb down, to resist by traditional forms of industrial militancy, or to develop their own political and, where required, militant strategies. Most unions would probably have found a way of climbing down through negotiation, perhaps securing important concessions in the process and living to fight another day. The NUM chose militancy and, although their leaders knew full well they were locked into a political conflict and were quite willing to pursue it, they were unable to escape from a tradition of trade unionism which has not equipped strikers with the tools to fight high-profile political strikes. Thus they ended up by getting the worst of both worlds: being blamed for projecting it as a political strike without actually mobilizing the necessary support successfully to *fight* it as one.

The strike was therefore a microcosm of the labour movement's weaknesses. But its strengths were shown too, especially in the miners' extraordinary determination which, in the face of massive hardship and uncompromising state power, was nothing short of heroic. If these strengths can be drawn upon and the new ways of organizing, particularly in the women's support groups, absorbed, then trade unionists may be able to apply the lessons of the strike with more success in the future.

'POLITICAL'
TRADE UNIONISM?

'Politically motivated' has been a charge levelled at British unions with increasing ferocity under Thatcherism, though it is also one which has cropped up throughout the history of the movement. It would be absurd to pretend that the activities of trade unions have no political *consequences*, either in terms of the balance of power between labour and capital, or the distribution of resources in society. But at the level of public debate the charge acts as a smear tactic, denying legitimacy to union action by implying ulterior motives and hidden agendas behind day-to-day trade union work.

For a fuller understanding of strikes, it is necessary to establish to what extent, if at all, an explicit political ideology has motivated British unions. This involves clearing away an undergrowth of mythology: while right-wing critics have exaggerated the political dimension of British trade union activity, many on the left have romanticized its potential for political change. Both have obscured what is – notwithstanding the link many unions have had with the Labour Party – a relatively 'non-political' tradition in British unions.

· 'INDUSTRIAL' AND 'POLITICAL' ACTION ·

However, the boundary between the 'industrial' and the 'political' is not always clear. One study identified three types of union political involvement and interest:

1. Involvement stemming from concern about government action or inaction in industrial matters (e.g. over wages, trade union rights, working conditions or the settlement of disputes).

2. Involvement arising from concern about government action or inaction in matters which, while not strictly industrial, are related to the protective function of unions (e.g. pensions, social security and other welfare provisions).

3. Involvement based on ideological or other commitments with little direct relevance to the industrial role of unions. Foreign policy would be included here; so would moral, constitutional or 'socialist' demands (such as the abolition of the House of Lords or nationalization without compensation).

But it added, 'The overlap between these categories is, of course, very great ... In fact, there is a shading off from matters which affect unions and their members on a daily basis, and issues which spring from the wider political idealism of union activists. The coexistence of these types of involvement is an important feature of British unionism.'[1] The question then becomes not so much whether British trade unions are 'political' or 'industrial', but which type of activity *predominates*. Another study suggests a fairly clear answer:

... when they have a choice, trade unions invariably prefer to rely on industrial rather than political methods to achieve their aims. This does not mean that they necessarily despise or disparage political action. On the contrary they are as a rule very ready to resort to it as a second string to their bow. What it means is that they are prepared to use political methods to support and to supplement their industrial methods, but never to supplant them.[2]

However, since that study was published in 1961, some public-sector unions have actually appeared to prefer 'political methods' to industrial action. Although they have shown no enthusiasm for political *strike* action, they have given a much greater priority than before to political campaigning – by organizing public rallies and marches, lobbying Parliament, distributing leaflets to the public, paying greater attention to press relations, and by linking their industrial concerns to social concerns. A good example was the £1 million advertising campaign against public expenditure cuts mounted in 1983 by the National and Local Government Officers (NALGO) – a union which has been less disposed to undertake major strikes than some others in the public sector.

Unions are also constrained by 'lower' and 'upper' limits on their use of political methods:

... as a minimum, trade unions must be involved in politics in order to establish and maintain the legal and economic conditions in which they can flourish. It makes the term 'non-political union', taken literally, a nonsensical description; there is no such animal . . . But . . . there is also a maximum, an upper limit to the aims they can follow in politics, which is also set by their institutional needs. They cannot, for example, adopt political aims which would seriously threaten their industrial unity. Their success in industry depends on their ability to organize all, or at least a large proportion, of the employees they claim to represent, regardless of their differences in politics. When political divisions within a trade union become too acute and occupy too much attention, the result is paralysis and possibly disruption.[3]

Whether such constraints on their political role are *inevitable* is another matter which will be discussed in the final chapter. But undoubtedly the relationship between the unions and politics as it has *actually evolved* over the decades has been highly pragmatic.

· ORIGINS ·

Part of the explanation for this pragmatism lies in the way in which working-class organizations developed. In the late eighteenth century, influenced by the French Revolution and the radical ideas of Tom Paine, 'political societies' were established all over the country; at least eighty such societies existed in England alone by the mid 1790s, their membership being drawn from both middle-class reformers and skilled artisans.[4] They overlapped to a degree with the trade union clubs which were emerging at the time, and state repression of trade unionists and political dissidents encouraged them to see they had common interests.

But working-class consciousness was extremely tenuous, and solidarity between workers and political activists continued to be limited through the early part of the nineteenth century.

Later, participation of trade unionists in demands for parliamentary reform was also fragmented. In the 1830s and 1840s, many trade societies felt the increasingly radical Chartist movement was damaging their attempts to win respectability. Some unions introduced 'no politics' rules and a few even prevented members who had participated in political activity from claiming out-of-work benefit. As has been shown:

Piecemeal and sectional action had been the hallmark of trade union action almost from the beginning. While there were undoubtedly minorities of workmen who at one time or another accepted visions for a Paineite, Owenite or Chartist reconstruction of society, they remained minorities.[5]

But if the majority backed away from a strategy which saw trade unions as agents of political change, they were nevertheless willing to bring political pressure to bear as and when they felt their ability to engage in collective bargaining could be advanced. After 1850, there was considerable trade union pressure for changes in trade union laws after attacks through the courts on their rights. They also supported political pressure to extend the franchise, though militant extra-parliamentary action was on the whole shunned: activity was mainly confined to lobbying through accepted channels.

By the early 1860s a group of 'new model' trade union leaders seemed to be advocating a more political dimension to trade unionism, though working-class politics in this period was of a quite different sort from the activity rejected by previous generations of trade unionists: it was much more reformist and focused on Parliament, and included quite close links with the Liberals.

Several of these 'new model' leaders wrote an 'Address to Trade Unions', arguing that they did not 'wish to turn our trades societies into political organizations, to divert them from their social objects; but we must not forget that we are citizens, and as such should have citizens' rights. Recollect also, that by obtaining these rights we shall be able more effectively to secure our legitimate demands as Unionists.'[6] They also helped to form a London Trades Council in 1860 with the prime aim of keeping 'watch over the general interests of labour, political and social, both in and out of Parliament'.[7] In 1862, they formed a Trade Union Political Union which three years later transformed itself into the National Reform League. Essentially an alliance between trade unionists and social reformers, the latter was orientated towards the Liberal Party and was dissolved after the passage of the 1867 Reform Act.

Unions now started to encourage their members to ensure that they were on the electoral register, since they organized only that small section of the working class who were at the time entitled to vote. The 1867 Act itself also encouraged pressure for working-class representatives in Parliament. The formation of the Trades Union Congress in 1868, and the accompanying efforts to secure legitimacy for unions as recognized groups in society, reinforced the instincts of their leaders to adopt the role of pressure groups seeking concessions from within the system rather than radical political changes. But such legitimacy as then existed had been won only for the better-off and most skilled sections of the working class. The vast majority remained virtually unorganized and voteless – and their interests continued to be ignored.

· THE BIRTH OF POLITICAL REPRESENTATION ·

For some years the unions relied on persuading the Liberals to achieve legislative change – partly through the TUC's Parliamentary Committee. The first trade unionists elected to Parliament in 1874 (both miners) stood as Liberals. It was not until the 1880s that there was real pressure for genuinely independent labour representatives to advance workers' interests in Parliament. Several factors were responsible for this gradual change of policy, including a worsening economy and persistent unemployment. But the greatest pressure came from political activists influenced by the spread of socialist ideas, and from the 'new unionism' of unskilled workers.

In 1888 a miners' activist called James Keir Hardie was unsuccessful in his attempt to win the Liberal nomination as a miners' candidate for a by-election in the Scottish seat of Mid-Lanark, and he set up a Scottish Labour Party. He failed to persuade the TUC that year to establish a national party of labour, but the idea was gaining ground. The formation of other socialist groups, such as the Fabians and the Social Democratic Federation, increased discussion of the idea, as did the intervention of socialist activists in key strikes. The stage was set for the forging of Hardie's 'labour alliance': of unions joining with socialist societies to form an independent party for labour.

The year 1889 was a watershed in the independent political development of labour. It saw the rapid growth of the 'new unionism' of unskilled and semi-skilled workers still outside existing unions, and

Since the latter showed relatively little interest in the task of organizing the unorganized, and the unskilled themselves found it difficult to provide from among their own ranks sufficient numbers of men with the education and administrative skills necessary to run an organization, socialists stepped in to fill the vacuum.[8]

They played a key role in London strikes by the match-girls, by gas workers and by dockers – the latter two prompting the formation of two new 'general' unions. The Gasworkers' and General Labourers' Union chose the socialist Will Thorne as its General Secretary. He had been taught to read by Karl Marx's daughter Eleanor, who became an officer of the union. The Dock, Wharf, Riverside and General Workers' Union had as its President the prominent socialist activist, Tom Mann. Other socialists held influential positions in both unions. Consequently these strikes encouraged forms of organization which began to change the nature of the trade union movement and point it in a more political and more socialist direction.

The 'new unions' still constituted only a small proportion of stable union membership and so their impact was limited. The established unions were unable to make the great break to political independence and so kept their links with the Liberals, ensuring that the TUC continued to distance itself from demands for a party of labour. But the depression of the 1890s, renewed legal attacks and hostile court judgments against picketing challenged the established unions' traditional reliance on their own bargaining strength. For the 'new unions' in particular,

the value of legislation for the consolidation of their industrial demands made them favourable to the Socialist demand for an independent labour party in Parliament. The new unionists had nothing to lose and a good deal to gain by a policy of political action such as the Socialists were advocating, involving as it did the legislative enforcement of what they were most anxious to win, and, having won, to preserve. It had very soon been made clear to them that their gains by industrial action were not easy to maintain.[9]

But this awareness did not produce an impetus for overt 'political', let alone 'socialist', unionism. It was a response to an immediate set of problems obstructing trade unionists from doing their job properly, and contained no challenge to the parliamentary system.

Much the same can be said about the formation of the Independent Labour Party (ILP) in 1893. It was a further step in Keir Hardie's wish to build a labour alliance, and his own Scottish Labour Party was dissolved. The new ILP brought socialist groups from all over the country together with many of those active in the 'new unions'. Its emphasis on, and relative success in, recruiting trade unionists distinguished it from other socialist groupings, notably the Fabians. The inclusion of 'Independent' in its title was a significant affirmation of a commitment to labour having its own party. However, its title was also significant in another respect: 'the word "socialist" had deliberately been excluded in order not to offend a trade union movement that still remained suspicious of socialism and socialists'.[10]

The extent of this suspicion is illustrated by the way that most unions frustrated moves to shift the TUC towards support for a labour party. For example, although Keir Hardie persuaded the TUC at its 1892 Congress to instruct its Parliamentary Committee to prepare a scheme for financing independent labour representation, nothing was done. Indeed, alarmed at the growth of socialist pressure within the unions, the TUC 'old guard' persuaded the 1895 Congress to introduce several major changes to consolidate their position. Trades councils (which often included a good number of 'new unionists' and socialists) were barred from direct representation in the conference. TUC delegates had to be either union officials or workers still engaged in their trade (designed to stop Hardie and other socialists from attending). Furthermore, rather than continuing to vote as individuals, a 'card' vote system was introduced under which delegates cast votes representing the size of their membership. The result of these changes was to strengthen the power of the already established leaders of large trade unions who often had close relations with the Liberal Party.

The ILP struggled to establish itself. All twenty-eight of its candidates, including Keir Hardie, were defeated at the 1895 general election. Its membership fell off in the late 1890s and it was close to bankruptcy by the turn of the century. But despite declining popular support for socialist ideas in this period, the ILP's influence among trade unionists was on the increase. This happened partly because socialist ideas offered new explanations for the depression of the time, but also because they 'implied a militant posture in relation to the employers'.[11] Another factor was that, with unions under strong attack, joining them required a positive commitment and those giving it were more likely to be attracted to the positive alternative offered by socialists.

As the support for socialism spread among trade unionists, events such as the 1894 Lanarkshire miners' strike clarified the class conflict with the Liberal Party, since the coal-owners were predominantly Liberals. For the most part, however, trade unionists were becoming more disenchanted with the Liberal leaders' shortcomings than with the ideological basis of Liberalism:

All along, there is little doubt that most non-Socialist trade-union leaders would have been happy to stay in the Liberal Party – which most of them had belonged to in the past – if the Liberals had made arrangements for a larger representation of the working class among their parliamentary candidates. Again and again it was the fault of the official Liberal Party constituency caucuses that this did not happen; and it was the behaviour of these caucuses that set many of the leaders of the workers thinking in terms of a separate party.[12]

·FORMATION OF THE LABOUR REPRESENTATION COMMITTEE·

By the late 1890s the case for workers to have their own political representatives had won wide support, and the 1899 TUC conference carried a resolution from the Amalgamated Society of Railway Servants to that effect. Socialists played a key part, both in organizing to ensure the railway union tabled the motion and in influencing the unions who supported it. Four of the seven main unions who voted in favour were new unions with socialist leaderships, and the ILP had influence in the other three.[13] But misgivings were expressed in the debate about the dangers of 'interfering in politics', and the relative closeness of the vote – 546,000 to 434,000 – indicated rather less than wholehearted enthusiasm for the idea of a working-class party.

The aim of the motion was quite cautious and pragmatic. Parliamentary representation rather than socialism was the order of the day, as its modest terms indicate:

That this Congress, having regard to its decision in former years, and with a view to securing a better representation of the interests of Labour in the House of Commons, hereby instructs the Parliamentary Committee to invite the co-operation of all the Co-operative, Socialistic, Trade Union and other working-class organizations to jointly co-operate on lines mutually agreed upon in convening a special congress of representatives from such of the above-named organizations as may be willing to take part to devise ways and means for securing the return of an increased number of Labour Members to the next Parliament.

The result was that the TUC's Parliamentary Committee convened a Special Conference on Labour Representation in the

Memorial Hall, Farringdon Street, London, on 27 and 28 February 1900.[14] Unions on the right wanted a Labour Group which would speak for workers' interests, but with a parliamentary wing which would be given a free hand on what they called 'purely political questions'. The left wanted a clear socialist position to be adopted, the Marxist Social Democratic Federation proposing a 'distinct party based upon the recognition of the class war and having for its ultimate object the socialization of the means of production, distribution and exchange'. But both right and left motions were defeated, Keir Hardie and the ILP successfully winning unity around a declaration that the new body's aim would be confined to the representation of working-class opinion 'by men [sic] sympathetic with the aims and demands of the Labour movement'.

The result was agreement to establish a Labour Representation Committee (LRC). Trade union dominance was maintained by its dependence on attracting union affiliations. There was no provision for constituency-based parties or for electoral machinery. Most union leaders wanted only a limited remit for the new organization: 'They were not consciously assisting at the birth of a Socialist Party; political action was more a matter of bread and butter than of ideology.'[15]

Early progress was slow. After a year, the union-affiliated membership stood at just 353,000 – less than the 570,000 members represented at the founding conference and only 29 per cent of the TUC's membership. Then things began to alter dramatically. The Taff Vale judgment by the House of Lords in July 1901 proved to be a turning-point, with union affiliations rising quickly to 626,000 by May 1902 and 847,000 by February 1903. The impetus to the growth of the LRC following the Taff Vale decision graphically underlined the way in which the trade union movement's links with politics were strengthened by attacks on its bargaining power. But this surge of support was still limited. The miners' union, the biggest in the country with over a third of TUC membership, was not affiliated and remained close to the Liberals. Less than 7,000 of the engineers' total membership of 85,000 participated in their affiliation ballot.[16] When the miners eventually affiliated in 1908, it was on a relatively narrow majority: 45 per cent of those voting were against.

· THE LABOUR PARTY TAKES ROOT ·

But support for an independent working-class party had deepened. The 1906 Trade Disputes Act, which overturned Taff Vale and gave unions new rights and immunities, did not check the rise in the number of affiliations. Still, the unions' ambivalence towards both political involvement and socialism remained. However much they agreed with independent political representation for their *union*, most workers then still thought of *themselves* as Liberals. Trade unions found a way around this, Keir Hardie maintained, by fixing 'upon a common denominator, that, when arguing in the House of Commons, they should be neither Socialists, Liberals, nor Tories, but a Labour Party'. Or as one historian aptly commented: 'The Labour Party represented a solution to the problem of party allegiances in that it distanced itself from existing political creeds and focused on labour representation as an end in itself.'[17] The 1906 conference of the LRC decided to change its name to the 'Labour Party', the choice of name being significant: the left wanted it to be called the 'Socialist Party', but most trade unionists 'wanted a name for the party which transcended politics'.[18]

· THE OSBORNE CASE ·

The unions had been using their 'general funds' to finance their affiliations and political activities such as securing parliamentary support. But the dominant class was becoming alarmed at the growth of the new political party. In 1904 a new Chief Registrar of Friendly Societies suggested that the promotion of labour representation in Parliament and other elected bodies lay outside the statutory definition of a trade union. This was followed by a number of court cases attempting to challenge unions' ability to spend their money on political activity.

These culminated in the momentous *Osborne* case preventing unions from financing political representation and activity from their general funds. The 1909 judgment handed down by the House of Lords was typically Delphic. The arguments given by their lordships owed more to the judiciary's hostility to working-class organization than to a fair interpretation of the relevant legislation on trade unions.[19]

Intense campaigning against the *Osborne* decision by the unions persuaded a Liberal Party anxious to retain workers' sympathy to bring in the 1913 Trade Union Act. This made provision for separate political funds from which union members could 'contract-out' if they did not wish to support their unions' political activities. (Other union expenditure continued to be financed from general funds.) Before a union could establish such a political fund it had to win an individual membership ballot. (A different procedure operates for actual affiliation to the Labour Party which can be done in accordance with unions' own rules, for example by a conference decision.)

Following the passage of the Act, the first political fund ballots took place in twenty-eight unions. These were conducted against a background of unprecedented industrial militancy, with strikes being denounced as acts of political subversion by government figures and a significant input of socialist activism in unions. Yet the first ballots under the 1913 Act showed the continuing weakness of trade union membership commitment to Labour and socialism.

Although there was a substantial overall majority in these unions for setting up political funds – totalling 605,437 in favour compared with 363,223 against – there were large 'no' votes in some unions. Furthermore, less than one third of the eligible membership actually voted, with some unions only achieving turnouts of 10 to 15 per cent.* This led to artificial levels of affiliation. For example, the 20,586 engineers voted 'yes' but their union affiliated about 120,000 to the Labour Party. The carpenters'

---

* However, it may be that the union membership levels claimed were higher than actually existed and that organizational weaknesses made it difficult to involve individual members in the ballots.

and joiners' 'yes' votes totalling 13,336 produced an affiliated figure of about 65,000. A significant exception was the miners who achieved a high poll and a reasonable majority.[20]

·CONSOLIDATION OF 'LABOURISM'·

Meanwhile working-class legitimacy was being strengthened, an indication of this being the Liberals' appointment of some 400 trade unionists to various public bodies or 'quangos' by 1912.[21] Then came the First World War which resulted instead in a consolidation of 'labourism' – of a more trade union and less socialist orientated working-class politics. The government needed union participation in the war effort and this had two important consequences. Unions were further co-opted into the system which in turn increased their public legitimacy. Afterwards the Webbs wrote:

Trade Unionism has ... won its recognition by Parliament and the Government, by law and by custom, as a separate element in the community, entitled to distinct recognition as part of the social machinery of the State, its members being thus allowed to give ... not only their votes as citizens, but also their concurrence as an order or estate.[22]

The war did have a radicalizing effect on many trade unionists, reinforcing their support for and role in the Labour Party: 'on the whole, the Labour Party was strong where trade unionism was strong and weak where trade unionism was weak'.[23] But the temporary collectivist policies used to solve wartime social and economic problems reinforced a labourist ideology which continued to dominate the political role of British unions.

Union leaders who were by now familiar with the corridors of power made explicit what had long been implicit in their organizations: a rejection of radical working-class politics in favour of a strict commitment to a parliamentary strategy of change. Labour's political and industrial leaders were 'equally determined ... not to stray from the narrow path of parliamentary politics'.[24] This was as true before all workers had the vote as it was afterwards, so that it had less to do with a commitment to *democracy* than to the virtues of the British parliamentary system.

It was perhaps not surprising therefore that the first Labour government elected in 1923 should take tough measures against strikers, such as the use of emergency powers against dockers and railwaymen. Few trade unionists seemed to expect that Labour's role in the 1926 General Strike should be more than marginal.* The party leadership's ambivalence was expressed by its leader, Ramsay MacDonald: 'I don't like it; honestly I don't like it; but, honestly, what can be done?'[26] In fact Labour's leaders 'had even less reason than their industrial colleagues to deplore the collapse of the General Strike, since it appeared to confirm the view . . . that in Parliament and Parliament alone lay the workers' salvation'.[27]

· CONSERVATIVE ATTACKS ·

Nevertheless, attacks on union rights to political representation showed that the labour movement was still seen as a threat to the Tories. The settlement around the 1913 Trade Union Act proved to be fragile. After the war, Conservative Party conferences passed motions in successive years calling for reforms of the system of union financing of politics, including substitution of 'contracting-in' for 'contracting-out' of paying the levy. Tory backbenchers pressed the matter in every parliamentary session between 1922 and 1925. As one Tory Cabinet minister recognized,

the major part of the outcry against the political levy is not motivated by a burning indignation for the trade unionist, who is forced to subscribe to the furtherance of political principles which he abhors. It is based on a desire to hit the Socialist party through their pocket . . . at least we should not delude ourselves as to our intentions.[28]

Tory leaders bided their time and, with the labour movement demoralized after the General Strike, introduced the 1927 Trade

* There is an uncanny similarity between the Labour leadership's attitude in 1926 and its reluctance to support the 1984–5 miners' strike.[25]

Disputes and Trade Unions Act which replaced 'contracting-out' with 'contracting-in'. It also prevented civil service unions from affiliating to bodies outside the civil service; part of the reason for this was Tory anger at financial support given in the General Strike by some civil service unions (none of them had actually gone on strike). As a result the Post Office Workers, the Tax Officers and the Civil Service Clerical Association were forced to disaffiliate from the Labour Party and wind up their political funds (they also had to withdraw from the TUC).*

While the Bill was passing through Parliament, the trade unions issued a May Day Manifesto explaining the threat to their members:

The Bill strikes a heavy blow at the political rights of trade unions ... The party of the rich is trying to cripple the party of the poor. A rich party financed by secret funds derived from the sale of honours and from large subsidies subscribed by wealthy men, is trying to disable a poor party which carries on its work by modest contributions from trade unionists.[30]

As the unions feared, the impact was dramatic. Between 1925 and 1938 the number of trade unionists affiliated to the party dropped from 75 per cent to 48 per cent of the total in the TUC, and between 1926 and 1929 the party's income dropped by a third; this was almost exclusively due to the Act.[31] If the levy on unions which remained affiliated had not been raised by a third and if the amount in union political funds had not accumulated during the war, then it is doubtful if Labour could have maintained its national organization intact and fought the following general election.

---

* The Post Office Workers did find ways of maintaining financial support for their sponsored Labour MPs and of channelling a little money towards the Labour Party. In 1930 the union set up a Direct Parliamentary Representation Society, with local 'centres' organized around its local branches and with annual meetings held at its annual conference.[29]

·LABOURISM IN THE 1930s·

But if the party lived to fight another day, the net result of this Tory attack was further to inhibit unions' readiness to interpret their role in political terms and to reinforce their predominant view that politics was something their representatives did on their behalf in Parliament rather than something integral to their own bargaining strategy.

Union sensitivity on their political activity was increased by further Tory attacks during the 1931 general election. And, in a manner which had echoes in the statements issued by Labour defectors to the Social Democratic Party in 1981, Ramsay MacDonald and his followers who split from the party in the 1931 crisis turned with venom on a union link from which they had been happy to benefit for decades. The former Labour Chancellor, Philip Snowden, accused the unions of being 'Labour's Little Lenins', claiming that the TUC had 'insisted on being the master' of the Labour government.[32]

Rather than reflecting an accurate picture of the unions' relationship with the 1929–31 Labour government, the extravagance of such rhetoric indicated the sense of pique felt by the defectors at the TUC's unwillingness to endorse the cuts strategy they had wanted to impose on the labour movement and the critique it produced of the bankruptcy of that strategy. If anything, the unions had become estranged from the government by its failure to repeal the 1927 Act (though as a minority administration it had some excuse for this) and by its failure to support the demands for better pay and conditions of various groups of workers, including miners, agricultural and textile workers, and weavers.

The rout of Labour at the 1931 election was to produce two broadly complementary effects. In the absence of a strong Labour parliamentary party the TUC leadership, notably Walter Citrine and Ernest Bevin, fashioned their own route to represent their interests directly to government. At the same time, they used their influence to try to establish control of the party, working partly through the National Council of Labour, a TUC–party liaison committee, which gained new authority.

The weakness of the parliamentary party created something of a vacuum which the unions tried to fill. Their bloc votes controlled the conference and, until 1937, the election of all members of the National Executive Committee. They sponsored thirty-five of the fifty-two Labour MPs and to a very large extent they initiated party policy development. Citrine, the T U C General Secretary, tried to clarify the unions' role in this situation, arguing that 'the General Council should be regarded as having an integral right to initiate and participate in any political matter which it deems to be of direct concern to its constituents', and he noted that

The G C . . . did not seek in any shape or form to say what the party was to do, but they did ask that the primary purpose of the creation of the party should not be forgotten. It was created by the trade union movement to do those things in Parliament which the trade union movement found ineffectively performed by the two-party system.[33]

Bevin put this even more bluntly, in a memorable speech to the 1935 Labour conference when he reminded delegates never to forget that their party had grown 'out of the bowels of the T U C'. In other words, so long as the party remained true to its birthright and reflected union interests, then union intervention in the party would be held in reserve. The problem arose when there was disagreement as to what exactly were the 'true interests' of the trade union movement. Then the careful distinction drawn by Citrine took on a different gloss, with many union leaders clashing with the left who accused them of class collaboration. Bevin retorted at the 1937 Labour conference that 'there are thousands of our members paying the political levy who are not conscious socialists', as he remonstrated with constituency party delegates.

Out of this tension the constituency delegates increased their power, winning both the right to vote for their own representatives on the party's National Executive Committee, and an increase in the number of these representatives from five to seven. The unions conceded these changes because they did not see them as a serious threat to their dominance of the party. By the end of the 1930s they had established a fairly firm grip on the party's policy-making process and its direction, with the left a minority force. If this was political trade unionism, it was hardly a radical challenge to the interests of the dominant class.

Furthermore, the 1930s were to emphasize a major feature of the unions' political role and their relationship with Labour in particular:

... whether under radical or moderate leaderships, whether engaging in syndicalist oratory or endorsing the mixed economy, unions have, save in exceptional circumstances, resisted political interference in their industrial autonomy ... Accordingly, the relationship between the party and the unions in the 1930s was a one-sided one ... the assertion of trade union control [over the party] was a gradual and halting process but at no point did the unions offer a share in industrial decision-making to the party, nor would they have entertained any such suggestion.[34]

This legacy holds the key to the politics of the labour movement and shows the extent to which unions, while being prepared to press their interests through their political arm, drew a firm line at any pressure in the other direction. They 'remained highly sensitive to what they regarded as political trespass by the party into their affairs; and in particular they resented those factions who wished to see the trade unions as political instruments'.[35]

Sometimes, however, this strict demarcation created a certain schizophrenia in members of the labour movement as they strove to wear the correct ideological clothing to fit their role for the occasion in question. As Attlee remarked: 'The same man in his capacity as a trade union official may take a slightly different attitude from that which he does as a member of the party Executive or Member of Parliament.'[36]

Whatever the nuances it contained, however, the essential pragmatism and parliamentarism of the unions' relationship with the party was cemented in the 1930s. Most unions with political funds had set them up immediately after the 1913 Act, but more continued to affiliate so that by 1939 over 200 had balloted and only thirteen had failed to obtain a majority for establishing a political fund.[37]

·THE SECOND WORLD WAR AND AFTER·

The Second World War created a new collectivist consensus favourable to the advance of labourism: the unions' participation in the war effort enormously enhanced their legitimacy within the established system, and thus their right to political representation. Although Tory agitation against the union–Labour link continued immediately after the war, the breadth of the consensus was shown by the conciliatory response from Churchill in the 1951 election campaign. While he did not regard as 'fair' the 1946 Trade Disputes and Trade Unions Act which Labour introduced to repeal the 1927 Act's bar on civil service unions and to switch back to 'contracting-out', he argued:

the Conservative and Liberal membership of the trade unions is growing so steadily, that a wider spirit of tolerance has grown up and the question may well be left to common sense and the British way of settling things.[38]

Of course the 1945–50 Labour government had done much to create this consensus too, by not going back to the pre-Osborne situation where unions did not need separate political funds. It accepted a middle way, for example rejecting an amendment in Parliament which would have enabled unions to transfer money from their general to their political funds.

Nevertheless, the 1946 Act proved immediately beneficial to the labour movement. The proportion of members in unions with political funds paying the political levy quickly rose from 48 per cent to 76 per cent: the change from 'contracting-in' to 'contracting-out' produced an extra two million contributors to the unions' political funds, an increase of about 25 per cent.[39] Between the end of the war and the end of Labour's period in office in 1951, the proportion of TUC members affiliated to the Labour Party had risen from 36 per cent to 63 per cent.

· POST-WAR LABOURISM ·

The numbers of trade unionists affiliated continued to rise in the 1950s – reaching its highest point in 1957 at 6.5 million or 68 per cent of TUC members. However, this was a decade for steady consolidation rather than spectacular advance. Union legitimacy was increased, militancy was largely restrained in a period of economic expansion, and influence on the Labour Party remained much in line with the principles reinforced during the 1930s.

The period was marked by deep left–right divisions within the labour movement: between the Bevanites and the old guard who included most union bosses. This was a conflict which went beyond the confines of party policy determination, touching on the heart of the relationship between Labour and its affiliated unions. The Bevanites angrily attacked the 'travesty' of the union bloc votes at party conferences, Aneurin Bevan claiming in 1954 on behalf of the left: 'Do not let the union leaders think that they alone speak for their members. We speak for them as much as they do.'[40] In one notable incident during the 1952 party conference, the right-wing leader of the National Union of Mineworkers, Sir William Lawther, shouted 'Shut your gob' at constituency party delegates.[41]

A more intellectual right took control of the party, supplanting the pragmatists of the Attlee era, and a 'revisionist' phase was ushered in. Hugh Gaitskell was elected leader in 1955 and Anthony Crosland's *The Future of Socialism* was published in 1956. Both men sought to shed Labour's traditional socialist goals and its 'cloth cap' image, arguing that a class-based analysis of British society was obsolete. There was debate among political scientists about 'the end of ideology', and Tory governments during this period seemed to share with Labour's right a belief in a new consensus. Although real differences remained, the Tories too were committed to full employment and the welfare state, and they did not challenge the post-1945 settlement on unions' rights of political representation.

The continuing Cold War and the exposure of the many crimes committed in the name of socialism by Stalin further served to isolate the left. Indeed, this was a time when the right seemed to want to drive the left out of the party. The powerful union-dominated National Executive Committee (NEC) was used as a virtual thought-police, with Nye Bevan and Michael Foot cast as the principal villains. The fact was that most large unions opposed the left because it challenged some of the traditions of labourism (though, unlike the 1980s, the 1950s Labour left was strictly parliamentarist).

But the unions' position was adopted more out of loyalty to the parliamentary leadership than for explicitly right-wing ideological reasons. The rationale for their behaviour was illustrated by their reaction to 'revisionism': basically they were uneasy about it. Although their hostility to the left continued, the new theories of revisionism, particularly the criticism of unions, cut across the traditions of the old Labour–union alliance.

In 1959 Gaitskell was defeated in his attempt to expunge the party's commitment to public ownership in Clause Four of the Constitution. Trade union opposition to his move was decisive. But although there had been hesitant signs of a shift in the unions' position, symbolized by the election of a left-winger, Frank Cousins, to the leadership of the TGWU in 1956, in reality 'union opposition to amending Clause Four represented the innate conservatism and sentimentality of the union leadership. They opposed the "revisionists" as they opposed the Bevanites because they were initiating change, and unsettling the party's traditions.'[42]

In other words their 'voluntarist', collective-bargaining traditions were threatened by 'revisionism'. When it came to reversing the 1960 party conference decision favouring unilateral nuclear disarmament, this was an issue outside the boundaries of their industrial role and union policies were changed more out of loyalty to the party leadership than anything else. That year, 1961, the dominant strand of union ideology was reasserted with a statement familiar in its tone: 'The TUC did not and could not start its examination of any problem as a Socialist, Liberal, Conservative or Communist. We start as trade unionists and we end as trade unionists.'[43]

But as the post-war boom began to ebb, the British economy entered a period of 'stop–go' and governments began to concentrate increasingly on the cost of labour in their economic policy equations. Holding down wages became a key part of the strategy of successive governments, Tory or Labour, drawing unions into the centre of political controversy and policy determination.

The Macmillan government inched towards planning of incomes, and in 1962 the Tory Chancellor, Selwyn Lloyd, introduced a 'pay pause' with a 'guiding light' of 2.5 per cent for wage rises. Though non-statutory, such tentative moves towards formal incomes policies posed a direct challenge to trade union autonomy and to free collective bargaining. In addition, union immunities were undermined by the courts in a case in 1964 known as *Rookes v. Barnard* in which the law lords ruled that unions could be sued for taking industrial action under the obscure tort of intimidation. This was a further example of the judiciary reinterpreting the law in a manner hostile to strikers (Parliament was forced to reverse the judgment in the 1965 Trade Disputes Act). With such attacks on their interests, the unions were encouraged to increase their contribution to Labour Party funds in the 1964 election; it jumped by 84 per cent over the previous election (compared with a 15 per cent rise in inflation over the same period).

·UNIONS AND LABOUR GOVERNMENTS·

But if the unions hoped that the election of Labour in 1964 and its re-election in 1966 would put an end to government pay curbs they were to be disappointed, for Harold Wilson's administrations went further down the road to controlling wages. The result was to force unions out of their preferred position in the shadows of politics and into the open, where they found themselves in conflict with Labour governments they had helped to put into office.

In 1965 Labour set up the National Board for Prices and Incomes (PIB) with trade union support. However, when the PIB was given compulsory powers to control wage increases, there was an open breach with the Transport and General Workers'

Union in particular. Its leader, Frank Cousins, who had been brought into the government as Minister of Technology, resigned in protest.

As wage restraint policies followed throughout the 1960s, the unity of the labour movement began to crack. In 1968 motions opposed to wage restraint legislation were moved by Frank Cousins at both the TUC and Labour Party conferences. They were overwhelmingly passed, by 7.7 million to 1 million votes at the TUC, and by 5 million to 1 million votes at Labour's conference despite strong opposition from the party Establishment. Some local union branches disaffiliated from the party, and in 1966 there was the biggest drop in numbers paying the political levy since 1928 (the year after 'contracting-in' had been introduced).[44] Although Labour's total vote rose by over a million and its share by 4.3 per cent in the 1966 election, the number of *trade unionists* voting Labour did not rise (since there had been an increase in total union membership, the proportion of trade unionists voting Labour actually *fell* by 2 per cent from 1964).

Many party members and trade unionists took the view that the Wilson government was pursuing an economic strategy little different from a Conservative one. The Labour Cabinet's apparent belief that strikes were at the root of Britain's economic problems provoked additional stresses and strains. In January 1969 the government proposed major new controls on unions and strike procedures in its White Paper *In Place of Strife*. There was a storm of protest from the TUC. Even union leaders on the right, such as the engineers' leader Jim Conway, believed the penal clauses proposed sounded 'the death toll of British trade unionism, they drive a wedge between the Labour Party and the trade unions'.[45]

The Labour–union alliance faced its most serious crisis since 1931 and eventually pressure from the unions and the party forced the government to back down and withdraw its plans. Commentators at the time spoke of unions as 'dictators' imposing their will on an elected government. In reality, 'The unions' desire was not to unseat the government, but to maintain the voluntarist system [of independent collective bargaining] intact.'[46]

The unions had always had some ambivalence towards Labour governments, from the first one of 1924. This was partly because, as J. R. Clynes, the Labour Lord Privy Seal, expressed it, Labour had to play 'the part of a national government, and not of a class government'.[47] Such a view came to characterize all subsequent Labour governments – Harold Wilson said much the same thing in 1966[48] – and it meant they had a basic conflict of interest with the unions.

In February 1924 the Labour government threatened to use troops and made preparations to use the Emergency Powers Act to resolve a strike by 110,000 dockers. The government's intervention eventually led to a settlement without the use of force. But Ernest Bevin, who was leading the negotiations for the Transport and General Workers' Union, expressed his frustration at Labour's role: 'I wish it had been a Tory government in office. We would not have been frightened by *their* threats. But we were put in the position of having to listen to the appeal of our own people.'[49]

Many union leaders in the 1960s felt the same, and there is no doubt that, while the trade union movement continued to give support to Labour in the 1970 general election, the return of the Wilson government was not anticipated with the burning enthusiasm apparent in 1964. In the event the Tories won.

The problems between the unions and the 1960s Labour governments both highlighted a basic contradiction in their relationship, and encouraged the leftward shift within the party in the 1970s.

· UNIONS AND LABOUR IN THE 1970s ·

With Labour now in opposition, the unions were determined not to repeat the experience of the 1960s. Most were flatly opposed to statutory incomes policies and this ensured that the party drew back from such an approach to economic management. There was equal determination to prevent any resurrection of the kind of proposals *In Place of Strife* had contained.

Consequently the unions, with positive proposals of their own, moved more firmly to shape party policy than at any time since the 1930s. But if such intervention was motivated by an anxiety to ensure that their 'own' government did not again challenge their traditional bargaining stance, another major factor involved was the anti-union programme of the 1970–74 Conservative government. Its 1971 Industrial Relations Act went much further down the road of government regulation of strikes and unions than Harold Wilson's 1969 proposals.

A new Labour Party–TUC Liaison Committee was established in January 1972, bringing together senior members of the TUC General Council, the party's National Executive Committee and Labour's Shadow Cabinet. This was the most formal tripartite representation of the industrial, political and parliamentary wings of the labour movement in one body since the National Council of Labour had been reconstituted in the wake of the 1931 election defeat. And it ensured that the party went into the 1974 election on the basis of a so-called 'social contract', under which a far-reaching programme of pro-union legislation would be introduced in return for union cooperation over general economic policy. Wages policy was glossed over, Labour's leader, Harold Wilson, saying that part of the agreement included a 'mood rather than a contract' for wage bargaining and the TUC promising to 'respond' positively.[50]

But by 1975 the failure to stick to the radical economic strategy in Labour's election manifesto forced the government into conventional remedies to combat soaring inflation. With the agreement of the TUC, two years of 'voluntary' pay policies, limiting increases to £6 weekly and then 5 per cent between a minimum and maximum of £2.50 and £4.00, were introduced. A third year imposing a 10 per cent limit, though not agreed formally by the TUC, was unofficially accepted. But meanwhile the pressure was building up. Revolts by British Leyland tool-makers in 1977 and 1978 highlighted the grievances of skilled workers who saw their differentials being squeezed by flat-rate incomes policies. The unprecedented strike by fire brigades workers in 1977 was a warning of looming public-sector unrest.

In 1978–9, the lid blew off when Labour tried to impose a

fourth year of pay restraint, this time against the steadfast opposition of the TUC. Tens of thousands of low-paid public service workers joined better-off lorry drivers, Ford car workers and others in a spate of strikes which eventually paved the way for the collapse of the government's credibility and its subsequent defeat by Mrs Thatcher's Tories in 1979.

The failure by the two wings of the labour movement to implement the common political strategy which had seemed to be agreed prior to 1974 resulted in electoral humiliation – including a serious loss of trade union voters. It also produced a shift in the balance of power within the party in which the unions played a significant role.

·UNIONS AND LABOUR'S 'NEW' LEFT·

In 1970 the left had seen the defeat mainly as a failure of *policy*. There was a widespread feeling in the constituencies that the Wilson governments had effectively adopted the policies of the 'revisionists'. Specific union disenchantment with the industrial policies of the Wilson governments also rebounded against the right of the party which was seen as largely responsible, having been the dominant force in those governments.

The left was therefore in an advantageous position to capture the initiative and appeal to the unions for support. Helped by the more progressive leaderships in the TGWU and the Amalgamated Union of Engineering Workers, the left captured a majority on the National Executive and pushed through the radical new policies contained in *Labour's Programme 1973*. These emphasized new systems of planning, democratic control and public ownership, as well as the repeal of the Tory Industrial Relations Act and comprehensive new rights for workers. The left's advance was also assisted by a background of confident extra-parliamentary trade union resistance to Tory rule, exemplified by defiance of the 1971 Act, by the 1972 miners' strike and by the release of the Pentonville dockers after widespread national strikes had been threatened.

But the 1974–9 Labour government quickly departed from the main planks of its left-leaning economic programme. By the time of its defeat, the fact that it had carried through far-reaching and unprecedented pro-union legislation as promised was buried beneath a mood of retribution about its confrontation with the unions over wages.

By now the constituency-based left did not see as its major obstacle the *policy* one identified after 1970. The policies upon which Labour had fought in 1974 were the left's policies. But the parliamentary leadership had not appeared to believe in them, let alone fight for them. The major problem was therefore seen as the lack of *democratic accountability* of the leadership, and it was decided to rectify this by constitutional changes to extend democracy within the party.

The left was able to construct an alliance based on *political* disillusionment in the constituencies and *industrial* disillusionment within the unions to win major reforms. These gave constituencies the right to change their MPs through mandatory re-selection and the right of the whole party, not just MPs, to elect the party leader and deputy. Furthermore, unlike 1979, Labour fought the 1983 election on a left-wing manifesto.

Undoubtedly, the left's steady advance through the 1970s – culminating in a position of 'stalemate'[51] in the balance of power inside the party after 1981 – was dependent on union support. And to an extent this was forthcoming because of an advance of the left inside the official structures of the unions themselves. Nevertheless extravagant claims made by right-wing critics and some on the Labour left of a major shift inside the unions were mistaken.

Although for a specific and limited period after the 1979 defeat more unions were prepared to back radical left positions, the votes which carried the reforms were still close. The tenuous basis of the left's strength was reflected both in the switch in control of the party's National Executive towards the right from 1981 and the growth of 'new realism' inside the TUC. It was also evident in the failure to mobilize extra-parliamentary action among rank-and-file workers to resist the strident anti-unionism of the

Thatcher government. True to their roots, the unions' role in this period sprang primarily from an *industrial* perspective influenced by unhappy experiences with Labour governments rather than any sudden lurch towards a left-wing ideology.

· THE 1984 TRADE UNION ACT ·

To a large extent Labour's 1979 and 1983 defeats exposed the illusion of a strong 'politically motivated trade unionism'. Indeed, the way was opened for the Thatcherites to attack the links between the unions and the party.

The 1984 Trade Union Act contained perhaps the most serious challenge to the labour movement's unity and strength this century. Following restrictions on the right to strike in the 1980 and 1982 Employment Acts, the 1984 Act marked a fresh step in the Thatcherite project to alter the balance of class forces in Britain.

It required unions to win an *individual* ballot of their members, first by March 1986 and at ten-yearly intervals thereafter, in order to retain their political funds and their party affiliation.

Furthermore, the new Act threatened even those unions without political funds. Their right to conduct public campaigns was challenged by updating the definition of 'political objects' originally contained in the 1913 Trade Union Act. That had allowed unions to use their *general* funds for campaigning activity of a broadly political kind, provided its 'main purpose' was to pursue unions' 'statutory objects' (i.e. members' industrial or economic interests). But under the new Act such activity had to be financed out of *political* funds if its 'main purpose' could be shown to be to persuade people either to vote or not to vote for a political party or candidate.

As the TUC pointed out, this left 'a number of grey areas concerning what may or may not be interpreted as party political expenditure'. For example, on the eve of the 1983 general election, the National Association of Local Government Officers (NALGO) ran a campaign which included very effective national newspaper advertisements against government public-spending cuts. Such action could have been stopped under the new Act, admitted a government junior employment minister during its committee stage in the Commons, because NALGO had no political fund. So could union campaigns against privatizing local council services, especially if these encroached upon the run-up to a local election.

In short, if any public initiative by a union could be construed as influencing support for or against a party – even if it happened to form the government of the day – then it could be caught by the legislation. This could only be avoided by unions having political funds and by financing such campaigns from them, which has rarely been the practice, since political funds have been directed almost entirely at supporting the Labour Party.

·POLITICAL FUNDS·

In 1983, forty-seven unions affiliated 6.1 million members to the party and contributed £2.9 million out of their political funds – nearly 80 per cent of the party's national income.

Having a political fund does not mean that unions are automatically affiliated to the Labour Party, though almost all have used theirs to do so. Establishing a political fund requires by law an individual membership ballot – deciding to use that political fund to affiliate to the Labour Party is a separate decision which can be taken according to unions' internal democratic procedures. When their union affiliates to the party, people contributing to the political fund through their regular union contributions become 'affiliated members'. 'Full members' join their local Labour Parties directly, though there is considerable overlap and most 'full members' are 'affiliated' through their unions as well.

By means of this affiliated status, unions are able to use their political funds to support the Labour Party, and in return are given rights and representation in the party's decision-making structures, the most visible of which is the wielding of union bloc votes at annual party conferences according to the number of members they have affiliated.

·A TACTICAL SWITCH·

The Tory right had begun to question the system of union affiliation to Labour with increasing regularity after Thatcher's 1979 election victory. A broader consensus for this position emerged in 1981, when the formation of the Social Democratic Party produced a barrage of criticisms from its leaders against the union link. In the autumn of 1982, the SDP published a document entitled *Reforming the Trade Unions* which attacked 'contracting-out'. Then the Tories issued a consultative document in January 1983. Entitled *Democracy in Trade Unions*,[52] it signalled the Thatcher government's intention specifically to legislate on the political levy, rather as in 1927.

In fact, the Act made no mention of the method of paying the political levy. Instead the government negotiated an agreement with the TUC under which 'contracting-out' remained, but unions promised to make more effort to inform members how to opt out. This was greeted by the Tory right as a considerable government climb-down, while many in the trade unions saw it as a victory secured by reasonable negotiation. In fact the switch in tactics brought several advantages for the Tories.

The 'compromise' stood a better chance of completely cutting the unions off from Labour and crippling the party financially. It deflected the charge of discrimination: of imposing restrictions on unions funding Labour while leaving untouched company financing of the Tories. But, perhaps most important, it put the labour movement on the defensive; by giving members the right to vote on a political link decided by their union generations ago, the Tories were able to disguise their attack on the link as an *extension* of democratic rights in unions. Even though their appeal to 'union democracy' was hypocritical – for example, it did not operate in GCHQ – the Tories struck a popular chord when they complained about the gap between the leaders and the led in the trade union movement. The Thatcher government had demonstrated some skill in exploiting this – its management of industrial relations resting in part on appealing through the media over the heads of union officials to individual members. And the system of individual balloting specified in the 1984 Act increased their opportunity to do this.

· 'AMERICANIZING' BRITISH POLITICS ·

However, the 1984 Act was not simply a punitive measure against an electoral competitor or an act of malice against trade unions. It was conceived as part of a much more ambitious political project designed to undermine the established institutions of the labour movement and thereby create a radically different political and industrial structure in Britian.

After the 1983 election, with Labour having just scraped into second place in the popular vote, political commentators began to canvass the prospect of the Alliance becoming the major Opposition. Reflecting the views of the business world, the *Economist* advocated 'a non-socialist, or barely socialist, opposition as the main alternative to the Tories'.[53] At the same time, Mrs Thatcher herself gave an interview to the *Director* magazine. Citing the USA as an ideal, she said she favoured two major British political parties operating 'within the same framework of free enterprise'.[54]

The objective was clear: to make Britain 'safe from socialism' by reducing Labour to a rump leftist group, with the implicit assumption that the SDP/Liberal Alliance would take its place. Just in case there was a temptation to dismiss all this as the fashionable talk of the 1983 summer, the Tory Chairperson, John Selwyn-Gummer, repeated the argument a year later. Discussing America's party system, he said: 'It is very valuable to have two sensible parties that both support capitalism. We have suffered in Britain from having the Labour Party.'[55] Around this time a conservative political columnist, Ronald Butt, echoed the same view: 'To become a significant political force, the Social Democrats must take and keep more votes from the Labour Party, aiming ultimately to replace it . . . it would be for the health of the nation to have a social democratic rather than a socialist party as the principal alternative to the Tories.'[56]

The new Tory right had become alarmed at the leftward shift in the Labour Party in the 1970s and the potential threat to their interests from a left Labour government. Restructuring the British party system to minimize this danger became about as important as retaining office, especially since it was a strategic ambition of Thatcherism to destroy the post-war social democratic consensus and replace it with a Thatcherite consensus. Achieving that ambition in turn required a different political system to support the new consensus, and because Labour would refuse to go along with this, Labour needed to be marginalized.

· 'AMERICANIZING' BRITISH UNIONS ·

In parallel with this 'Americanization' of British politics has been a desire to 'Americanize' British unions too. The Thatcherites persistently criticized 'politically motivated' trade unionism, contrasting this with a desirable form of trade unionism in which defence of sectional interests is the guiding principle. The influential Tory minister, Norman Tebbit, became fond of reminding the public of his role as a trade union negotiator in his previous career as an airline pilot, where he 'stood up for his members' interests', while simultaneously criticizing union leaders for playing a political role through their influence in the Labour Party.

The 'business unionism' practised widely in the USA is attractive to the Thatcherites, both because it de-politicizes trade unionism and because it is less militant. They have encouraged 'no-strike' agreements and look favourably upon any initiatives in that direction. Leaders of the Amalgamated Union of Engineering Workers (AUEW) and the Electrical, Electronic, Telecommunication and Plumbing Union (EETPU) have obliged by promoting 'no-strike' deals, especially in 'sunrise' industries and at new Japanese electronics and car manufacturing plants. The EETPU actually applied to affiliate to the Confederation of British Industry in 1984 (though they were not accepted) and invited Norman Tebbit to open a new training centre in 1985.

The Thatcherites had also become increasingly concerned at the rise from the late 1960s onwards of a more campaigning style of unionism, notably in the public sector. Unions like the National Union of Public Employees (NUPE), NALGO and the Post Office Engineering Union (POEU) sought to defend their interests by going outside the traditional territory of free collective bargaining to mobilize public support. Such campaigns were directly opposed to a central objective of Thatcherism – reducing the scope of the public sector – and the 1984 Act was intended to limit their effectiveness. The redefinition of 'political expenditure' under the Act meant that unions without political funds could be prevented from financing campaigning activity on issues of public policy.

· RECOMPOSITION OF CLASS ·

A greater opportunity was presented to the Thatcherites to carry through their attack on the political unity of the labour movement by its failure to adapt to post-war changes in the class system. This recomposition produced important changes in the class make-up of unions, notably the growth of white-collar and public-sector TUC members. But the link with the Labour Party was not kept in harness with these changes and, by the late 1970s, the trade union movement was divided almost evenly between 'Labour trade unions' and 'non-Labour trade unions'.

Between 1957 and 1977, for example, the proportion of TUC-organized trade unionists affiliated to the Labour Party declined from about 70 per cent to 50 per cent. (Over a longer time-span the picture is even more dramatic, since the proportion of TUC members in the party stood at 93 per cent in 1913.) From 1964 to 1979 – a period when Labour was in power for all but four years – TUC membership shot up by 46 per cent, but the number of trade unionists affiliated to the Labour Party rose by only 18 per cent (see Table 1).

The fall in TUC union membership of the party reflected itself electorally, too. In 1964, 73 per cent of trade unionists voted Labour; in 1966, 71 per cent; and in 1970, 66 per cent. By 1974

Table 1   *Recent Labour/TUC membership changes*

| | Percentage increase in trade union members since 1964 | |
	Affiliated to Labour	Affiliated to TUC
1966	0.7	6.5
1970	0.3	12.9
1974	5.2	20.1
1979	18.3	45.7

this had fallen to 55 per cent, by 1979 to 51 per cent, and by 1983 to just 39 per cent. The overall shift in trade union voting is illustrated in Table 2.

Table 2   *1964–83: How trade unionists voted (percentages)*

	1964	1966	1970	1974	1974	1979	1983
Labour	73	71	66	55	55	51	39
Tory	22	25	28	30	23	33	32
Others	5	4	6	15	16	13	28

If the actual numbers of trade unionists voting Labour over this period is taken, the picture is quite stark: between 1964 and 1983 the number dropped by 2 million while the number of TUC members rose by 2 million. In addition, closer inspection of the nature of Labour's affiliated trade union membership hardly suggests a fighting force for socialism: in 1983, for instance, about 3.3 million trade unionists voted Labour – 2.7 million *fewer* than the party's affiliated union membership (see Table 3).

Table 3   *Voting and affiliated membership (millions),
with percentage of total TUC membership*

	Trade unionists voting Labour	Trade unionists affiliated to Labour
1964	5.3 (73%)	5.5
1966	5.3 (71%)	5.5
1970	5.1 (66%)	5.5
1974	4.8 (55%)	5.8
1979	5.3 (51%)	6.5
1983	3.4 (39%)	6.1

·WEAKNESS OF LABOUR–UNION LINKS·

Thatcherism's instinct that the Labour connection with the unions was vulnerable is underlined by evidence that rank-and-file trade union support for the party is much weaker than is often assumed by those active in the labour movement.

For instance, a 1974 study of a major union, the Union of Post Office (now Communication) Workers, showed massive member ignorance and lack of interest in the political activity of their union.[57] Only half of those paying the political levy realized they were doing so. There is no reason to suppose that this was untypical of the movement as a whole.[58] The traditional practice in most unions of making it hard to 'contract-out' amounted to a short-term expedient which encouraged a passive political relationship with rank-and-file members, and therefore one susceptible to being undermined.

The evidence suggests that throughout the post-war period – and quite likely before then as well – apathy about politics was normal in local union branches, with political discussion at meetings very rare and then almost exclusively about the Labour Party.[59] This was even the pattern at the time of a general election. During the 1964 election, for example, less than 2 per cent of union members could recall a union representative approaching them and asking them to vote.[60]

Additionally, unions became less influential and less active within local parties. This was partly a demographic problem: unions with the strongest Labour ties historically tended to be those based mainly around urban areas with close links between industries and communities. Their connections with the party were quite strong for cultural and geographical reasons – the miners are the classic example. But these (mainly manual manufacturing) unions were declining in numbers and influence, while others (mainly white-collar and public-sector) were growing. Furthermore, 'Whilst it is clear that there are mining constituencies, and may once have been "railway" constituencies, or "engineering" towns, it is doubtful whether there are ASTMS cities, or NUPE counties.'[61]

There has also been a declining proportion of party activists from manual unions, and a predominance on constituency General Committees (GCs) of members from white-collar or public-sector unions sometimes not affiliated to the party. This has meant that constituency parties steadily have become more culturally and politically distant from their union base.

In any case, very little life has flowed through the system of union affiliation to these GCs. (GCs are the main decision-making bodies of local parties and consist of delegates from ward branches and from affiliated groups such as local branches of unions nationally affiliated to Labour.) Many affiliated union branches have found it hard to persuade one of their members to be their delegate to the local GC. In the 1950s there were cases of communists and even a Tory councillor being approached to be delegates because nobody else could be persuaded.[62] Frequently Labour Party activists become union delegates on GCs because they cannot get elected from the local branch of their party.

Even bona fide union delegates tend to be divorced from the mainstream of union branch life. The evidence suggests that such trade union delegates to GCs 'are often more "political" than their branch members, since many industrially active members have little time for political activities too'.[63] It is rare for GC delegates to report party decisions back to, or get mandates from, their union meetings, often because crowded agendas leave no time for discussion like this which is not seen as central to the branch's activity. There are exceptions, of course, but the general picture is one in which the local union connection is a paper one: 'Many a local Labour Party carries out its work in isolation from the organized trade union movement and the mainstream of trade union thought.'[64]

In real terms, unions are mainly bound to the party *nationally* by financial links and by the direct representation which they have on Labour's National Executive and at annual conference. The base of their political involvement has been neglected. Even then, the situation at national level remains far from satisfactory.

The role of sponsored MPs used to be at the heart of the link with the Labour Party: these MPs acted as their unions' political representatives and tended to speak mainly or only on industrial matters in Parliament. This did not mean that the MPs' relationship with their unions was free of problems; indeed at least one union was 'unable to define clearly what they expect MPs to do'.[65] But gradually their role evolved into a more independent one, so that by the 1950s, 'Once the spearhead of his union's industrial–political activity, the trade union MP now stands on the side-lines.'[66]

Additionally, there has been little membership participation in union decision-making on Labour Party policies. The leaders, national executives and party conference delegations of unions have almost always taken the initiative, invariably determining the line adopted. When the results are reported back to annual union conferences, 'All too often political issues are discussed at the end ... when delegates are racing through the agenda, speakers are limited to three minutes, and debate is discouraged.'[67] Nor has this occurred, as right-wing union critics suggested, because of a deliberate attempt to exclude the membership from participation in determining their organization's political policies. On the contrary, many union leaders would welcome the chance to have full debates at annual conference. The problem is rather a product of the 'de-politicized' nature of unions and the priority given to bread-and-butter issues.

The net result has been not simply to offer a series of *political* hostages to fortune, but almost to invite criticisms of the *democratic* legitimacy of union members' link with Labour. This link is in truth an ossified one, held together by historic institutional ties. The absence of opportunities for rank-and-file – as opposed to activist – participation became a major handicap as the labour movement found itself under political attack, especially in the 1970s and 1980s.

Ironically, however, the 1984 Act did the labour movement something of a back-handed favour. By instituting a political fund ballot it effectively encouraged political activity and discussion within trade unions, and this could well prove a positive consequence of the legislation. By forcing unions to win arguments to retain their political funds, it forced union officials to give priority to political education which, instead of being a luxury option, started to become a necessity. And by altering the definition of political expenditure it encouraged unions traditionally opposed to having political funds to try to set them up – which is the first step towards recognizing a more political role, even if it does not initially result in affiliation to Labour. And finally, by giving rank-and-file members a chance to participate directly in a key political decision, the Tories opened the way to much more active and democratic support for Labour in the working class.

The first major organization to ballot under the 1984 Act, the printers' union SOGAT '82, voted by three to one to retain its political fund, with a high turnout of 57 per cent. Another bonus, SOGAT officials admitted, was that the ballot campaign 'forced the union to rediscover itself: in some areas the union found little organization at all below branch committee level. The vote forced on the union has made it strengthen itself by finding its roots again at workplace level.'[68] Soon afterwards the Union of Communication Workers won with a three to one vote – almost identical to their previous vote in 1946 but, on a turnout of 69 per cent, nearly twice as much.

This early momentum continued, with other unions notching up even bigger victories (see Table 4). *Every* union won its ballot comfortably. Significantly, two new political funds were established when both the Inland Revenue Staff Federation and the Hosiery Workers voted overwhelmingly in favour. The turnouts were generally very high and the results far surpassed those achieved when most unions first established their political funds seventy years before. Despite the post-war erosion of support for Labour among trade unionists, members were effectively asked in these ballots to show loyalty to their unions and to defend their right to a political voice. There was also evidence that the membership resented the one-sided way in which the legislation left company contributions to the Conservatives untouched. Most unions ran well-organized campaigns with professionally produced literature urging a 'Yes' vote. The government (and indeed many of those within the labour movement who had been pessimistic about the outcome) clearly

Table 4   *Political fund ballot results 1985–1986*

	Turnout (percentage of membership)	Yes	(percentage)	No	(percentage)
SOGAT '82	57	91,760	(78)	25,947	(21)
ISTC	68	28,633	(87)	4,404	(13)
FTAT	30	11,410	(72)	4,269	(28)
UCW	69	102,546	(76)	33,337	(24)
NCU	79	77,183	(81)	17,757	(19)
GMBATU	61	448,426	(89)	54,637	(11)
APEX	60	39,465	(73)	14,380	(27)
BFAWU	62	19,954	(90)	2,237	(10)
AUEW (ENG)	37	238,604	(84)	44,399	(16)
EETPU	45	140,913	(84)	26,830	(16)
NUR	61	71,907	(87)	10,580	(13)
PLCWIWU	89	2,242	(75)	697	(25)
ASLEF	85	19,110	(93)	1,491	(7)
NUS	34	6,179	(87)	963	(13)
TSSA	67	22,975	(69)	10,017	(30)
CERAMIC TU	73	17,967	(77)	5,383	(23)
SCALEMAKERS	54	460	(77)	135	(23)
TGWU	51	511,014	(81)	119,823	(19)
COHSE	40	81,012	(91)	7,731	(9)
NTGW	87	52,634	(91)	4,968	(9)
NUDAGO	68	2,388	(84)	439	(16)
Blind DL	83	2,218	(90)	221	(9)
NUFLAT	84	20,956	(77)	5,963	(22)
USDAW	40	134,952	(88)	17,824	(11)
ACTT	49	7,149	(59)	5,043	(41)
NGA	72	68,559	(78)	18,931	(22)
TWU	76	7,790	(90)	905	(10)
NACODS	76	9,930	(87)	1,481	(13)
TASS	55	91,389	(76)	29,467	(76)
NUPE	59	329,442	(84)	60,332	(16)
RUBSSO	40	1,244	(78)	358	(22)
GUALO	92	928	(84)	176	(16)
MU	37	10,492	(76)	3,237	(24)
NUM	76	96,226	(90)	9,958	(10)
FBU	87	30,607	(80)	7,652	(20)
ASTMS	40	102,236	(81)	23,996	(19)
UCATT	30	56,733	(92)	5,295	(8)

Two non-fund holders voted 'Yes' for the first time:

NUHNW	90	35,017	(83)	6,616	(83)
IRSF	87	39,776	(82)	8,862	(82)
Total		2,957,235	(82)	656,534	(18)

misjudged the position; what had been a serious attack rebounded, with the labour movement's confidence enhanced.

The unions jointly formed and funded a Trade Union Co-ordinating Committee for the ballot campaign. It had an initial budget of £150,000 and agreed in consultation with Labour Party leaders on a 'rolling programme', with unions holding their own ballots consecutively between March 1985 and March 1986. The TUCC produced professionally designed publicity material for unions to use or adapt. It also provided a forum for tactics to be discussed and agreed.

In keeping with their traditions, almost all the unions concentrated entirely in their ballot campaigns on the advantages of having political representation of their *industrial* interests through their own voice in Parliament. The question of the Labour Party was deliberately played down, even by left-wing-controlled union executives like the National Communications Union (formerly the POEU). Some on the left argued that the opportunity should be taken to argue the case positively for Labour and for socialist ideas.[69] But the only major union to make the Labour link more of an 'up front' issue in their campaign was the National Union of Public Employees.

· BRITISH UNIONS AND POLITICS ·

The assertion that British unions are political beyond the call of their industrial interests is simplistic. The picture is a much more complex one and there is certainly no evidence for claims that strikes are in general called for political rather than industrial reasons.

The main motivation has remained the defence and advance of unions' ability to engage in free collective bargaining.[70] Unions in Britain have tended to adhere to what has been described as 'voluntarism', namely: 'preference for free collective bargaining as opposed to state legislation; complete autonomy for the parties; and a non-legalistic type of collective bargaining'.[71] It follows that trade union political activity must be seen in terms of the defence of the doctrine of voluntarism: and ... union–party relations must be considered within that context ... when governments have no longer been prepared to accommodate to the voluntarist ideology of the trade union movement ... unions have extended their political activity both in its scope and content. The defence of voluntarism has provided the dialectics of change both within the movement, and within the state.[72]

In many ways the union role is best understood as that of a *pressure group* rather than a direct participant in politics in its own right. Obviously such a role is more easily facilitated through the link with Labour, but it has not ruled out political representation independent of Labour. It has also meant a 'stand off' stance in relation to political action in general, in which politics becomes something others engage in through Parliament.

Furthermore, although unions may play a political role by exercising influence inside the Labour Party, they deny the right of party members to exercise any political influence back into their unions *as party members*; such influence should be exercised through the 'proper channels', in their capacity as individual members of their union. This 'one-way street' politics imposes another major obstacle in the way of a successful socialist strategy which presupposes a direct link between political action through the Labour Party and industrial action through the trade unions, linking parliamentary politics with extra-parliamentary action.[73]

Unlike other socialist groups in Britain – the Communist Party and the Socialist Workers Party, for instance – Labour has no industrial organizer and the party has not normally campaigned on behalf of a union on strike; it remains to be seen whether the unprecedented support work organized by local parties around the 1984–5 miners' strike will have any long-term effect. The distinct lack of enthusiasm shown by union organizations for the idea of Labour Party 'workplace branches', officially endorsed by the party in 1982, should perhaps have come as no surprise. Despite this, by 1985 over a hundred workplace branches had been established through local initiative; reports suggested they had some success in drawing more workers into Labour Party involvement, though many branches had difficulty in sustaining momentum and interest beyond a year or two, partly because they lacked the institutional support of the party and the unions nationally.

A key characteristic of the labour movement has been the demarcation between what is seen as the 'industrial' and the 'political', creating a false division:

A *de facto* division of 'labour' exists between trade union leaders and leaders of the Labour Party. The task of the former is to deal with those industrial and workplace matters that concern trade unions as such: wages, conditions of work and so on. The task of the latter is to ensure adequate Labour representation in Parliament and to engage in matters of government . . . Extra-parliamentary activity, including trade union activity, becomes relatively de-politicized; and political activity becomes focused on events within Parliament.[74]

The labour movement's legacy of pragmatic parliamentarism encouraged union leaders to turn up to Labour Party conferences, become politicians for a week, and wield their bloc votes almost in isolation from their membership. It was said even of the socialist leadership of the 'new unionism' at the end of the last century that 'the leader had to be a trade unionist first, and a socialist in his spare time'.[75] That became more so as the decades rolled by, except that a commitment to 'labourism' rather than 'socialism' became increasingly evident.

From their beginnings there has been an insistent belief that unions 'were not to be instruments of political change. The lobbying of Parliament and the recruitment of political allies was legitimate; extra-parliamentary agitation was not . . . a highly peculiar definition of politics . . . that has traditionally been associated with conservatism: people who were prepared to accept the status quo and work within it for piecemeal reform were not political; people who wanted to overturn the established order were . . . "politically motivated".'[76]

The unions originally won their members' agreement to affiliate to the Labour Party more because of the external climate of hostility, including events such as the Taff Vale decision of 1901, than the arguments of socialist activists in their ranks. Unions which did not affiliate then subsequently found it more and more difficult to achieve affiliation. Ballots by NALGO in 1982 and the Civil and Public Services Association (CPSA) in 1983 showed majorities of eight to one and two to one respectively against establishing political funds and Labour links. (The forerunner to the CPSA had in fact been affiliated before the 1927 Act barred this.) The only major new affiliation since the war was that of the Post Office Engineering Union, which won a political fund ballot in 1964. (It, too, had been affiliated before 1927.)

The absence of consistent socialist education inside union structures and at workplace level proved to be a serious problem in retaining working-class support for the Labour Party and for its policies. The fact that all unions overcame the hurdles erected by the 1984 Act to maintain their *political funds* does not mean that they would have won individual membership ballots to maintain their *Labour Party affiliation*.

Nor does it mean that the attack on Labour–union links has ended. As overwhelming 'Yes' votes mounted up, frustrated Conservatives, Social Democrats and the Institute of Directors called for the introduction of a system 'contracting-in' to paying the political levy such as existed between 1927 and 1946.

Mrs Thatcher's Ministers had maintained a relatively low profile during the ballots, though they did criticize unions for failing to emphasize the Labour Party dimension. They were also openly hostile to attempts by Civil Service unions to set off political funds in order to defend their ability to campaign on public issues. But public criticism by Ministers of the Inland Revenue Staff Federation seemed to have the opposite effect when its members favoured setting up a fund for the first time with an 87 per cent 'Yes' vote in March 1986.

· DEMOCRACY ·

Far more legal restrictions have been placed on *labour* than on *capital* in supporting the political party of its choice. Companies make considerable donations to the Conservatives (and latterly to the Liberals and the SDP) without having to consult their shareholders, and without the necessity for a political fund separately financed from their general income. Not only is Labour discriminated against in this way, but it also suffers by receiving far less in financial support from unions than the Conservatives obtain from company donations. In the 1983 general election it was estimated that the Tory Party had between £15 and £20 million available to it, while the comparable figure for Labour was £2.5 million.[77]

The way in which British politics developed during this century meant that the Labour–union connection became a central cog in the country's system of liberal democracy, because it facilitated relatively free competition between parties by supporting a major opposition to the Tories, with (until recently) a two-party system reflecting the class structure. As has been argued,

the fact remains that no other organizations have appeared in British society which have emerged from the lives of [workers] . . . and which try actively to prosecute an interpretation of their interests where these conflict with others in the society. To advocate the end of all links between the Labour Party and the unions is nothing less than to advocate the end of political pluralism in Britain, for there is no other social cleavage within the society to support a major degree of party competition than that which is represented by the conflict between organized labour and capital.[78]

Defence of Labour's historic link with the trade unions is thus a defence of *democracy*. But whether this can be transformed and become the instrument for the advance of *democratic socialism*, as the left has argued from the beginning, will depend on unions becoming more 'political' in their daily activity.

A NEW UNIONISM

'Unions and strikes are "old-fashioned", relics of a bygone age of "real" class politics', was the increasing cry from media commentators and politicians on the right and centre during the Thatcher era. They seemed to have forgotten that this sort of thing had been said before.

An influential book published in Britain in 1961 argued that unions had 'an increasingly dated, "period" flavour. The smell of the music-hall and the pawnshop clings to them, and this more than anything else alienates the middle classes and the would-be middle classes from them.'[1] As a prediction it proved to be completely wrong. Although TUC membership had remained virtually stagnant between 1950 and 1960 (the proportion of the workforce in unions actually fell from 44.1 per cent to 43.1 per cent), in the following two decades the 'middle classes' joined as never before and union membership rose to its highest-ever level. The fact is that unions have enjoyed troughs and peaks of membership throughout their history, in accordance with the environment in which they found themselves.

'The strike has been going out of fashion', argued a 1960 study of strikes in fifteen Northern European countries, including Britain, in the 1950s; it also predicted the 'withering away of the strike'.[2] In fact this proved to be wrong for every one of the countries surveyed, including Britain where days lost through strikes in the 1960s and 1970s reached some of the highest levels ever.[3]

So long as class divisions remain and with them inequalities in the ownership and control of capital, strikes will continue to occur. The threat to withdraw their labour is the ultimate sanction workers possess, and consequently strikes are an essential means by which the working class defends its interests and seeks to improve its position. As one study shows, 'in the broad sweep of social history there is little doubt that strikes have contributed positively to the nurturing and sustenance of trade union organization, to advance wages, and to wrest more democratic controls over working conditions and managerial decision-making, throughout industry'.[4]

From their beginnings trade unions have played a crucial role in improving the general living standards and conditions of working people. They have maintained labour's share of national income, despite the crisis of profitability British capital has experienced during the last thirty years in particular.[5] They have achieved increases in earnings, reductions in working time, improved holidays, better pensions and allowances, higher health and safety standards, and a workplace environment in which workers' rights could be defended against arbitrary decisions of management.

During the 1970s a more progressive trade unionism started to emerge. Although the pace of change remained slow, the needs of women workers at last began to be taken more seriously. For example in 1975 the public-sector manual workers' union NUPE commissioned an independent study of its structure, as a result of which changes were made to give positive encouragement to women who formed the majority of its members but who were badly under-represented in decision-making positions within the organization.

The white-collar union ASTMS made the running on health and safety issues, especially in 'new technology' industries. Most public-sector unions began to organize campaigns in defence of public services, rather than relying simply on bargaining with their employers. The Transport and General Workers' Union and the National Union of Seamen blacked dumping of nuclear waste at sea. Post Office workers tried to black mails and operator-controlled telephone calls to South Africa in a week of protest against apartheid in 1977. Much of this activity represented a blurring of the divide between industrial and political action.

However, these considerable advances and achievements

obscured a number of problems which the trade union movement did not really tackle and which left it exposed to the new right's attack when it came in the 1980s. The first batch of problems concerned the changing nature of union membership and social base; the second involved the reappearance of historic weaknesses.

·CHANGES IN UNION MEMBERSHIP·

By 1979–80, trade union membership in Britain had reached its highest-ever level, both in absolute and relative terms. Over 12 million workers were affiliated to the TUC and the proportion of the labour force organized by unions stood at an historic high-point of 55.4 per cent – a higher figure than any other Western country of comparable size.

The big surge in membership occurred between 1969 and 1979, when some 3.2 million workers joined unions. Reasons for this included the relative success of union bargaining, the ability to strike effectively, and worker anxiety at rising inflation after the 1973 oil crisis. Perhaps the most important factor was the new legislation introduced by the 1974–9 Labour government which enormously boosted union recognition, organization and recruitment. But 85 per cent of the new members recruited in this 1969–79 period worked in already well-unionized areas of manufacturing industry and the public sector.[6] Effectively, there-fore, unions consolidated their support in their *existing base*. They were less successful in the poorly organized areas of construction, agriculture, distribution, hotel and catering and other service industries, and still less in the 'sunrise' sector of 'new technology' industries.

Then between 1980 and 1984 unions lost an average of 500,000 members a year; the total TUC membership in 1985 fell to 9.9 million – the lowest since 1972. The collapse of manufacturing industry in the Thatcherite era (especially in such traditionally well-organized areas as shipbuilding, engineering and metal trades, and textiles), together with the

squeeze on the public sector, were particular factors in the decline of unions.

The restructuring of production has also undermined union
power. This was built in Britain's industrial heartlands, specifically in the strongholds of the North and generally in the cities.
Since the 1960s, however, capital, industry and population have
moved out of the city centres to the suburbs and beyond to
country towns. This dispersal of manufacturing industry has
complicated the process of creating trade union solidarity, which
has traditionally been forged around factories in the big conur-
bations with their workers living nearby.[7] The trend has been for
unions to be more isolated in areas with no strong working-class
tradition. One study showed that industry's shift from the old
strongholds of union activism in the big cities to smaller towns
was part of 'capitalist restructuring' to avoid conditions where
labour militancy could thrive: 'It's better here. It's a different
type of labour . . . It's about being able to manage,' explained one
manager.[8]

This geographical diversification of British industry has been
accompanied by industrial diversification, with firms having
plants on many different sites, often making a variety of products.
Although ownership of manufacturing industry has been concentrated in fewer and fewer companies, these giants are not to be
found in one place: they spread their activities around. Many are
foreign-owned, so that key managerial decisions may be taken
outside the country. In addition, new technology has reduced the
need for labour and has made it possible to have small plants,
which has not in the past produced strong unions.

The labour movement's traditional strength was based in the
old heartlands and the sense of community which grew up there
was important in creating the kind of class solidarity needed to go
on strike against formidable odds. Although the mining communities were always unique in the closeness of the bond between
their pits and the villages around them, their strength was based
on something much more than their industrial muscle, as the
former miners' leader Will Paynter made clear in his description
of the South Wales miners in the 1930s:

It was a lot more than a trade union; it was a social institution providing through its local leaders an all-round service of advice and assistance to the mining community on most of the problems that could
arise between the cradle and the grave. Its function became a combination of economic, social and political leadership . . . After all, these
communities existed in narrow valley concentrations, were dependent
upon a pit for their existence, and were tightly bound together by this
common interest.[9]

It was notable that the South Wales area was the most solid in
support of the 1984–5 miners' strike, the residue of that strong
community solidarity still persisting. Other pit areas, though being
much more tightly-knit than is generally the case in Britain today,
had experienced a sharper fragmentation of their once-strong
communities.

·CLASS CHANGES·

As would be expected, the restructuring of the British economy
has resulted in a re-composition of the working class. The post-
war decline of the manufacturing sector, accelerating rapidly in
the Thatcher years, reduced the number of manual workers, so
that they now form under half of the workforce (the proportion
was 80 per cent in 1911). In parallel there has been a significant
growth of white-collar and public-sector workers, and this has
been reflected in the composition of the trade union movement.
Another important trend has been the steady rise in women's
employment. The number of married women going out to work
rose from 10 per cent in 1931 to 42 per cent in 1971. In the
growth decades of trade unionism in 1960–80, while male
membership rose by 18 per cent, women's membership jumped
by 110 per cent.

   The scale of the change is illustrated by comparing the character
of trade union membership in the mid 1970s with that in the mid
1980s. The total remained the same at 10 million (having risen to
12 million in 1979 and then fallen). But within that unchanged
total there were:

- one million more white-collar members, and one million fewer blue-collar members;
- 700,000 more members working for local and national government, and half a million fewer members in traditional heavy industries;
- half a million more women and half a million fewer men;
- one million more home-owners and one million fewer council and private tenants.[10]

But the labour movement did not keep abreast of these changes in the working class. It remained overwhelmingly orientated, in its priorities, policies and organizational style, towards the male manual worker in manufacturing industry. Not surprisingly, therefore, its ability to deliver class solidarity on the basis of an obsolete class appeal became increasingly problematic, with obvious consequences for strikes.

· WOMEN ·

Women now constitute one in every three trade unionists, but union organizations have until comparatively recently only paid lip-service to their rights and grievances. For much of their history, unions excluded women from membership. Although the TUC adopted an equal-pay policy as long ago as 1888, union collective bargaining gave no priority to its implementation. For a long time male workers resisted equality – they were even prepared to strike occasionally against women being brought in to do 'men's' work because they believed this would be used to undermine their own conditions.[11]

During the 1970s some progress was made by women workers in terms of pay and job rights – though it was patchy and the recession later undermined much of it. But the evidence suggests that this was mostly achieved by legislative changes, particularly the 1970 Equal Pay Act and the 1975 Sex Discrimination Act.

Women were prepared to strike, however. One example was the four-month strike in 1976 at the West London firm of Trico. The employers had been able to win a case against equal pay at an industrial tribunal, but the workers refused to accept this and went on strike, forcing the women's claim to be conceded. The Grunwick workforce which went on strike in 1976 contained a majority of women, and there was a breakthrough during mass picketing of the factory in 1977 when miners and other male trade unionists linked arms with feminists, 'many of whom had never before been involved in industrial action'.[12] In 1981, women successfully occupied the Lee Jeans factory in Greenock to maintain their jobs. In 1984–5, women cleaners went on strike at Barking Hospital in East London over an attempt by a private contractor to cut their hours by 41 per cent. Although they maintained a picket line for over a year and produced their own 'workers' plan' for domestic services at the hospital, they were unable to win the strike. In 1984, women sewing-machinists at Ford's went on strike and eventually won the full equality which had just eluded them during their famous strike in 1968.

For the most part, however, union collective bargaining priorities did not alter noticeably to reflect women's needs and their growing importance in the unions. The idea of the 'family wage' – that men require a wage large enough to support a family whereas women's wages merely supplement family income – still dominates collective bargaining. Yet fewer than one in five male workers is now the sole breadwinner. One child in eight lives with a single parent, usually a woman. Women's wages form an increasingly important part of family incomes – in their absence, at least a further million families would be forced below the poverty line.[13]

Women invariably have a quite different perspective on bargaining priorities. They do not necessarily share the traditional concentration on wages: reduced working time, more flexible hours, part-time work, job-sharing and child-care facilities are more important. Most unions retort that their long-term objectives include achieving these aims. But collective bargaining priorities are determined by pressure from within unions, and the most immediate and vociferous pressure comes from male activists who virtually always choose a wage increase above improvements in conditions of the type women need.

Women remain badly under-represented within union decision-making structures from local to national level, their interests are not given a real priority, and few hold high office.[14] They are subject to sexual harassment within their unions, the style of male-dominated branch meetings is alienating, and the timing and venue of branch meetings is frequently inconvenient for women with domestic responsibilities.

It is important to note that women workers are concentrated in jobs which unions have traditionally found hard to organize.[15] Over half women manual workers are cleaners, caterers, hairdressers and service workers, and 40 per cent of all women are part-timers. Many white-collar women workers are in jobs in the private sector where there is little or no union tradition.

The position of women also has significant implications for traditional methods of bargaining and strike action, as one study points out:

> Trade unions have a highly masculine image in the public mind. Men in overalls, men shouting on picket lines, men in suits talking on the television, miners with blackened faces ... Women are invisible ... There are two assumptions behind the image. There is the idea that what men do is 'real' trade unionism. Also, many people think that militant action is the most important sign of a strong trade union.[16]

The argument here is *not* that militancy is an inherently male phenomenon. It is firstly that women are mostly in jobs which lack the industrial muscle and economic power to make strikes effective, and secondly that the masculine image and *style* of trade union bargaining is a tough, aggressive one with which women do not identify. A trade union strategy which gives a disproportionate emphasis to *traditional* strike action may therefore be unable to mobilize the women who make up a third of union members, or appeal to the 60 per cent of all women workers who still need to be recruited.

Low-paid workers (who by the early 1980s numbered over 7 million, or 30 per cent of those employed) have also consistently lost out through traditional union collective bargaining strategies. The majority are women and their position has deteriorated as

they have found themselves disproportionately hit by the taxation system. The labour movement has ducked the problem of
low pay, only recently moving towards policies, such as a statutory minimum wage, which might overcome it. Black workers,
too, have grown in numbers, yet have found themselves under-
represented in their unions, with racism remaining a serious
problem in practice despite the trade union movement's opposition to it in principle. They experience higher levels of unemployment and those in work are trapped in the worst-paid
jobs.

·UNIONS AT THE CROSSROADS·

By attacking it politically, Thatcherism reopened traditional
questions about the role and purpose of British trade unionism.
The Thatcherites set out to 'Americanize' Britain's trade union
movement, either by limiting its role to purely sectional bargaining or by removing any perceived need for unions at all.
This provoked two main responses. The trade union right
pressed through the TUC for a 'new realism', which emerged
clearly after the Tories' 1983 election landslide and which was
directed at the art of the possible in the face of a powerful,
rejuvenated and uniquely hostile government. The traditional
union left vigorously reasserted the virtues of free collective
bargaining.

Although attractive to most of the left and axiomatic to some,
the commitment to what may be described as old-style free collective bargaining reproduces many of the problems which have
traditionally dogged the British trade union movement. It appears
a strong and effective weapon for the *defence* of the interests of
union members. But its capacity to *advance*, especially in the face
of a direct political challenge, can be severely limited. To argue
for more 'left-wing policies', more traditional bargaining, more
vigorous leadership in response to the Thatcherites and the new
realists is inadequate:

If trade unionism does not evolve in the direction of larger social ambitions, demanding the pursuit of wider goals, there is no evidence at all that it will be allowed to linger on in its present state, defensively adapting itself to conditions which no longer correspond in the slightest degree to those with which it was designed to contend.[17]

Those words were written in 1971, and proved remarkably prophetic. Going even further back, to 1886, the words of Tom Mann seem just as relevant a hundred years later:

To Trade Unionists, I desire to make a special appeal. How long, *how long* will you be content with the present half-hearted policy of your unions? I readily grant that good work has been done in the past by the unions, but in Heaven's name, what good purpose are they serving now? All of them have large numbers out of employment ... None of the important societies have any policy other than of endeavouring to keep wages from falling. The true unionist's policy of *aggression* seems entirely lost sight of; in fact the average unionist of today is ... hopelessly apathetic, or supporting a policy that plays directly into the hands of the capitalist exploiter.[18]

The key weakness of British unions is thus their lack of a coherent *political* strategy. As they developed, they had a narrow conception of political change being won mainly through parliamentary procedures. Even when they formed the Labour Party, they saw their political interests being advanced and defended largely through Labour representatives in Parliament. There was a reluctance to mobilize trade unionists themselves in a strategy of active political struggle which complemented the fight in Parliament.

In practice, the left has offered what amounts to a more vigorous version of this traditionally defensive approach. While correctly stressing the importance of wage struggles and wage militancy, the trade union left has rarely gone beyond this. Even the shop stewards' movement after the First World War – though the shop stewards constituted a powerful group strongly influenced by socialists – was hidebound by tradition. Its collapse, said G. D. H. Cole, had much to do with its failure to shift its attention from the shopfloor upwards to 'the higher reaches of control ... especially the control over investment'.[19] More recently, as Tony Benn argues,

wage claims alone – however successful – do not necessarily alter the balance of power in industry. High wage settlements can be neutralized by inflation, offset by redundancies or clawed back in taxation, while industrial and political power remain in the same hands. Trade unionism confined narrowly to wage claims can become something of a dead-end. Moreover, because industrial disputes about wages involving the withdrawal of labour are essentially negative in character, they may not always command wholehearted support amongst the workforce and may alienate public opinion, without getting to the root of the problem, which is the uneven distribution of power between capital and labour.[20]

Hyman adds in his major study, *Strikes*: 'It is therefore difficult to imagine that strikes could ever spontaneously develop into a mechanism of open assault on managerial authority, let alone broader political authority. If workers' struggles should acquire a higher rationale than they at present possess, they would almost certainly need to transcend purely industrial forms of organiza-tion.'[21]

The limitations of traditional wages militancy have also been underlined by the experience of disadvantaged groups, notably women, the low-paid and black people. *Traditional* wages mili-tancy has been a male strategy from which women workers have benefited hardly at all.[22] Similarly, the low-paid (mostly women as well), who are badly organized and neglected by the trade union movement, have found their interests consistently taking second place to higher-paid workers, particularly those with the in-dustrial muscle which the low-paid do not possess.[23]

Unions, partly through strikes, have more than held their own over the years and that has been a considerable achievement. They have successfully defended their members and have made gains when economic conditions permitted. They have contested management's 'right to manage' and their strength has prevented a serious erosion of working-class living standards, even during the Thatcher years. But they have not challenged the basic power structure of industry. On the contrary, the share of wages in national income has remained roughly constant for the last hundred years, and there has been little redistribution in the ownership of capital this century.[24]

There are many on the left who have elevated wage struggles and strikes as the supreme strategy for socialist transformation, in a syndicalist fashion. But in Britain strikes have primarily been instruments of *economic defence* rather than of *political advance*. As the Marxist scholar, Perry Anderson, pointed out:

The trade union's . . . maximum weapon against the system is a simple *absence* – the strike, which is a *withdrawal* of labour. The efficacy of this form of action is by nature very limited. It can win wage increases, some improvements in working conditions, in rare cases some constitutional rights. But it can never overthrow a social regime. As a political weapon, strikes are nearly always profoundly ineffectual . . . The strike is fundamentally an economic weapon, which easily boomerangs if used on terrain for which it is not designed.[25]

It is important to recognize that strikes are overwhelmingly acts of last resort by unions defending their interests. With very few exceptions, unions have only indulged in industrial action when their rights are under attack or when they have exhausted normal negotiating procedures. Furthermore, they have rarely set an alternative agenda for how their industry should be run. Claims for better conditions are usually set within traditional boundaries. For example, demands for higher wages are pursued with relish, while potentially more important issues such as investment decisions are regarded as management's responsibility. British unions have been insular, cautious and fairly conservative. As one industrial relations study put it:

Trade unions may be a force for progress, but in their actual functioning they are, in the literal and unusual meaning of the word, 'reactionary' bodies. They react very closely to their members and their members in the main react to their everyday industrial experience. That is how union traditions have been formed over the years to express the lessons of group experience.[26]

A shop steward at Vickers explained: 'At the moment we just react [to company decisions] and it's usually too late.'[27] Or, as the

TUC General Secretary, Len Murray, said in the 1970s, 'We have always been very good at stopping what we don't like, but not at starting anything.'[28]

·ECONOMISM·

Strikes which remained 'economistic' – that is to say, concerned with sectional issues of wages and workplace conditions alone – were relatively successful in the growth period of the 1960s and early 1970s. Even strikers who were defeated sometimes found that they benefited subsequently: for instance, Post Office workers were driven back after their seven-week strike in 1971, only to be granted a special pay increase in 1974 which effectively settled their grievances. But as economic crisis closed in, union militancy had to be resisted uncompromisingly. When the Thatcherites made union militancy a political issue and turned major strikes into political ones, unions found themselves badly placed to protect themselves.

A study by the Department of Employment showed that strikes between 1966 and 1976 were overwhelmingly concerned with pay,[29] and, in an important article in September 1978 entitled 'The Forward March of Labour Halted?', the Marxist historian Eric Hobsbawm pointed to the fact that trade union militancy at the end of the 1970s had become increasingly 'sectional' and 'economistic' in character.[30] There had been a decline in class consciousness and the grip of sectionalism and economism actually undermined class solidarity, helping to pave the way for the victory of Thatcherism in 1979. As research into police trade unionism showed, it is

important to distinguish between *industrial* militancy and class consciousness in a wider sense. Despite the apparent radicalism of the slogans that may accompany militancy over essentially narrow, economistic demands, it is quite possible for workers to combine militant trade unionism or industrial action with wider social and political attitudes and practices of a conservative or even reactionary character.[31]

The argument here is not one antagonistic to wage struggles. They remain major vehicles to defend working-class interests. Most wage claims and struggles implicitly concern job control, and to the extent that they limit the accumulation of capital at the expense of labour, they can have important political consequences too. The left argument [32] that workplace wage struggles are part of the 'daily struggle for power' by the working class is therefore valid. The problem is that, although 'economistic' and 'political' activities are inextricably linked in principle, in practice they remain segregated because neither wing of the labour movement has made bridging the ideological gap between them a priority. Thus workers involved do not see their own interests within a broader context. [33]

There has been too ready a tendency by Labour's right to disparage wage militancy, particularly when it upsets their policies in government. For example, Ramsay MacDonald wrote in 1924: 'Strikes for increased wages ... not only are not socialism, but may mislead the spirit and the policy of socialism.' This is wrong. The real issue is the *limited nature* of the trade union movement's almost entirely economistic tradition of collective bargaining and, when it breaks down, strike action. Lenin described the inability of 'economism or "strikeism" ' to alter the structure of industrial power. [34] As a strategy it has been only partially successful and remains continually vulnerable to a political attack.

There is an alternative which maintains an *absolute commitment* to independent trade union bargaining, wage struggles and militancy where appropriate, but which supplements it with other strategies; together they constitute a 'new unionism'. But before discussing this it is necessary to examine other obstacles preventing the advance of the trade union movement.

Although many on the left seem at times obsessed with blaming 'compromises' and 'betrayals' by union *leaders* as the major reason why greater political advances have not been made, this does not stand close examination. [35] The very structure and character of the British trade union movement has discouraged the kind of *class solidarity* between trade unionists necessary to make political advances.

·SECTIONALISM·

A key problem is the sectionalism which has dominated the trade union movement since it was formed by skilled craft workers anxious to preserve their own status. This was displayed, for example, by the failure of attempts to bring together workers from different trades into one union in the early 1830s. In 1829 a National Association for United Trades for the Protection of Labour was formed and at one stage attracted affiliations from 150 societies spread over twenty trades, with a total membership of 100,000. But it quickly disintegrated, the real problem being

the incoherent market structure of the industries in which the affiliated trade societies were operative. Each of the various societies had, understandably, joined with the large body in the belief that it would get support from other workers for its struggles. When the National Association found that a large proportion of its constituents all needed to fight at the same time it found its task impossible. Not only did the various sections not understand the complexity of the environment in which they collectively worked, but market circumstances ensured that operatives, far from making their own initiatives, were forced to respond to those of their employers. Such was the diversity of trades, and the diversity within trades as between localities, that sectionalism and in-discipline rather than strategically planned action became the dominant mode of activity.[36]

Another attempt during the 1830s to overcome sectionalism was the formation of the Grand National Consolidated Trade Union (GNCTU) by followers of one of the early English socialists, Robert Owen. It had a radical programme for the re-placement of capitalism by a cooperative system under workers' control, indicating that some trade unionists at least saw the need to build a broader class consciousness to improve their strength. It emphasized the importance of *solidarity* between different groups of workers in struggles. But this brave attempt was short-lived and the GNCTU disintegrated into its constituent trades again.

During the period between 1850 and 1890, as unions spread

and their organization developed, power started to be concentrated in central union leaderships, and rank-and-file members reacted by asserting their parochial interests. This 'localist' reaction occurred in the absence of a strong socialist or class perspective which might have provided an alternative vehicle for grass-roots disquiet at bureaucratic centralization to express itself. And the legacy of that period is still very much with the trade union movement today:

That the working class was divided into a large number of competing sectional groups meant that working-class organizations had failed to overcome *politically* what were *economic* facts. This is to say that sectionalism was the direct outcome of a labour market differentiated by industry, by variations among firms within industries, and by the division of labour within particular workplaces ... the division of labour within the national labour market ensured sectionalism between broad industrial groups, the division of labour in a workplace ensured sectionalism between groups housed under the same roof.[37]

The lack of a broader political dimension which could have given workers a sense of common class interest meant that

the collectivity of producers was dissolved into a fragmented mass of consumers where the individual was exalted. Thus strikes were often as bitterly denounced from within the working class as from without: a strike of one section inhibited the ability of others to consume. And the fact that today's complainants were often tomorrow's strikers seemed in no way inconsistent ... [because] one group of workers could affect the ability to consume of other groups, the others had little choice but to emulate them if they wanted to retrieve their situation.[38]

This phenomenon has been especially divisive in the public sector, which experienced an unprecedented wave of strikes in the 1970s. Strikes in the 1978-9 'Winter of Discontent' could easily be portrayed as the product of union 'self-interest' and 'callousness', even though the workers involved were among the poorest in the country, and their militancy sprang from the failures of Labour's incomes policy. This was because it was fellow members of the working class who were most badly hit: people, especially the old, who could not afford private treatment and depended upon strike-hit hospitals; parents (mainly women) penalized by striking caretakers closing schools and teachers refusing to supervise lunches. Savings could actually be made by local health and council services from unpaid wages, releasing the pressure on public finances and managers. The dilemma for public-sector trade unionists is that, while strikes are aimed at those in authority, it is working-class people most dependent upon state services who suffer most from their withdrawal.[39]

To point out these consequences of strikes by public employees is not to deny their *right* to strike. Nor is it to ignore the conditions which often leave them with no alternative but to take industrial action. It is rather to underline the consequences, as Hobsbawm points out:

... it now often happens ... that the strength of a group lies not in the amount of loss they can cause to the employer, but in the inconvenience they can cause to the public, that is, to other workers ... This is a natural consequence of a state-monopoly capitalist system in which the basic target of pressure is not the bank account of private employers but, directly or indirectly, the political will of the government. In the nature of things such sectional forms of struggle not only create potential friction between groups of workers, but risk weakening the hold of the labour movement as a whole.[40]

Conscious of the dilemma they face, health service unions adopted 'selective strike' tactics in the national NHS dispute in 1982. The same approach was adopted by teachers in 1985. Civil service unions in 1981 concentrated on pulling out key computer staff in order to disrupt the government machine. But the dilemma is not simply one for public-sector workers. Since they now constitute about half the TUC's membership, the whole trade union movement has been affected.

Most workers today seem to have an 'instrumental' view of trade unionism. They support their own trade unions and are prepared to push hard for their own wage increases, sometimes to the point of striking themselves. But they are antagonistic to other workers' unions, frequently regard other workers' pay claims as greedy and are quick to condemn disruption by other workers' strikes. Opinion polls conducted by MORI in the early 1980s showed that a clear majority of members were 'satisfied' with the job being done by their own trade union leaders, but thought that 'most unions' (presumably other people's) were 'controlled by a few extremists and militants'.

There have been repeated instances of the grip of sectionalism being broken. For example, the triple alliance of rail, steel and mine workers after the First World War did present a stronger and more united front to the government. And miners joined picket lines at Grunwick in 1977 and in the 1982 health workers' dispute. But these instances have been relatively rare.

Perhaps the best modern example of the potential of inter-union solidarity was the strike action undertaken after the imprisonment for contempt of court of five London dockers in a dispute over 'containerization' in the summer of 1972. They were eventually released after other workers had either gone on strike or threatened to do so. The day before their imprisonment, the dockers had been involved in a bitter sectional dispute with lorry drivers who were actually members of the same union. Dockers' pickets had been stopping lorries at container terminals and the drivers retaliated by picketing docks in protest. But the day the dockers were jailed, the drivers called off their action and decided to support the dockers. The action of the government had turned the dispute into a political conflict which threatened the interests of every trade unionist. In the face of this common threat and, crucially, the willingness of unions to react in an essentially political fashion, sectionalism dissolved and the strikers were victorious.

· UNION CO-OPTION ·

Another barrier to a more progressive and political trade unionism is the extent to which unions have been absorbed into capitalist modes of production so that they perform functions compatible, rather than in conflict, with it. The progress of capitalism in the nineteenth century increasingly required a workforce which was stable and which bargained within routines that were orderly. Unions could assist with that objective since they substituted bureaucratic systems of industrial relations for situations that were unstable and prone to spontaneous strikes.

Back in 1869, the minority report of the Royal Commission on unions concluded that the effect of unions was generally

to diminish the frequency and certainly the disorder of strikes and to guarantee a regularity of wages and hours rather than to engage in constant endeavours to improve them . . . It appears that the strongest, richest and most extended of all the unions are to be found in those trades in which the wages and the hours of labour show the greatest permanence, and in which on the whole the fewest disputes occur.[41]

Other evidence supported that general proposition as the century drew to a close. And in 1912, a Conservative leader, Bonar Law, echoed this: 'I should like to see the trade unions become stronger, because I think that, as a rule, they tend to the diminution of disputes.'[42] At a time of great industrial crisis in 1919, Bonar Law told the Cabinet that 'trade union organization was the only thing between us and anarchy, and if trade union organization was against us the position would be hopeless'.[43]

Studies by political scientists and sociologists after the Second World War showed how unions could become 'managers of dis-content' and 'serve to integrate their members into the larger body politic and give them a basis for loyalty to the system'.[44] This occurred because of the institutional role of unions under British capitalism and it was assisted by the 'co-option' of union leaders into the Establishment. The labour correspondent of *The Times* wrote in 1961 that they 'had become part of the body of the state . . . instead of, as they once were, something outside the state and in some senses a rival power'. He added: 'Belonging as they now did implied loyalty.'[45]

This was especially true of the TUC which, ever since it was formed in 1868, had sought a close relationship with governments and employers, and frequently acted to dampen down worker militancy and strikes, well-known examples including the 1926 General Strike and the 1983 Stockport Messenger strike. Nor have union officials been co-opted at national leadership level alone. Even during the 1960s, a period in which shop stewards exercised considerable power, the Donovan Commission reported:

... it is often wide of the mark to describe shop stewards as 'trouble-makers'. Trouble is thrust upon them ... shop stewards are rarely agitators pushing workers towards unconstitutional action ... Quite commonly they are supporters of order exercising a restraining influence on their members in conditions which promote disorder.[46]

Consequently, private capital has adopted a contradictory attitude towards unions. On the one hand, union *militancy* is a threat and strikes have to be opposed or legally curbed. On the other, strong union *organization* has certain very real advantages to employers. Union discipline provides a means of dealing with the workforce as a whole and avoids having to negotiate contracts with individual workers. They provide information about workers' intentions and beliefs which would otherwise have to be researched. The relatively relaxed attitude towards the closed shop taken by the Confederation of British Industry, despite the bitter opposition to it by the Thatcherites, illustrates this employer ambivalence. Another contradictory view is the periodic one that unions are too powerful. As one study argued, 'critics of unions ... cannot have it both ways. If they want the unions to be strong enough to maintain the peace by controlling members' behaviour, they should not complain of excessive union power.'[47]

Unions have been intrinsically liable to co-option. It is not primarily a question of 'sell-outs' by leaders. For unions 'do not *challenge* the existence of a society based on a division of classes, they merely *express* it ... By their very nature they are tied to capitalism. They can bargain with the society, but not transform it.'[48]

· UNION ORGANIZATION ·

Reflecting capitalist society as they do, British unions have tended to have similar hierarchical structures which have been obstacles to membership participation, even if the members (in turn social- ized by the society to be passive) actually want to be active in the first place.

Union branch meetings are poorly attended. On average less than one tenth of union members now turn up regularly to branch meetings – roughly 2 per cent of the national electorate. The most active members form an even smaller proportion, so that their claims to represent the working class can be questioned, especially since only a half of workers are registered union members. When it comes to undertaking strike action this problem can become acute, and certainly acts as a brake on union militancy.

But there is no evidence that indirect democracy based on individual member ballots will make much difference to levels of participation (though it seems to undermine militancy). With the exception of the miners, whose ballots tend to have high turnouts, those unions which do have systems of balloting individual members on key issues rarely, if ever, achieve more than a third of members voting; normally, far fewer bother to vote.[49]

A persistent complaint is that branch meetings are boring, bogged down in business and bureaucracy, and dominated by full-time officials or lay representatives; there are few op- portunities for ordinary members to become involved. Women make up the group most alienated from the conventional cycle of branch life and there have recently been devastating critiques of workplace trade unionism, showing that it is overwhelmingly orientated to men's interests and men's life-styles.[50] The fact that women constitute such a large proportion of the wage-earning workforce – 40 per cent – makes this shortcoming a potentially crippling one for what one feminist writer, Bea Campbell, terms 'the men's movement'.[51]

The lack of class consciousness at the base of the labour movement has been accentuated by organizational changes. For example, 'check-off' systems (automatically deducting union subscriptions from pay) now cover 75 per cent of manufacturing industry and almost all the public sector. Although an advance in that they reduce the administrative load on a movement still largely dependent upon voluntary effort, regular contact between the union and the individual member has declined. Union collectors of old would reinforce the ideas and values of the labour movement on their weekly rounds. Now many trade unionists lack this counterweight to the opinions and interpretations pumped out through a media and absorbed from a culture deeply hostile to union militancy. Similarly, while the closed shop has been beneficial for union organization it has not necessarily increased member commitment to trade unionism. By the early 1980s, one worker in four was in a closed shop, and some of these hardly realized that they were actually union members. Together, the check-off and the closed shop have helped to 'depoliticize' the idea of union membership.

Against this background the huge expansion of union membership in the 1960s and 1970s did not automatically mean a strengthening of class solidarity. Workers were increasingly recruited on a sectionalist basis, with many – particularly in traditionally under-unionized white-collar jobs – joining for pragmatic reasons. They did so to protect their interests just as they took out life insurance or became members of the Automobile Association.

The fact that white-collar professions and jobs have become much more unionized clearly offers the *potential* for building a broader class consciousness into the middle classes. The large number of women in unions also offers an opportunity to broaden the movement's class appeal, as does the relatively new dominance achieved by public-sector unions. But so far the tendency has been to assume that this will occur *automatically*, 'now that these groups are part of the organized working class'. Very little has been done to alter the approach of the labour movement to acknowledge that there is now a *new working class*, drawn partly from its traditional blue-collar, manual base and partly from these new sources. Capital has been restructured, production has been restructured, and the working class has been restructured; but, by and large, unions have not.

Another factor which needs careful assessment is the professionalization of trade union organization from the 1960s onwards. While strengthening unions organizationally, injecting greater expertise and providing more member services, dependence on professionals shifted the focus away from the workplace. Far too many union branches now exist only on paper and are run by full-timers in district or regional offices. On the other hand, by employing more full-time staff and organizers unions have been better able to contact members and maintain a flow of information between local and national levels.

Partly because of the decline in branch life, shop stewards have become more important. Members can relate better to them since they are near by in the workplace, whereas branch membership has increasingly spread out geographically with industry rationalizing and communities disintegrating. They also deal with issues and grievances on a direct basis, in contrast with the bureaucratic style of branch machinery. However, as power has become concentrated in shop stewards, they have in turn developed specialist skills and become absorbed into union structures and are sometimes 'co-opted' by management. Even during the 1960s and early 1970s, when shop stewards' organizations were responsible for organizing strikes and winning many advances for their members, 'it was still an error to treat the activist minority as if they were simply coterminous with the membership at large'.[52]

· A NEW UNIONISM ·

The trade union movement has experienced great changes since the early 1960s, and the new right's political attack has undoubtedly reduced its power to advance, as well as its ability to strike. However, the alternative is not to abandon strikes on the spurious pretext that their time has passed. They remain the ultimate right of a worker and an integral part of the trade unionist's armoury. Indeed there is a need to organize strikes more effectively and with greater care for a sense of tactics and strategy suited to the available circumstances.[53]

But they are just one feature of a 'new unionism'. Workers must look to the future, building upon existing collective bargaining procedures, to tackle a much wider range of company decisions guarded under the umbrella of 'the right to manage'.[54] Full disclosure of information, investment priorities, production plans, research, marketing, profit distribution, future planning – all these are potentially more important than waiting to see what is left to pick up during annual wage negotiations. Joint control over staff pension funds – which contain deferred wages – is another key objective.

Industrial health and safety policies and the nature of the workplace environment should also be given greater emphasis. So should the demands raised by the women's movement for child-care facilities, flexible working patterns, provision for regular screening and other aspects of personal health and medical care. These issues are not just 'women's issues' and they are not only important in their own right. They also offer a greater opportunity for *popularizing* trade unionism – for making its apparently sectional objectives appeal to a wider political and social audience. Striking for demands like these could well win greater support than striking over wages. Feminists have challenged the way in which trade unions invariably focus only on *workers'* interests, isolating them from the wider community. As Sheila Rowbotham argues, this tradition

obviously excludes women working in the family just as it excludes other groups who are not on the cash nexus, children or old people for example. It also tends to disregard areas of life which are crucial in women's lives, around welfare legislation for instance, or around personal and sexual relationships . . . There is also a tendency to see workers possessing a true consciousness intact underneath the encrustment of treacherous leaders and the beguilements of the leaders. (This can be transplanted to women.) Once the crust is cut off the true consciousness becomes apparent. This implies that the people cutting the crust off are somehow not part of the problem.[55]

The trade union movement's emphasis on struggle within the system of *production* has not been connected into struggles within the associated systems of *reproduction* and *consumption*. The process of reproduction involves having children, raising them to become future workers, and supporting the labour force through education, health, housing and social services: it throws up what are often called 'community' issues. Capital depends upon all three systems: production is dependent on the reproduction of labour which in turn involves the consumption of goods provided both by private capital and by the state. Modern capitalism has consequently become increasingly interdependent.[56] Yet, by and large, unions have continued to act as if this was not the case, even though their own interests would clearly be strengthened by linking up with the interests of consumers and the community. The traditional insistence on the primacy of the industrial struggle in the workplace, rather than a broader class struggle in alliance with other social movements, has contributed to this one-dimensional trade unionism, as some socialists have recognized.[57]

It is probably normal for even militant, politically conscious shop stewards to say as one did in a recent study, 'Trade unionism ends for me when I go out of the gate at night.' And sometimes, the study adds, 'that literally means a particular factory gate', since a connection is seldom made to the concerns of even workers in neighbouring plants.[58]

Every worker is affected by 'community' issues – not just matters of clear public policy like welfare and housing, but personal ones connected with relationships at home, including the distribution of domestic work. Every worker is a consumer too. Exploitation does not occur simply at the workplace. Equally, what may be seen as relatively narrow issues of workplace concern, such as safety and amenities, are in practice linked not merely to profitability but to wider environmental issues.

· WORKPLACE/COMMUNITY LINKS ·

The evidence suggests that the linking of 'industrial' to 'community' action can strengthen both, by enabling a more com-

prehensive challenge to be mounted against the existing system of
power and resource allocation. A classic example occurred in 1915
when munitions workers threatened industrial action in support
of a rent strike on the Clyde and in Glasgow; the rents campaign
was largely successful as a result and the power of the workers
rose as well.[59] In Australia in the early 1970s, the New South
Wales Builders' Laborers' Federation blacked new property developments, particularly office blocks, which threatened the interests of the local working-class community and were opposed by
environmentalists. As a result the community campaign was enormously strengthened, and the political power of the building
workers was enhanced by their alliance with local residents.[60]

The campaign to defend the Inner London Education Authority in the 1980s from government threats to dismantle it or cut
its budget is an excellent example of mobilizing the maximum
political pressure by linking the interests of ILEA teachers and
staff with those of parents and the wider community, including
local Labour Parties. Although they caused some irritation and
inconvenience, it was interesting that ILEA 'days of action' including school strikes were relatively sympathetically received by
parents because they were involved in the action too. In recent
years many Labour councils have made an effort to promote joint
action between the consumers of their services and the workers
who provide them to oppose cuts.

Workers occupying their workplace to fight redundancies or
closures have found the active support of the local community
can be crucial in determining whether or not the law is invoked
against them, and also in circumscribing the role of the police.[61]
Employers, governments and agents of the state like courts and
the police are all quite sensitive to the political environment.
Strikes by Asian workers being exploited in London's East End
were boosted by community support which helped to isolate the
employers politically and socially.[62] The 1984–5 miners' strike
was most solid in South Wales, where community support for the
miners was strongest.

Indeed, throughout the history of the British trade union
movement the level of public and political support has been a

critical factor in the outcome of strikes, especially those where the government is effectively the employer.[63] Public-sector unions have recently given a much greater priority to mobilizing public opinion, particularly over cuts in provision. Postal workers striking against local post office closures have distributed leaflets to the public and lobbied politicians. Staff in hospitals due to be closed have occupied them and mounted joint campaigns with local people. Joint action to resist privatization of council or health services has come much nearer to linking the community's interest in decent standards with the interests of workers not to have forced upon them the reductions in pay and conditions of service which privatization has always produced.

For all its shortcomings in contending for *general* public support, the 1984–5 miners' strike showed vivid possibilities for alliances to be built with the newer *social movements*, particularly women's groups. Had it not been for the support work around the strike organized by women, the strike could not have been sustained over a full year. Here in action was a fusion between 'old' and 'new' class struggles which cut across the assertion that strikes, industrial muscle and free collective bargaining are necessarily counterposed against struggles by these newer social movements.

· POLICIES FOR POPULARIZING TRADE UNIONISM ·

Unions need to extend their policy horizons as well. Far too often they appear simply to defend their own interests in a narrow fashion, allowing governments, employers and the media to play them off against the 'public interest'. For instance, rather than simply defending an existing and perhaps declining company, unions should also be involved in pressing for a more effective regional policy for the country, for this provides a *general* vehicle for engaging the wider public in a defence of a *specific* interest: the jobs of the workers concerned. Significantly, when the National Union of Teachers took industrial action in 1985–6, although their primary motive was pay, they linked this to educational cuts in order to demonstrate that teachers were suffering *individually* from the same government squeeze on resources that was hitting children, students and parents *collectively*.

Of course, some conflicts of interest are irreconcilable. And some trade unionists would argue that they do always try to win the public to their case. But a qualitatively different approach is needed to popularize the cause of unions, especially when they take industrial action.

If, for example, the miners had gone beyond their traditional approach of free collective bargaining and pressed for industrial democracy in their industry, they would have been encouraged to formulate a 'workers' fuel policy' based on a proper evaluation of the social costs of various fuels and a common strategy for defending the interests of workers in other sectors of energy supply. As the Institute for Workers' Control (IWC) argued in 1968, 'Such a policy would require that the miners broke out of their narrowly "industrial" thinking and approached workers in oil, gas and electricity with proposals for the preparation of joint policies and coordinated action to implement them.'[64]

The IWC also argued in 1984 for the miners to link their case against pit closures to pensioners' needs for fuel, but this was never given any prominence in the strike. The miners could also have gained a sympathetic response by challenging the government's switch to placing greater reliance on nuclear energy partly as a method of undermining the miners' union. There is a wide section of public opinion opposed to expanding capacity for nuclear power generation, including thousands of anti-nuclear and environmental activists who could have been recruited to give practical support for the strike. Although union officials did raise the issue, it was always as an afterthought. It was never given the priority it needed over the daily issues crowding in on the union as it became increasingly embattled. Yet it could have been the basis of projecting a practical alternative to the government's run-down of the coal industry, placing the NUM in a positive position rather than the negative one it was pushed into.

Strikers are often seen to be defending a status quo which, while it may protect their immediate job interests, is generally unpopular. This has frequently been the case in the public sector where union campaigns against many of the cuts introduced by the Thatcher government fell on deaf ears (at least in its first term), partly because council tenants and those dependent on welfare were fed up with the service they had been getting over the years – a service often made worse by protectionist working practices developed by unions.

Women's groups have been particularly critical of this and, in campaigning against cuts, have explicitly argued for improvements to services such as nursery schools and child-care facilities. In this way campaigns which necessarily begin by being defensive can become progressive, enabling the workers and parents threatened to go on to the offensive together. This occurred when women campaigning to keep open the Elizabeth Garrett Anderson Hospital in 1977 received extra support by suggesting imaginative ways in which its services could be better tailored to the needs of women.

Such campaigns may not succeed. Under the pressure of government cuts in public expenditure in the late 1970s and 1980s, few have been victorious – but then neither has traditional trade union resistance. What this strategy of building wider alliances offers is not a guarantee of success, but a better prospect of mobilizing broader support and thereby transforming the *political conditions* surrounding attacks on working-class interests. There are no magic formulas, especially not in circumstances of sharper class conflict as in recent years. But there are more effective strategies.

· COUNTER-PLANNING ·

These strategies can also go beyond acts of protest to challenge the whole authority of management. For instance, when the highly skilled workforce at the armaments firm, Lucas Aerospace, was threatened with redundancies, they drew up their own corporate plan for the company in 1975 and 1976. Through their 'combine committee' – comprising shop stewards from different plants and unions – they came up with a programme for utilizing their skills and resources to create new socially useful products. Potentially this represented a major extension of workers' power. Yet it also required serious community consultation to ensure that people actually wanted and needed the alternative goods being produced. As the Lucas workers' experience showed, the other advantage of the 'workers' plan' strategy is that it points

to a way out of the impasse that many trade unionists find themselves in when defending a declining industry against management's attempts to restructure and 'modernize'. Such a defensive stand has often been the only way to defend jobs, but in the long run it is a hopeless struggle in industries like the car industry where the market for the type of cars being produced is virtually saturated. Workers' plans are in effect proposing a form of restructuring, but a restructuring in the interests of labour rather than capital. They anticipate and identify new markets and consumption patterns, and by their political pressure they attempt to back social needs with the purchasing power of local or national government.[65]

However, the Lucas experience also shows that winning popular support is a necessary but not sufficient condition for success. In the end, the workers needed the backing of government. But their appeals, first to the Labour government and then Mrs Thatcher's administration, were unsuccessful. In Labour's case at least this was partly because of the opposition of their national trade union organizations which felt threatened by the new direction taken by this expression of shopfloor power and which discouraged Labour ministers from offering assistance.[66]

More recently, the work of local authority enterprise boards – in London, Sheffield and the West Midlands, for example – has shown the need for unions to concentrate much more on industrial strategy. There is enormous scope for unions locally to formulate their own proposals for the future employment trajectory of their industry, how it should meet social needs, what local labour skills are available, where investment would come from, and so on. Struggles over wages essentially involve *distributional* issues, and they had some success in conditions of economic growth. But *production* issues have become increasingly important as the country's manufacturing base and capacity to generate wealth has collapsed. Unions can cooperate with local councils in planning a future for their industrial sector or looking to different production possibilities for their members' skills.

It is necessary to close the traditional gap between government industrial planning and workplace initiatives, and what has been described as 'counter-planning' offers a way of doing this. It need not involve grandiose alternative plans like the Lucas one, but more 'nuts and bolts' work, planning ahead, anticipating employment, production and consumer developments, anticipating new technology and using collective bargaining methods to do this.[67]

· WORKERS' CONTROL ·

In the 1970s, a complementary strategy emerged in a spate of factory occupations and sit-ins. As in the well-known case of Upper Clyde Shipbuilders in 1971 – where the workers occupied the shipyard and conducted a country-wide political campaign to save their jobs – these usually occurred in response to mass redundancies or plant closures. They gave a glimpse of trade unionism as a vehicle for workers' control rather than as an agency simply for collective bargaining.[68] They were also associated with the establishment of publicly funded workers' cooperatives to run industries where private capital and management had failed.

The interest shown in workers' control and industrial democracy by socialist trade unionists during the late 1960s and early 1970s drew on a strand in the labour movement which, though it had been dormant for many decades, has strong roots.[69] It has been associated with the tradition of libertarian socialism which emphasizes decentralization, workers' control and community control, rather than the centralized 'statist' ideas dominant in labour movements across the world.[70]

But it stands outside the mainstream of British trade unionism by being willing to participate in the management of enterprises as a first step to winning full control. By focusing on the *power* relations of industry, it also seeks to transcend the limitations of traditional wages militancy. It is no more liable to co-option by employers than trade unions have traditionally been in practice. On the contrary, it poses a much more serious challenge to management's right to manage unilaterally.

·THE POLITICAL DIMENSION·

But a 'new unionism' needs a clear political dimension. The 1970s and early 1980s confirmed that even workers' occupations, alternative plans and struggles conducted with the broadest feasible support will eventually crumble if there is not a positive political response from the Labour Party in and out of power. Labour governments need to introduce statutory workers' rights to vote for the conversion of small firms into cooperatives. There also needs to be legislation to encourage and support industrial democracy in industry.

Equally, however well-meaning government policies may be they cannot succeed against the power of private capital unless workers' organizations have been involved from the outset in formulating them and in struggling for them. Looked at in this way, industrial strategies and economic programmes become less shopping lists for governments to implement from on high and more *vehicles for struggle*, giving trade unionists the leverage and the opportunity to organize at workplace level and win greater control.

An important study by four trades councils on the 1974-9 Labour government's industrial policy showed how even its minimal proposals for planning agreements between workers and management failed because these proposals were not understood on the shopfloor. Generally, there was no grass-roots demand for them and, where there was, the government was not sufficiently responsive.[71] Much the same message came out of the workers' report by the shop stewards' 'combine committee' of the multinational company, Vickers.[72]

This experience underlined again the key necessity for linking extra-parliamentary action by trade unionists to parliamentary action which is responsive to such struggles.[73] New trade unionism will involve extended collective bargaining and counter-planning. It will include positive strikes where they are required to gain increased control. Such strikes – for example against an obdurate private employer who resists disclosure of information or proposals for industrial democracy – will need the support of Labour ministers, so that the authority of government is harnessed with shopfloor power.

Policies for purchasing from the private sector the goods and services needed by the public sector must require the supplying companies to grant full trade union rights, to promote equal opportunities and to adopt ecologically sound methods such as energy conservation, recycling of waste, and so on.

· UNION REFORMS ·

For such a strategy to be established, the trade union movement will also have to put its own house in order and, although a detailed discussion of internal union reforms lies outside the scope of this book, a number of key areas need highlighting.

First, the sectionalism endemic in the movement could be eroded by a more rational structure of union organization. Because the trade union movement took root among skilled workers in craft societies, relatively few 'industrial' unions emerged. The historic pattern of 'craft', 'general' and 'industrial' unions survives to this day. But the issue is not so much the number of unions: this declined from 184 to 109 between 1960 and 1980, during which time total membership rose from 8 to 12 million, and about three-quarters of all trade unionists are in the eight biggest unions. The problem is rather the *ad hoc* way in which unions moved into new areas of recruitment, failing to adapt to the restructuring of production and ending up by competing for members in many of the same areas. This has bred inter-union rivalry of an intensity which sometimes surpasses hostility to management, obviously weakens the strength of workers and leads to inter-union disputes which are extremely damaging. It would therefore be desirable to set the objective of one union for each industry or main area of work, and an agreement between the big general unions on the areas they cover.

Second, it is essential to revitalize union branch life. Too many branches are now organized on a geographical basis and maintained either by full-timers or a handful of activists. The aim should be to replace geographical branches with workplace branches where possible. Concerted effort is needed to make meetings more attractive and accessible to the membership, taking place in work time where possible, or at least having crèche facilities, arranging cheap transport, and avoiding clubs or pubs as venues. There has been a growing demand from women for alternatives to formal meetings, such as informal discussions, and for officers on a rota system.

There has also been an acceptance by some of the more perceptive and progressive trade union leaders that the left has relied for too long on 'paper armies' behind the small core of activists which effectively *are* the unions, and that new ways must be found to involve the whole membership, and to extend democracy and accountability.[74] This is quite different from the reform programme based on balloting and introduced by the Thatcherites in the 1984 Trade Union Act in order to encourage a passive, *individualized* concept of trade unionism which would undercut unions' only source of strength: their capacity for *collective* action and solidarity.

Building on the success of the political fund ballots, it will be necessary to breathe new life into the links between the unions and the Labour Party so that the system of affiliation provides a channel through which the two can interact properly, breaking down the labour movement's demarcation line between the industrial and the political. This implies a more political role by unions, just as it requires Labour Party members to support local trade unions by campaigning actively around local workplace issues.

In addition, progressive national trade union leadership is necessary. Although the argument in this book has shown that a fixation on the failures of leaders is mistaken, the cautious pragmatism and conservatism of even 'left' trade union leaders is completely unsuitable for tackling British trade unionism's crisis. Whether by giving support to strikes on principle or by reforming union organizations, radical and imaginative leadership is required to alter the whole direction of the movement.

·CONCLUSION·

The new right's political attack has exposed the central dilemma of the British trade union movement. Organizationally it has survived intact and is much stronger than in the late 1920s, the last time it suffered such a major attack. Britain still has a higher proportion of workers – just under 50 per cent – in unions than any other Western country except Sweden. Unions are still willing to engage in extraordinarily heroic strike action, as shown by the miners at least. Strikes continued in the Thatcher years, despite stringent legal restrictions and despite an ideological attack through the media probably unsurpassed in the country's history.

But, by using authoritarian state powers against unions and by dragging major strikes even more firmly on to the political battleground, Thatcherism may well have done the trade union movement a back-handed favour. The movement's fundamental political weakness has been placed on the agenda again. The question is whether this weakness will be seriously addressed or whether it will be relegated, as in the past, to 'any other business'.

The choice before the labour movement could be stark. Either there will be greater 'Americanization' of British trade unions through 'no-strike' deals and aggressive management techniques which by-pass local officials. Or Britain's unions can try to overcome their historic limitations by constructively politicizing their activities, broadening their sectional interests into community-wide ones, mobilizing public support, revitalizing and democratizing their structures to involve their members more effectively, and, most important, campaigning for industrial democracy as a step towards *real* workers' control.

REFERENCES

CHAPTER I POLITICAL STRIKES

1. *The Times*, 23 August 1984; *Daily Mirror*, 27 August 1984; and Nicholas Ridley, Minister of Transport, *Guardian*, 29 August 1984.
2. *Observer*, 5 August 1984.
3. *Sunday Times*, 18 November 1984.
4. *The Times*, 20 July 1984.
5. Ben Pimlott and Chris Cook (eds.), *Trade Unions in British Politics* (Longman, 1982), p. 70.
6. Eric Wigham, *Strikes and the Government 1893–1981* (Macmillan, 1982), p. 28.
7. V. L. Allen, *Trade Unions and the Government* (Longman, 1960), p. 151.
8. Tony Lane, *The Union Makes Us Strong* (Arrow, 1974), p. 17.
9. V. L. Allen, *The Militancy of British Miners* (Shipley, Moor Press, 1981), pp. 238, 242.
10. Robin Blackburn and Alexander Cockburn (eds.), *The Incompatibles* (Penguin, 1967), pp. 187, 190.
11. *Guardian*, 23 August 1984.
12. Richard Hyman, *Strikes* (Fontana, third edition, 1984), p. 35.
13. John McIlroy, *Strike!* (Pluto, 1984), p. 18, and Robert Taylor, *The Fifth Estate* (Pan, 1980), p. 43.
14. Allen (1960), op. cit., p. 117, and reference in Hyman, op. cit., p. 17.
15. J. E. T. Eldridge, *Industrial Disputes* (Routledge & Kegan Paul, 1968), p. 3.
16. McIlroy, op. cit., pp. 86–104.
17. Taylor, op. cit., p. 41.
18. Lane, op. cit., p. 277.
19. See, for example, Sarah Boston, *Women Workers and the Trade Unions* (Davis-Poynter, 1980), pp. 35, 68.
20. Ken Coates and Tony Topham, *Trade Unions in Britain* (Spokesman, 1980), p. 217.
21. Hyman, op. cit., p. 183.

22. Michael Silver, 'Recent British Strike Trends: A Factual Analysis', *British Journal of Industrial Relations* (March 1973), p. 77.

23. Hyman, op. cit., p. 36.

24. Friedrich Engels, *The Condition of the Working Class in England in 1844* (Allen & Unwin, 1968 edition), p. 218.

25. Allen Hutt, *British Trade Unionism* (Lawrence & Wishart, 1975 edition), p. 13.

26. Quoted in Allen (1960), p. 146.

27. Lane, op. cit., p. 263.

28. Hyman, op. cit., p. 82.

29. Lane, op. cit., p. 113.

30. Fenner Brockway, quoted in Christopher Farman, *The General Strike* (Panther, 1974), p. 300.

31. For a summary of the evidence, see McIlroy, op. cit., pp. 20–22.

32. V. L. Allen, *Militant Trade Unionism* (Merlin Press, 1966), p. 27.

33. J. W. Durcan *et al.*, *Strikes in Post-War Britain* (Allen & Unwin, 1983), p. 403, and Coates and Topham, op. cit., p. 223.

34. For a useful analysis, see Paul Thompson, *The Nature of Work* (Macmillan, 1983), pp. 236–45.

35. Hyman, op. cit., pp. 176–7.

36. Allen, op. cit. (1960), p. 214.

37. Hyman, op. cit., p. 189.

38. Bob Rowthorn, *Capitalism, Conflict and Inflation* (Lawrence & Wishart, 1980), and Michael Barratt-Brown, *From Labourism to Socialism* (Spokesman, 1972).

39. Keith Smith, *The British Economic Crisis* (Penguin, 1984), p. 29.

40. ibid., p. 55.

41. Ralph Miliband, *The State in Capitalist Society* (Weidenfeld & Nicolson, 1969), p. 271.

42. ibid., p. 54.

43. For a discussion of this topic, see L. J. MacFarlane, *The Right to Strike* (Penguin, 1981), pp. 159–60.

44. Keith Jeffrey and Peter Hennessy, *States of Emergency* (Routledge & Kegan Paul, 1983), pp. 262–3.

45. Hyman, op. cit., p. 170.

46. ibid., p. 160.

47. ibid., p. 168.

48. Ralph Miliband, *Capitalist Democracy in Britain* (Oxford University Press, 1982), pp. 5–7.

49. Keith Middlemas, *Politics in Industrial Society* (André Deutsch, 1979).

CHAPTER 2   LIMITS ON 'THE RIGHT TO STRIKE'

1. *The Times*, 4 March 1978.
2. See Ralph Miliband, *Capitalist Democracy in Britain* (Oxford University Press, 1982), p. 18.
3. Geoffrey Marshall, 'The Armed Forces and Industrial Disputes in the United Kingdom', *Armed Forces and Society* (February 1979), p. 271.
4. E. Wade and G. Phillips, *Constitutional and Administrative Law* (Longman, 1977), p. 506.
5. Joe Rogaly, *Grunwick* (Penguin, 1977), p. 141.
6. Jeremy McMullen, *Rights at Work* (Pluto, 1983), p. 415.
7. Quoted in V. L. Allen, *Trade Unions and the Government* (Longman, 1960), p. 130.
8. ibid., p. 132.
9. ibid., p. 138.
10. ibid., p. 141.
11. Quoted in Peter Tatchell, *Democratic Defence* (GMP, 1985), p. 85.
12. ibid.
13. Alan Ward, 'The British Army and Civilian Trade Unions: A Marriage of the Incompatible?', *Political Quarterly*, Vol. 50, No. 4 (October–November 1979), p. 461.
14. Sir Basil Thomson, head of the Special Branch, quoted in Tony Bunyan, *The Political Police in Britain* (Julian Friedmann, 1976), p. 119.
15. Ward, op. cit., p. 465.
16. Tatchell, op. cit., pp. 80–81.
17. Steve Peak, *Troops in Strikes* (Cobden Trust, 1984), p. 14.
18. L. J. MacFarlane, *The Right to Strike* (Penguin, 1981), pp. 130–32.
19. Robert Reiner, *The Blue-Coated Worker* (Cambridge University Press, 1978), pp. 19–21.
20. ibid., pp. 21–3.
21. Thom Young, *Incitement to Disaffection* (Cobden Trust, 1976), p. 58.
22. Reiner, op. cit., p. 6.
23. ibid., p. 268.
24. Allen, op. cit., p. 124.
25. Eric Wigham, *Strikes and the Government 1893–1981* (Macmillan, 1982), p. 192.
26. Department of Employment, *Trade Union Immunities*, Cmnd. 8128 (HMSO, January 1981), pp. 80–82.
27. Alan Clinton, *Post Office Workers* (Allen & Unwin, 1984), p. 463.
28. See Counsel's Opinion to the UPW, 25 March 1977. This shows that all industrial action short of a national all-out strike is illegal.

Counsel also argued that even a national strike could be caught, though the Attorney-General implied that that was not the case in Parliament in 1981 and 1984.

29. Allen, op. cit., p. 79.
30. MacFarlane, op. cit., p. 143.
31. Eric Wigham, *From Humble Petition to Militant Action* (Civil and Public Services Association, 1980), p. 138.
32. ibid., p. 152.
33. *The Times*, 15 November 1983.
34. *Labour Weekly*, 3 August 1984.
35. ibid.
36. *Sunday Times*, 17 March 1985.
37. *Guardian*, 21 May 1985.

CHAPTER 3   AN HISTORIC CONFLICT

1. Quoted in V. L. Allen, *Trade Unions and the Government* (Longman, 1960), p. 4.
2. Henry Pelling, *A History of British Trade Unionism* (Penguin, 1969), p. 19.
3. ibid., p. 21.
4. ibid., p. 25.
5. Sheila Lewenhak, *Women and Trade Unions* (Ernest Benn, 1977), p. 22.
6. Tony Lane, *The Union Makes Us Strong* (Arrow, 1974), p. 35.
7. ibid., p. 34.
8. E. P. Thompson, *The Making of the English Working Class* (Penguin, 1979 edition), p. 199. See also pp. 458–61.
9. Quoted in Roy Lewis, 'The Historical Development of Labour Law', *British Journal of Industrial Relations* (March 1976), p. 2.
10. Lane, op. cit., pp. 54–5.
11. Pelling, op. cit., p. 30.
12. Sidney and Beatrice Webb, *The History of Trade Unionism* (London, 1920), p. 292.
13. Joyce Marlowe, *The Tolpuddle Martyrs* (Panther, 1974), p. 78.
14. ibid., p. 91.
15. ibid., p. 81.
16. Quoted in Pelling, op. cit., p. 41.
17. Sarah Boston, *Women Workers and the Trade Unions* (Davis-Poynter, 1980), p. 15.
18. Lewenhak, op. cit., p. 26.
19. Boston, op. cit., p. 16.
20. ibid., pp. 23–4.

21. Figures given by E. H. Hunt, *British Labour History 1815–1914* (Weidenfeld & Nicolson, 1981), pp. 192–3, 250.

22. Friedrich Engels, *The Condition of the Working Class in England in 1844* (Allen & Unwin, 1952 edition), p. 224.

23. Lane, op. cit., p. 62.

24. ibid., p. 69.

25. ibid., p. 76. See also Pelling, op. cit., p. 60.

26. Lane, op. cit., pp. 84–5.

27. The term 'labour aristocracy' is, however, the subject of considerable controversy: see Robert Gray, *The Aristocracy of Labour in Nineteenth Century Britain* (Macmillan, 1981).

28. Lewis, op. cit., p. 1.

29. Lane, op. cit., p. 89.

30. Boston, op. cit., pp. 41–2.

31. ibid., p. 46.

32. ibid., pp. 51–4.

33. John Saville, quoted in Lane, op. cit., p. 92.

34. Allen, op. cit., p. 120.

35. Keith Middlemas, *Politics in Industrial Society* (André Deutsch, 1979), p. 58.

36. Eric Wigham, *Strikes and the Government 1893–1981* (Macmillan, 1982), p. 1.

37. ibid., p. 13.

38. Quoted in Pelling, op. cit., p. 125.

39. E. J. Hobsbawm, *Labouring Men* (Penguin, 1964), pp. 324–5.

40. Hunt, op. cit., p. 336.

41. E. J. Hobsbawm, *Worlds of Labour* (Weidenfeld & Nicolson, 1984), p. 163.

42. Allen, op. cit., p. 121.

43. Wigham, op. cit., p. 25.

44. Allen Hutt, *British Trade Unionism* (Lawrence & Wishart, 1975 edition), pp. 63–4.

45. ibid., p. 65.

46. Lane, op. cit., p. 110.

47. Middlemas, op. cit., p. 56.

48. Hutt, op. cit., pp. 66, 68.

49. See George Dangerfield, *The Strange Death of Liberal England* (Granada, 1972 edition).

50. Middlemas, op. cit., p. 123.

51. Boston, op. cit., pp. 126–7.

52. ibid., pp. 122–3.

53. ibid., pp. 137, 152–3.

54. Hutt, op. cit., p. 129.

55. Middlemas, op. cit., pp. 127–8.

56. ibid., p. 143.
57. Hutt, op. cit., p. 126.
58. Allen, op. cit., p. 151.
59. ibid., p. 174.
60. Keith Jeffrey and Peter Hennessy, *States of Emergency* (Routledge & Kegan Paul, 1983), p. 20.
61. ibid., pp. 5–6.
62. ibid., p. 21.
63. Allen, op. cit., p. 185.
64. Jeffrey and Hennessy, op. cit., pp. 78, 80–81.
65. Allen, op. cit., p. 191.
66. Henry Phelps Brown, *The Origins of Trade Union Power* (Oxford, Clarendon Press, 1983), p. 82.
67. ibid.
68. Robert Spicer, *Conspiracy* (Lawrence & Wishart, 1981), p. 66.
69. Allen, op. cit., p. 194.
70. ibid., p. 195.
71. Boston, op. cit., pp. 174–5.
72. Christopher Farman, *The General Strike* (Panther, 1974), pp. 240–42.
73. ibid., p. 247.
74. Jeffrey and Hennessy, op. cit., p. 118.
75. Tony Bunyan, *The Political Police in Britain* (Julian Friedmann, 1976), p. 263.
76. Jeffrey and Hennessey, op. cit., p. 140.
77. Farman, op. cit., pp. 230–50.
78. Jeffrey and Hennessy, op. cit., p. 119.
79. Allen, op. cit., p. 199.
80. See Middlemas, op. cit., pp. 202–5, 374.
81. Ben Pimlott and Chris Cook (eds.), *Trade Unions in British Politics* (Longman, 1982), p. 111.
82. Ralph Miliband, *Parliamentary Socialism* (Merlin Press, 1973 edition), p. 236.
83. Middlemas, op. cit., p. 323.
84. See ibid., pp. 243, 265.

CHAPTER 4   MODERN GOVERNMENTS AND STRIKES

1. See J. W. Durcan *et al.*, *Strikes in Post-War Britain* (Allen & Unwin, 1983), p. 353.
2. Ralph Miliband, *The State in Capitalist Society* (Weidenfeld & Nicolson, 1969), p. 81.

3. ibid., pp. 81–2.

4. Keith Middlemas, *Politics in Industrial Society* (André Deutsch, 1979), p. 279.

5. Ralph Miliband, *Parliamentary Socialism* (Merlin Press, 1973 edition), p. 272.

6. *Hansard Parliamentary Debates*, 17 February 1943, cl. 1818.

7. Paul Addison, *The Road to 1945* (Quartet, 1982), pp. 234–5.

8. Middlemas, op. cit., p. 301.

9. Durcan *et al.*, op. cit., p. 26.

10. Eric Wigham, *Strikes and the Government 1893–1981* (Macmillan, 1982), pp. 98–9.

11. See Samuel Beer, *Modern British Politics* (Faber, 1965), p. 215.

12. Henry Pelling, *A History of British Trade Unionism* (Penguin, 1984), p. 218.

13. Sarah Boston, *Women Workers and the Trade Unions* (Davis-Poynter, 1980), pp. 209–10.

14. ibid., p. 188.

15. ibid., p. 196, and see Penny Summerfield, *Women Workers in the Second World War* (Croom Helm, 1985).

16. Boston, op. cit., p. 242.

17. Keith Jeffrey and Peter Hennessy, *States of Emergency* (Routledge & Kegan Paul, 1983), p. 156.

18. ibid., p. 159.

19. ibid., p. 180.

20. ibid., p. 193.

21. ibid., p. 206.

22. Wigham, op. cit., p. 104.

23. ibid., p. 103.

24. Jeffrey and Hennessy, op. cit., p. 191.

25. ibid., p. 192.

26. ibid., p. 197.

27. ibid., p. 215.

28. Middlemas, op. cit., p. 404.

29. Pelling, op. cit., p. 231.

30. Middlemas, op. cit., p. 372.

31. Tony Lane, *The Union Makes Us Strong* (Arrow, 1974), p. 155.

32. Wigham, op. cit., p. 106.

33. ibid., p. 112.

34. ibid., p. 114.

35. ibid., p. 117.

36. ibid., p. 119.

37. V. L. Allen, *Trade Unions and the Government* (Longman, 1960), p. 201.

38. Wigham, op. cit., p. 130.

39. Perry Anderson, 'The Limits and Possibilities of Trade Union Action', in R. Blackburn and A. Cockburn (eds.), *The Incompatibles* (Penguin, 1967), p. 278.
40. Paul Foot, 'The Seamen's Struggle', in Blackburn and Cockburn, op. cit., p. 187.
41. ibid., p. 185.
42. Lane, op. cit., p. 135.
43. Middlemas, op. cit., p. 441.
44. Wigham, op. cit., p. 149.
45. Harold Wilson, *The Labour Government 1964–1970* (Weidenfeld & Nicolson, 1971), p. 209.
46. Middlemas, op. cit., pp. 451–2.
47. Boston, op. cit., p. 264.
48. ibid., p. 265.
49. Sheila Lewenhak, *Women and Trade Unions* (Ernest Benn, 1977), p. 247.
50. Boston, op. cit., pp. 278–9.
51. Guy Arnold, *The Unions* (Hamish Hamilton, 1981), p. 21.
52. Durcan *et al.*, op. cit., pp. 4, 402.
53. J. A. G. Griffith, *The Politics of the Judiciary* (Fontana, 1981), p. 76.
54. ibid., p. 77.
55. Wigham, op. cit., p. 179.
56. Robert Taylor, 'The trade union "problem" since 1960', in Ben Pimlott and Chris Cook (eds.), *Trade Unions in British Politics* (Longman, 1982), p. 189.
57. David Coates, 'The Question of Trade Union Power', in D. Coates and G. Johnston (eds.), *Socialist Arguments* (Martin Robertson, 1983), p. 69.
58. David Coates, *Labour in Power?* (Longman, 1980), p. 203.
59. *Report of a Court of Inquiry under Lord Scarman*, Cmnd. 6922 (HMSO, 1977).
60. Jack Dromey and Graham Taylor, *Grunwick: the Workers' Story* (Lawrence & Wishart, 1978), p. 188.
61. Joe Rogaly, *Grunwick* (Penguin, 1978), pp. 110–11.
62. Wigham, op. cit., p. 195.
63. ibid., p. 199.
64. ibid., p. 205.
65. Arnold, op. cit., pp. 93–4.
66. ibid., pp. 20–21.
67. ibid., p. 30.

CHAPTER 5   THE THATCHERITE ATTACK

1. See Stuart Hall and Martin Jacques (eds.), *The Politics of Thatcherism* (Lawrence & Wishart, 1983).
2. For an analysis of 'new right' ideology on this point, see Geoff Hodgson, *The Democratic Economy* (Penguin, 1984), p. 124.
3. *Guardian*, 11 October 1984.
4. Richard Hyman, *Strikes* (Fontana, 1984), pp. 199, 221–5.
5. Keith Jeffrey and Peter Hennessy, *States of Emergency* (Routledge & Kegan Paul, 1983), p. 255.
6. ibid., p. 235.
7. ibid., p. 238.
8. *Labour Research*, June 1980, p. 137.
9. See John Gennard, *Financing Strikers* (Macmillan, 1977).
10. Mark Dickinson, *To Break a Union* (Manchester, Booklist, 1984), p. 10.
11. For details, see ibid.
12. ibid., p. 189.
13. Bob Fine and Robert Millar, *Policing the Miners' Strike* (Lawrence & Wishart, 1985), p. 8.
14. Huw Beynon (ed.), *Digging Deeper* (Verso, 1985), p. 36.
15. Michael Crick, *Scargill and the Miners* (Penguin, 1985), p. 88.
16. Beynon, op. cit., p. 37.
17. Crick, op. cit., p. 96.
18. *Morning Star*, 7 February 1985.
19. Crick, op. cit., p. 140.
20. J. Coulter, S. Miller and M. Walker, *State of Siege* (Canary Press, 1984), p. 183.
21. *Guardian*, 10 September 1984.
22. *Financial Times*, 16 March 1984.
23. *The Times*, 29 March 1985.
24. *New Statesman*, 8 March 1985.
25. Alex Callinicos and Mike Simons, *The Great Strike* (Socialist Workers Party, 1985), pp. 153–4, 157.
26. *New Socialist*, March 1985, and Andrew Glyn, *The Economic Case Against Pit Closures* (NUM, 1984).
27. *Guardian*, 23 October 1984.
28. *Guardian*, 29 June 1984.
29. Fine and Millar, op. cit., p. 2.
30. Andrew Gamble, 'This Lady's Not for Turning: Thatcherism Mark III', *Marxism Today* (June 1984), pp. 13–14.
31. *New Statesman*, 14 December 1984; *Morning Star*, 7 February 1985; *Labour Research*, February 1985; Beynon, op. cit., pp. 61–3.

32. *Guardian*, 23 January 1985, and 'Today', BBC radio, 23 January 1985.
33. *The Times*, 26 January 1985.
34. *The Times*, 1 April 1985.
35. Eric Batstone, *Working Order: Workplace Industrial Relations Over Two Decades* (Oxford, Basil Blackwell, 1984).
36. *The Times*, 13 February 1985.

CHAPTER 6   MILITARY INTERVENTION IN STRIKES

1. Allen Hutt, *British Trade Unionism* (Lawrence & Wishart, 1975), p. 11.
2. V. L. Allen, *Trade Unions and the Government* (Longman, 1960), p. 118.
3. See Steve Peak, *Troops in Strikes* (Cobden Trust, 1984), pp. 21–3.
4. ibid., pp. 26–7.
5. Quoted in ibid., p. 30.
6. ibid., p. 31.
7. ibid., p. 31.
8. Christopher J. Whelan, 'Military Intervention in Industrial Disputes', *Industrial Law Journal* (December 1979), p. 222.
9. Christopher Farman, *The General Strike* (Panther, 1974), p. 118.
10. Peak, op. cit., p. 47.
11. ibid., p. 84.
12. ibid., p. 116.
13. Keith Jeffrey and Peter Hennessy, *States of Emergency* (Routledge & Kegan Paul, 1983), p. 236.
14. Peak, op. cit., p. 118.
15. Tony Bunyan, *The Political Police in Britain* (Julian Friedmann, 1976), pp. 272–4; Carol Ackroyd *et al.*, *The Technology of Political Control* (Penguin, 1977), pp. 141–5; and Barrie Penrose and Roger Courtiour, *The Pencourt File* (Secker & Warburg, 1978), pp. 240–42.
16. Peak, op. cit., p. 123.
17. ibid., pp. 129–30.
18. ibid., p. 131.
19. ibid., p. 133.
20. ibid., p. 131.
21. Quoted by Whelan, op. cit., p. 222.
22. Peak, op. cit., p. 139.
23. ibid., p. 148.

24. ibid., p. 153.
25. ibid., p. 156.
26. Jeffrey and Hennessy, op. cit., pp. 249–52.
27. Peak, op. cit., p. 40.
28. Jeffrey and Hennessy, op. cit., pp. 215–16.
29. Peter Tatchell, *Democratic Defence* (GMP, 1985), pp. 157–76.
30. Jeffrey and Hennessy, op. cit., p. 253.
31. Ralph Miliband, *The State in Capitalist Society* (Weidenfeld & Nicolson, 1972), p. 129.
32. Quoted by Whelan, op. cit., p. 232.
33. ibid.
34. ibid., p. 233.
35. *Guardian*, 5 April 1980.
36. Penrose and Courtiour, op. cit., pp. 10–11, 241, 324.
37. *Guardian*, 26 June 1985.
38. Ackroyd, op. cit., p. 110.
39. ibid.
40. Penrose and Courtiour, op. cit., pp. 243–4.
41. Bunyan, op. cit., p. 277.
42. Ackroyd, op. cit., p. 59.
43. Peak, op. cit., p. 12.
44. ibid., p. 169.
45. Brian Sedgemore, *The Secret Constitution* (Hodder, 1980), p. 132.

CHAPTER 7   POLICING THE WORKERS

1. Tom Bowden, *Beyond the Limits of the Law* (Penguin, 1978), p. 221.
2. Quoted by E. P. Thompson, *The Making of the English Working Class* (Penguin, 1968), p. 60.
3. ibid., p. 89.
4. Tony Bunyan, *The Political Police in Britain* (Julian Friedmann, 1976), p. 61.
5. ibid., p. 60.
6. Bowden, op. cit., p. 225.
7. D. Philips, 'Riots and Public Order in the Black Country 1835–60', in J. Stevenson and R. Quinault (eds.), *Popular Protest and Public Order* (Allen & Unwin, 1974), pp. 159–60.
8. Quoted in Bowden, op. cit., p. 225.
9. Tony Lane, *The Union Makes Us Strong* (Arrow, 1974), p. 92.
10. Bowden, op. cit., p. 226.
11. ibid., p. 21.

12. T. A. Critchley, *A History of the Police* (Constable, 1967), p. 163.

13. See Christopher Farman, *The General Strike* (Panther, 1974), pp. 229–32, 238–40, 243, 247.

14. Bowden, op. cit., pp. 226–7.

15. Critchley, op. cit., pp. 232–3.

16. Bunyan, op. cit., p. 270.

17. See Joanna Rollo, 'The Special Patrol Group', in Peter Hain (ed.), *Policing the Police*, Vol. 2 (John Calder, 1980), p. 172.

18. ibid., p. 173.

19. Robert Mark, *In the Office of Constable* (Collins, 1978), p. 224.

20. Rollo, op. cit., pp. 181–4, and Jack Dromey and Graham Taylor, *Grunwick: the Workers' Story* (Lawrence & Wishart, 1978).

21. Bob Fine and Robert Millar (eds.), *Policing the Miners' Strike* (Lawrence & Wishart, 1985), p. 28.

22. Lane, op. cit., pp. 283–4.

23. Bunyan, op. cit., p. 114.

24. *Guardian*, 1 March 1985, and *Labour Weekly*, 8 February 1985.

25. Bunyan, op. cit., p. 144.

26. ibid., pp. 143–4.

27. *New Statesman*, 1 February 1980.

28. *The Times*, 22 February 1985.

29. J. Coulter, S. Miller and M. Walker, *State of Siege* (Canary Press, 1984), p. 47.

30. Patricia Hewitt, *The Abuse of Power* (Martin Robertson, 1981), p. 32.

31. *Observer*, 22 July 1984.

32. *Guardian*, 1 March 1985.

33. Quoted in Huw Beynon (ed.), *Digging Deeper* (Verso, 1985), pp. 101–2.

34. Report of an Inquiry by Lord Scarman, *The Brixton Disorders*, Cmnd. 8427 (HMSO, 1981), para. 4.58.

35. Gillian Susan Morris, 'The Police and Industrial Emergencies', *The Industrial Law Journal*, Vol. 9, No. 1 (March 1980), p. 3.

36. Robert Reiner, *The Blue-Coated Worker* (Cambridge University Press, 1978), p. 140.

37. ibid., pp. 141–3.

38. See Peter Hain, *Political Trials in Britain* (Allen Lane, 1984), Chapter 2.

39. Fine and Millar, op. cit., p. 32.

40. See Martin Kettle, 'The Politics of Policing and the Policing of Politics', in Peter Hain (ed.), *Policing the Police*, Vol. 2 (John Calder, 1980), pp. 9–62.

41. Kettle, op. cit., p. 13.

42. Robert Mark, *Policing a Perplexed Society* (Allen & Unwin, 1977), pp. 258–9.
43. Coulter *et al.*, op. cit., p. 17.
44. ibid., p. 18.
45. *Guardian*, 23 June 1984.
46. *Guardian*, 11 August 1984.
47. *The Times*, 5 February 1985.
48. Fine and Millar, op. cit., p. 31.
49. *Economist*, 24 March 1985.
50. Coulter *et al.*, op. cit., p. 23.
51. *Guardian*, 17 October 1984.
52. Fine and Millar, op. cit., p. 159.
53. Coulter *et al.*, op. cit., p. 22.
54. *Observer*, 16 December 1984.
55. *Observer*, 24 June 1984.
56. Sheffield Policewatch, *Taking Liberties* (Sheffield, 1984), p. 9.
57. ibid., pp. 6–7.
58. National Council for Civil Liberties, *Civil Liberties and the Miners' Dispute* (NCCL, 1984).
59. *Guardian*, 8 February 1985.
60. Fine and Millar, op. cit., p. 193.
61. *Guardian*, 10 October 1984.
62. Sheffield Policewatch, op. cit., pp. 5–6; Coulter *et al.*, pp. 25–34.
63. Coulter *et al.*, op. cit., pp. 90–93.
64. ibid., p. 35.
65. BBC TV, 'Open Space', 8 November 1984.
66. *Guardian*, 3 December 1984.
67. *New Statesman*, 17 August 1984; *Morning Star*, 18 May 1984.
68. Coulter *et al.*, op. cit., pp. 81–6.
69. *Daily Mirror*, 29 August 1984.
70. *Guardian*, 3 July 1984.
71. *Guardian*, 5 March 1985.
72. Coulter *et al.*, op. cit., pp. 101–4.
73. *Observer*, 24 June 1984.
74. *Observer*, 19 August 1984.
75. *Guardian*, 4 June 1984.
76. *Guardian*, 10 October 1984.
77. *Guardian*, 3 October 1984.
78. *Guardian*, 23 June 1984.
79. *Guardian*, 11 August 1984.
80. *New Statesman*, 22 March 1985.
81. *The Times*, 5 February 1985.

CHAPTER 8   THE LAW AND UNIONS

1. Lord Gifford, QC, *et al.*, *Labour Herald*, 19 October 1984.
2. Ralph Miliband, *Capitalist Democracy in Britain* (Oxford University Press, 1982), pp. 120–21.
3. Chris Ralph, *The Picket and the Law* (Fabian Research Series 331, 1977), p. 9.
4. ibid., p. 10.
5. *Trade Union Immunities*, Cmnd. 8128 (HMSO, 1981), para. 14.
6. Roy Lewis, 'The Historical Development of Labour Law', *British Journal of Industrial Relations* (March 1976), p. 2.
7. See Peter Hain, *Political Trials in Britain* (Allen Lane, 1984), Chapter 4.
8. Robert Spicer, *Conspiracy* (Lawrence & Wishart, 1981), p. 29.
9. Peter Wallington, 'Criminal Conspiracy and Industrial Conflict', *Industrial Law Journal* (June 1975), pp. 83–5.
10. Ralph, op. cit.
11. Wallington, op. cit., pp. 69, 72–3.
12. Spicer, op. cit., pp. 173–4.
13. C. H. Rolph, 'The Uses of Conspiracy', *New Statesman*, 3 August 1973.
14. Ralph, op. cit., p. 7.
15. *Observer*, 23 October 1977.
16. Eric Wigham, *Strikes and the Government 1893–1981* (Macmillan, 1982), p. 190.
17. *The Times*, 4 March 1978.
18. Robert Taylor, *The Fifth Estate* (Pan, 1980), pp. 281–2.
19. ibid., p. 277.
20. Hain, op. cit., p. 97.
21. Quoted in Lord Wedderburn, 'Industrial Relations and the Courts', *Industrial Law Journal* (June 1980), p. 91.
22. J. A. G. Griffith, *The Politics of the Judiciary* (Fontana, 1981), p. 225.
23. ibid., p. 223.
24. See Griffith, op. cit., p. 227, and Wedderburn, op. cit., p. 91.
25. W. E. J. McCarthy, *New Society*, 4 September 1980.
26. *New Society*, 20 November 1980.
27. *Guardian*, 5 November 1980.
28. Wedderburn, op. cit., p. 78.
29. *Labour Herald*, 19 October 1984.
30. Henry Pelling, *A History of British Trade Unionism* (Penguin, 1984 edition), pp. 63–4.

31. See Steve Peak, *Troops in Strikes* (Cobden Trust, 1984), pp. 55–9, for an interesting analysis.
32. ibid., p. 23.
33. Hain, op. cit., pp. 129–30.
34. ibid., p. 122.
35. ibid., p. 125.
36. For a detailed account, see Louise Christian, 'Restriction Without Conviction', in Bob Fine and Robert Millar (eds.), *Policing the Miners' Strike* (Lawrence & Wishart, 1985).
37. *New Statesman*, 31 August 1984.
38. *Legal Action*, August 1984.
39. *Guardian*, 12 September 1984.
40. *Labour Weekly*, 14 and 28 September 1984.
41. Hain, op. cit., p. 133.
42. *Observer*, 2 September 1984.
43. *The Times*, 14 November 1984.
44. *Guardian*, 9 July 1984.
45. *New Statesman*, 4 January 1985.
46. *Guardian*, 13 April 1985.
47. Robert Moore, *Racism and Black Resistance* (Pluto, 1975), p. 70.
48. Hain, op. cit., p. 279.
49. *The Times*, 19 July 1984.
50. ibid.
51. *Guardian*, 9 October 1984.
52. *Guardian*, 13 October 1984.
53. Hain, op. cit., p. 126.
54. *Financial Times*, 13 August 1984.
55. Christian, op. cit., pp. 132–3.
56. *Guardian*, 8 February 1982.
57. *Morning Star*, 3 September 1984.
58. *Guardian*, 8 October 1984.
59. See Fine and Millar, op. cit., and Huw Beynon (ed.), *Digging Deeper* (Verso, 1985).
60. ibid.
61. *Guardian*, 20 July 1984.
62. Hain, op. cit., pp. 94–5.
63. Ralph Miliband, *The State in Capitalist Society* (Weidenfeld & Nicolson, 1972), p. 142.
64. See Griffith, op. cit., and Hain, op. cit.
65. Lewis, op. cit., pp. 13–14.
66. Home Office, *Review of Public Order Law*, Cmnd. 9510 (HMSO, May 1985).

CHAPTER 9   LESSONS FROM THE MINERS

1. This chapter draws heavily on discussion within the Labour Co-ordinating Committee which resulted in its statement, *After the Strike* (9 Poland Street, London WIV 3DG).
2. *Sunday Times*, 20 May 1984.
3. Alex Callinicos and Mike Simons, *The Great Strike* (Socialist Workers Party, 1985), pp. 10–15, 80.
4. See Hywel Francis, 'NUM United', *Marxism Today*, April 1985.
5. Mick McGahey, NUM Vice-President, *The Times*, 7 March 1984.
6. See Michael Crick, *Scargill and the Miners* (Penguin, 1985), pp. 100–109.
7. *Sunday Times*, 31 March 1985.
8. *New Statesman*, 22 March 1985.
9. Mark Hollingsworth, 'Press Partisans', *New Socialist*, April 1985.
10. Beatrix Campbell, 'Politics Old and New', *New Statesman*, 8 March 1985.
11. Crick, op. cit., p. 61.
12. See, for example, repeated demands made in *Socialist Worker*, and the analysis in Callinicos and Simons, op. cit.
13. *Economist*, 1 September 1984.
14. See Lee Diggins *et al.*, 'The Comfort of Strangers', *New Socialist*, February 1985; Doreen Massey and Hilary Wainwright, 'Beyond the Coalfields: the Work of the Miners' Support Groups', in Huw Beynon (ed.), *Digging Deeper* (Verso, 1985), pp. 149–68.
15. The labour staff on the *Guardian*, 5 March 1985.
16. Kim Howells, 'Stopping Out: the Birth of a New Kind of Politics', in Beynon, op. cit., p. 146.
17. See Barnsley Women, *Women Against Pit Closures* (c/o NUM, Sheffield); Loretta Loach, 'Women in the Miners' Strike', in Beynon, op. cit., pp. 169–79; also articles in *New Socialist* and *Marxism Today* in 1984 and early 1985.
18. Beatrix Campbell, *Wigan Pier Revisited* (Virago, 1984), pp. 97–115.
19. *New Statesman*, 18 January 1985.
20. *Marxism Today*, April 1985.
21. Kim Howells, op. cit., and Hywel Francis, 'Mining the Popular Front', *Marxism Today*, February 1985.
22. *Guardian*, 5 March 1985.
23. *Guardian*, 20 May 1985.
24. Andrew Glyn, *The Economic Case Against Pit Closures* (NUM, 1984).
25. Ken Coates and Tony Topham, *The New Unionism* (Penguin, 1974), pp. 120–21.

26. Arthur Scargill, 'The Case Against Workers' Control', *Workers' Control*, No. 37 (Institute for Workers' Control, 1977), pp. 13–14.
27. Raphael Samuel, 'A Managerial Power Cut', *New Socialist*, April 1985.
28. *Morning Star*, 14 May 1984.
29. V. L. Allen, *Trade Unions and the Government* (Longman, 1960), pp. 170, 306–8.

CHAPTER 10 'POLITICAL' TRADE UNIONISM?

1. Ben Pimlott and Chris Cook, *Trade Unions in British Politics* (Longman, 1982), pp. 2–3.
2. Allan Flanders, *Management and Unions* (Faber, 1970), pp. 26–7.
3. ibid. pp. 30–31.
4. John Stevenson, 'Early Trade Unionism: Radicalism and Respectability 1750–1870', in Pimlott and Cook, op. cit., p. 22.
5. ibid., p. 31.
6. Henry Pelling, *A History of British Trade Unionism* (Penguin, 1965 edition), p. 62.
7. Roger Moore, *The Emergence of the Labour Party* (Hodder, 1978), p. 20.
8. John Lovell, 'Trade Unions and the Development of Independent Labour Politics 1889–1906', in Pimlott and Cook, op. cit., p. 39.
9. Henry Pelling, *Origins of the Labour Party 1880–1900* (Oxford, Clarendon Press, 1965), p. 84.
10. Lovell, op. cit., p. 44.
11. ibid., p. 47.
12. Pelling, *Origins*, op. cit., p. 222.
13. Lovell, op. cit., p. 48.
14. For detailed accounts, see Bill Simpson, *Labour, the Unions and the Party* (Allen & Unwin, 1973), pp. 38–43, and Ralph Miliband, *Parliamentary Socialism* (Merlin Press, 1973 edition), p. 17.
15. Martin Harrison, *Trade Unions and the Labour Party since 1945* (Allen & Unwin, 1960), p. 12.
16. See Lovell, op. cit., pp. 51–2.
17. ibid., p. 56.
18. Simpson, op. cit., p. 61.
19. K. D. Ewing, *Trade Unions, the Labour Party and the Law* (Edinburgh University Press, 1982), pp. 22–32.
20. Lewis Minkin, 'Polls Apart', *New Socialist*, No. 22 (December 1984), p. 8.
21. David Rubinstein, 'Trade Unions, Politicians and Public Opinion', in Pimlott and Cook, op. cit., p. 60.

22. Quoted by Chris Wrigley, 'Trade Unions and Politics in the First World War', in Pimlott and Cook, op. cit., p. 81.

23. ibid., p. 87.

24. Miliband, op. cit., p. 13.

25. See David Howell, 'Where's Ramsay MacKinnock?', in Huw Beynon (ed.), *Digging Deeper* (Verso, 1985).

26. Miliband, op. cit., p. 136.

27. ibid., p. 151.

28. Ewing, op. cit., p. 51.

29. Alan Clinton, *Post Office Workers* (Allen & Unwin, 1984) pp. 407–8.

30. Simpson, op. cit., p. 155.

31. Ewing, op. cit., pp. 61–2.

32. Richard Shackleton, 'Trade Unions and the Slump', in Pimlott and Cook, op. cit., p. 125.

33. See Anthony Fenley, 'Labour and the Trade Unions', in Chris Cook and Ian Taylor (eds.), *The Labour Party* (Longman, 1980), p. 62.

34. Shackleton, op. cit., p. 121.

35. Fenley, op. cit., p. 60.

36. Shackleton, op. cit., p. 136.

37. Harrison, op. cit., p. 23.

38. ibid., p. 30.

39. ibid., p. 36.

40. ibid., p. 129.

41. Labour Party, *Report of the 1952 Annual Conference*, p. 79.

42. Fenley, op. cit., p. 69.

43. ibid., p. 51.

44. ibid., p. 71.

45. ibid.

46. ibid., p. 72.

47. V. L. Allen, *Trade Unions and the Government* (Longman, 1960), p. 232.

48. Miliband, op. cit., p. 357.

49. Allen, op. cit., p. 231.

50. Robert Taylor, 'The Trade Union "Problem" since 1960', in Pimlott and Cook, op. cit., p. 204.

51. See Peter Hain, *The Democratic Alternative* (Penguin, 1983), pp. 137–41.

52. *Democracy in Trade Unions*, Cmnd. 8778 (HMSO, 1983).

53. *Economist*, 18 June 1983.

54. *The Times*, 26 August 1983.

55. BBC radio, 'Today', 23 August 1984.

56. *The Times*, 6 September 1984.

57. M. Moran, *The Union of Post Office Workers: a Study in Political Sociology* (Macmillan, 1974).

58. Harrison, op. cit., pp. 41–2.
59. ibid., pp. 112–13, 119–25.
60. David Butler and Donald Stokes, *Political Change in Britain* (Penguin, 1971), p. 202.
61. Ken Coates and Tony Topham, *Trade Unions in Britain* (Spokesman, 1980), p. 306.
62. Harrison, op. cit., p. 116.
63. ibid., p. 118.
64. ibid.
65. Clinton, op. cit., pp. 405–9.
66. Harrison, op. cit., p. 296.
67. ibid., pp. 165–6.
68. *Financial Times*, 8 May 1985.
69. See Peter Hain, 'An Unhappy Marriage?', *Marxism Today* (November 1984).
70. Colin Crouch, *Trade Unions: the Logic of Collective Action* (Fontana, 1982), pp. 190–91.
71. Fenley, op. cit., p. 52.
72. ibid., p. 51.
73. See Hain, *The Democratic Alternative*, op. cit.
74. Geoff Hodgson, *Labour at the Crossroads* (Martin Robertson, 1981), p. 18.
75. Tony Lane, *The Union Makes Us Strong* (Arrow, 1974), p. 112.
76. ibid., p. 287.
77. *Financial Times*, 17 April 1985.
78. Crouch, op. cit., pp. 202–3.

CHAPTER 11 A NEW UNIONISM

1. Michael Shanks, *The Stagnant Society* (Penguin, 1961), p. 73.
2. A. M. Ross and P. T. Hartman, *Changing Patterns of Industrial Conflict* (New York, Wiley, 1960).
3. Richard Hyman, *Strikes* (Fontana, third edition, 1984), pp. 86–7.
4. Ken Coates and Tony Topham, *Trade Unions in Britain* (Spokesman, 1980), p. 228.
5. See Andrew Glyn and Bob Sutcliffe, *British Capitalism, Workers and the Profits Squeeze* (Penguin, 1972).
6. R. Price and G. Bain, 'Union Growth in Britain: Retrospect and Prospect', *British Journal of Industrial Relations* (March 1983), p. 53.
7. See Tony Lane, 'The Unions: Caught on the Ebb Tide', *Marxism Today* (September 1982), and Doreen Massey and Nicholas Miles, 'Mapping out the Unions', *Marxism Today* (May 1984).

8. Quoted in Chris Mulhearn, *Urban Decline and Labour Movement Response* (Department of Town Planning, Polytechnic of the South Bank, 1985).

9. Quoted in Tony Lane, *The Union Makes Us Strong* (Arrow, 1974), p. 186.

10. Figures given by Peter Kellner, *The Times*, 9 July 1984.

11. See Sarah Boston, *Women Workers and the Trade Unions* (Davis-Poynter, 1980).

12. Jenny Beale, *Getting It Together* (Pluto, 1982), p. 5.

13. ibid., p. 9.

14. ibid., pp. 7–9.

15. ibid., pp. 20–21.

16. ibid., p. 31.

17. Ken Coates and Tony Topham, *The New Unionism* (Penguin, 1974), p. 19.

18. Quoted in ibid., p. 20.

19. Quoted by Huw Beynon and Hilary Wainwright, *The Workers' Report on Vickers* (Pluto, 1979), p. 175.

20. Tony Benn, *Arguments for Democracy* (Cape, 1981), p. 165.

21. Hyman, op. cit., p. 143.

22. Anna Coote and Beatrix Campbell, *Sweet Freedom* (Pan, 1982), p. 157.

23. Philip Pearson, *Twilight Robbery: Trade Unions and Low Paid Workers* (Pluto, 1985).

24. Victor Allen, 'The Paradox of Militancy', in R. Blackburn and A. Cockburn (eds.), *The Incompatibles* (Penguin, 1967), pp. 243–4, and Robert Taylor, *The Fifth Estate* (Pan, 1980), p. 243.

25. Perry Anderson, 'The Limits and Possibilities of Trade Union Action', in Blackburn and Cockburn, op. cit., pp. 265–6.

26. Allan Flanders, *Management and Unions* (Faber, 1970), p. 293.

27. Beynon and Wainwright, op. cit., p. 175.

28. Quoted in Taylor, op. cit., p. 150.

29. Taylor, op. cit., p. 43.

30. Eric Hobsbawm, *The Forward March of Labour Halted?* (Verso, 1981).

31. Robert Reiner, *The Blue-Coated Worker* (Cambridge University Press, 1978), p. 274.

32. See, for example, Steve Jeffreys, in Hobsbawm, op. cit., pp. 103–13.

33. Peter Fairbrother, *All Those in Favour* (Pluto, 1984), pp. 71–72.

34. Lenin, *Collected Works*, Vol. 23, p. 28.

35. See Lane, *The Union Makes Us Strong*, op. cit., p. 28, for a useful discussion.

36. ibid., p. 58.

37. ibid., p. 174.

38. ibid.

39. For a sensitive socialist analysis of the problem, see London Edinburgh Weekend Return Group, *In and Against the State* (Pluto, 1980), p. 88.

40. Hobsbawm, op. cit., p. 14.

41. Quoted in Henry Phelps Brown, *The Origins of Trade Union Power* (Oxford, Clarendon Press, 1983), p. 25.

42. Ben Pimlott and Chris Cook (eds.), *Trade Unions in British Politics* (Longman, 1982), p. 4.

43. Ralph Miliband, *Capitalist Democracy in Britain* (Oxford University Press, 1982), p. 57.

44. For a review of the literature, see Hyman, op. cit., pp. 78–85.

45. ibid., p. 83.

46. *Royal Commission on Trade Unions and Employers' Associations*, Cmnd. 3623 (HMSO, 1968), pp. 28–9.

47. Quoted in Hyman, op. cit., pp. 50–51.

48. Anderson, op. cit., pp. 264–5.

49. Roger Undy and Roderick Martin, *Ballots and Trade Union Democracy* (Oxford, Basil Blackwell, 1984).

50. Beatrix Campbell, *Wigan Pier Revisited* (Virago, 1984), and Anna Coote and Beatrix Campbell, *Sweet Freedom* (Pan, 1982).

51. Campbell, op. cit.

52. Bob Fryer, 'Trade Unionism in Crisis: the Challenge to Union Democracy', in Huw Beynon (ed.), *Digging Deeper* (Verso, 1985), p. 76.

53. See John McIlroy, *Strike!* (Pluto, 1984), for an excellent guide to organizing strikes.

54. Ken Coates and Tony Topham, *The New Unionism* (Penguin, 1974), pp. 72–4.

55. Sheila Rowbotham et al., *Beyond the Fragments* (Merlin Press, 1979), pp. 95–6.

56. For a review of the literature, see Peter Hain, *Neighbourhood Participation* (Temple Smith, 1980), pp. 173–81.

57. Cynthia Cockburn, *The Local State* (Pluto, 1977).

58. Paul Thompson, *Working the System* (Pluto, 1985), p. 103.

59. B. Moorhouse et al., 'Rent Strikes – Direct Action and the Working Class', in *The Socialist Register 1972* (Merlin Press, 1972), pp. 133–56.

60. P. Thomas, *Taming the Concrete Jungle* (Sydney, New South Wales branch of the Australian Building Construction Employees' and Builders' Laborers' Federation, 1973).

61. T. Clarke, 'Redundancy, Worker Resistance and the Community', in G. Craig et al., *Jobs and Community Action* (Routledge & Kegan Paul, 1979), p. 95.

62. P. Morris, 'Race, Community and Marginality', in Craig, op. cit., pp. 100–112.

63. V. L. Allen, *Trade Unions and the Government* (Longman, 1960), pp. 206, 213.

64. Coates and Topham, *The New Unionism*, op. cit., p. 122.

65. Hilary Wainwright and Dave Elliott, *The Lucas Plan* (Allison & Busby, 1982), pp. 245.

66. ibid., pp. 176–82.

67. Thompson, op. cit., pp. 131–5.

68. Ken Coates, *Work-ins, Sit-ins and Industrial Democracy* (Spokesman, 1981).

69. See Ken Coates and Tony Topham (eds.), *Workers' Control* (Panther, 1970).

70. See Peter Hain, *The Democratic Alternative* (Penguin, 1983).

71. Coventry, Liverpool, Newcastle, N. Tyneside Trades Councils, *State Intervention in Industry* (Spokesman, 1980).

72. Beynon and Wainwright, op. cit.

73. For a discussion of this topic, see Hain, *The Democratic Alternative*, op. cit.

74. Tom Sawyer, 'Politics will Make the Unions Strong', *New Socialist* (September 1984).

INDEX

College of Ripon & York St. John. STUDENT LIBRARY. Industrial

College of Industrial
Relations.
STUDENTS' LIBRARY.